THE JOY OF

HEALTHY PASTA

PASTA IS AS GOOD FOR YOU AS IT IS GOOD TASTING...
HERE'S HOW TO KEEP IT THAT WAY!

JOE FAMULARO

BARRON'S

PHOTOGRAPHER: Thom DeSanto
FOOD STYLIST: Andrea B. Swenson

All inquiries should be addressed to:
Barron's Educational Series, Inc.
250 Wireless Boulevard
Hauppauge, New York 11788
http://www.barronseduc.com

International Standard Book No. 0-7641-5102-9

Library of Congress Catalog Card No. 97-52142

Library of Congress Cataloging-in-Publication Data
Famularo, Joseph J.
The joy of healthy pasta / Joe Famularo.
p. cm.
Includes index.
ISBN 0-7641-5102-9
1. Cookery (Pasta) I. Title.
TX809.M17F34 1998
641.8'22—dc21 97–52142
CIP...

PRINTED IN HONG KONG
9 8 7 6 5 4 3 2 1

CONTENTS

ACKNOWLEDGMENTS

Thanks to Eileen Canzoneri who had infinite patience with the detailed and numerous nutritional analyses; Sue Garufi for her care and devotion to the typing of the manuscript; Helen and Tony Crimmins who tested many recipes; my nieces, Carolyn Famularo Patton and Susan Imperiale Guillen, who watch over my physical well-being, who insist on healthier eating habits, and who have consistently shown their interest in my work; Christopher Laus, my assistant, who is of Filipino ancestry but cooks pasta like an Italian; Bernie Kinzer, who never refuses a plate of pasta and contributes valuable critiques of my recipes; and special thanks to Mark Miele and Grace Freedson, my editors.

INTRODUCTION

Americans love pasta. Americans want to eat more healthfully. These two facts are the reasons for this book. Food trends may come and go, but cooking pasta is routine in most American homes. Some call pasta an American national cuisine.

The most noticeable food trend today is the link between diet and health. New government food guidelines, new nutritional analyses printed on food packages, manufacturers' commitments to creating low- or nonfat products, and new studies on diet, obesity, and health, all document the shift to healthier eating.

From a health standpoint, nutritional labeling information required for store-bought food should be available for the food we prepare and eat in our homes. This is why this book gives a nutritional analysis for each recipe, in addition to offering tips that are vital to cooking pasta healthfully.

Diet has been implicated in two of the three major risk factors related to heart disease (high cholesterol and hypertension; the third is smoking). Diet also has been linked to some forms of cancer. There is a consensus as to which dietary elements play a role in promoting or preventing disease. Experts recommend a diet low in saturated fat, to help prevent heart disease, and high in fruits, grains, pasta, and vegetables, especially those containing antioxidants, which have been shown to reduce the risk of some types of cancer and heart disease.

The recipes in this book have been developed with United States Department of Agriculture (USDA) dietary pyramid guidelines in mind and provide nutritional analyses for each recipe. Foods such as lean meats and spray oils have been suggested to help reduce saturated fats. Many of the recipes are based on traditional Mediterranean diets, which are high in vegetables and complex carbohydrates and low in animal foods.

I have cooked pasta for many years and have learned that anyone who wants to eat healthier pasta, without sacrificing flavor, has to modify how he or she prepares it, especially the way one sauces the pasta. I wrote this book to show how modifications, such as using little or no butter and cream, less oil, leaner and less meat, and so on, will maximize health benefits without sacrificing flavor, a concept not found in most pasta books.

As a child, I watched my mother and grandmother, father and grandfather, cook pasta. I still can smell the eggplant, onions, and garlic they added to their dishes. As a teenager, I thought a day at the beach or in the country was incomplete without a lukewarm dish of pasta.

My first apartment, on West 11th Street in Manhattan, had the tiniest kitchen, and there I prepared pasta with almost every vegetable I could find in Balducci's, a well-known food shop in lower Manhattan in New York City. Through time and experience, I, too, have grown more convinced of the connection between health and a low-fat diet and, therefore, rarely use butter or cream these days. I eat moderate amounts of beef, use more turkey and fish in my pasta recipes, and allow vegetables, pasta, and fruits to play a dominant role in meal planning.

Most of the recipes in this book contain only ten or fewer grams of total fat, with saturated fat levels well below five grams. Most pasta books ignore nutritional content, and the resultant pasta dishes are laden with fat. For example, where traditional recipes use four to eight tablespoons of olive oil, mine use one, two, or sometimes three tablespoons. Almost every recipe is flavored with herbs, spices, and vegetables to perk up the flavor. These are ingredients such as garlic, onion, scallions, and all types of peppers, with food values that won't compromise fat and calorie counts, and with flavors that make a big impact. Portion sizes also have been trimmed. Such guidelines are basic to each recipe.

Pleasure is what good eating is all about, and with this book in hand, you won't have to use a slide rule to figure out tonight's menu. Just look at the nutritional analysis following each recipe for guidance; in other words, the complex computations have been done for you, and you are spared the drudgery of figuring milligrams of saturated fat.

No one wants to stop enjoying his or her favorite pasta dish. Because pasta is one of America's favorite foods, how do we continue to prepare it and be reasonably healthy in our efforts? The trick is to reduce the consumption of certain high-fat foods, increase the use of spices and herbs to augment flavor, and take advantage of the natural sweetness found in most foods. You may be familiar with the routine of practically starving yourself all day and then giving in to munching rich chocolate chip cookies before going to bed. Why? You have not satisfied your appetite with a decent, healthy meal.

Over the years, I've learned a few lessons about dieting: if you deprive yourself of the good kinds of food, you'll end up eating the wrong foods when your willpower is weak. But if you eat foods that are good for you to start with, you won't have to worry about feeling hungry and deprived later on. I find that pasta has the visual appeal, well-founded taste, and nutritional value that most people are looking for in a healthy diet.

Italy is a country of dark green palms and blue-gray olive trees. There, the oleander blooms in multiple shades of pink against fields of deep red poppies, and the lantana on the countryside is a sign of eternal spring. The worn, gray stone houses are filled with history, silhouetted by trees bent to suit the wind. In these Italian homes, there is usually a big bowl of just-prepared pasta waiting to be brought to the table.

The image of America as a melting pot is stronger than ever when it comes to food, and especially when it comes to pasta. Today, pasta is more like a tossed salad, in which diverse ingredients do not necessarily surrender their original flavor and character. Although pasta, Neapolitan style, or pasta with Bolognese ragú sauce, for example, are classics, and still popular today, the number of pasta choices is exploding.

Good and great taste in pasta is hot again, except that the emphasis is on lower fat. The food police are out there, for sure. But we all want to put the zip back into our pasta dishes with the enhanced flavor of fat free. The book's overriding objective is to offer 150 tested low-fat pasta recipes of irresistible flavor to satisfy the cook's desire for a pasta dish that is healthy, light, and loaded with the pleasures of the Italian kitchen.

Here's healthy delicious pasta. Put your water on to boil, and let's get started.

Joe Famularo
Key West, Florida

A Special Note: Please take a few minutes to glance at the index. This cookbook contains helpful information on many essential ingredients.

NOTES ON NUTRITIONAL ANALYSES

Nutritional analyses have been included for each recipe as a general guideline to help you and your family track the amount of fat and other nutrients.

- If a recipe gives a range of servings, such as six to eight servings, the largest number of servings is usually used, but check each nutritional analysis for serving size.
- If an ingredient is optional, it is NOT included in the analysis.
- If a recipe calls for nonfat sour cream, or low-sodium soy sauce, such ingredients were used in the analysis and are so indicated in the list of ingredients.
- In some cases, the number of grams and milligrams of key nutrients analyzed were rounded off.
- Some of the calories and other nutrients may differ slightly for you, depending on the brands or types of pasta you use as ingredients or whether you make a substitution.

SOME THOUGHTS ABOUT LOW FAT AND DIETS

According to the United States Department of Agriculture, the average American diet is now 33 percent fat. It was considerably higher, but since the 1970s red meat consumption has been greatly reduced, and at the same time, sales of yogurt and lower-fat milk and cheeses have soared. It has been reported that the number of deaths due to heart disease has significantly decreased in the last 20 years. Improved medical techniques have surely helped, but the change in diet has also been credited.

It seems that people are still somewhat confused, or at least the health message seems misguided, because total fat intake may not be the full culprit—it is the amount of saturated fat that really matters. This theory gets its support from the American Cancer Institute, American Heart Association, and the National Heart, Lung and Blood Institutes. In other words, recent research claims that specific fats, rather than fat in general, are the things which should concern us. In November 1977, *The New England Journal of Medicine* reported a study about nurses who ate more than 45 percent of their calories as fat; they did not increase their risk of heart disease provided that these fats were not saturated or trans fats (those fats that are solid at room temperature, or the partially hydrogenated vegetable oils found in margarine and some other processed foods).

There is obvious disagreement among the experts. The Harvard School of Public Health (Department of Nutrition) says that the *type* of fat is important for heart disease, that the total amount of fat is not important if people watch *total caloric intake*. They believe the Mediterranean diet based on monounsaturated fats (i.e., olive oil) keep heart disease rates low in those Mediterranean areas. This is one of my reasons to keep some olive oil in pasta; another is for flavor. I have also paid more attention to saturated fat amounts and have included some recipes with 30 percent or more fat from calories if the saturated fat is reasonably low. It is important to understand that if there is one high-fat food in a given meal, it can be balanced with low-fat choices for that meal or other meals that day.

1. Figure your fat limit based on the calories you need each day.

2. Try to plan your meals accordingly and do not exceed 10 percent of calories from saturated fat in any one day.

This simple chart may help guide you:

Calories Needed Each Day	**Fat Limit Per Day** 30 Percent of Total Calories (fat intake in grams)*
1,200	40
1,500	50
1,800	60
2,100	70
2,400	80

* To compute, determine 30 percent of calories needed daily (30 percent of 1,200 calories equals 360); divide 360 by 9 (there are 9 calories per fat gram) to equal 40 (i.e., 360 divided by 9 equals 40).

If you need 1,200 calories daily, do not exceed 40 grams of fat.

CONSIDER DIETARY FIBER LEVEL

Adults should get about 25 grams of dietary fiber a day. Meals that combine pasta with legumes (beans, chickpeas, lentils, peas) and vegetables offer a wide variety of healthy, tasty, and interesting meals, rich in fiber. In using this book, note the fiber level of any particular recipe. For example, the linguine with clam sauce on page 25 has 9 grams of fiber (more than one third of the daily requirement). The chickpea, tomato, and pasta soup on page 53 has 7 grams of fiber. Tomato puree is very high in fiber—see the roasted tomato and onion sauce with 6 grams of fiber per serving on page 82, and the tomato, cheese, and herb sauce on page 87. The fresh tomato sauce on page 81 has 8 grams per serving.

CHAPTER 1
THE PASTA BASICS

INTRODUCTION

Pasta, the most omnipresent component of Italian cuisine, is in itself a remarkable food. The pasta in this book is firm, supple, full of personality, and a sheer pleasure to chew. Al dente does not mean simply undercooked as so many American cooks have come to interpret it. Al dente means something that can stand up to the tooth, pasta with a little spring and life to it. As a rule, Italians often cook the pasta separately and add the sauce to the pasta just before serving it.

Pasta in any form is also a dish of great simplicity. Italians have created many shapes of it and an extraordinarily high number of ways to use them. It has been said often that Italians are at their best when it comes to pasta. In the United States, of the foreign dishes that have now become part of our national cuisine, probably the most popular is pasta. Stores everywhere carry shelves full of the dried type and, a more recent phenomenon, long and wide refrigerated units overflowing with fresh pasta. Most dried and fresh pasta is made in factories either owned or managed by Americans of Italian descent (although many of these firms have now been swallowed by giant corporations); fortunately for us, their products hold up well against the Italian imports. Italians have used pasta dough (basically made of semolina mixed with water) to create hundreds of fanciful and decorative shapes. The names of the small pastas go on *ad infinitum*—some of the more popular pastas are in the shapes of seeds, stars, wheels, tiny shells, small tubes, and small elbows. Some of the stuffed pastas are ravioli (small squares filled with a variety of fillings such as ricotta), cappelletti (called little hats because when they are cut, they form peaks), and tortellini (the ends of the stuffed pasta are brought together, twisting them around the finger to form a ring).

Until I was a teenager, I didn't know that pasta could be bought in a grocery store. In my home and in the other homes I knew, the wooden pole dripping with pasta was as permanent a piece of furniture as the kitchen table. Like the family's cleavers that cut across many chicken necks, the family pasta board received special care and safekeeping. The pasta board in our home, made by an Italian carpenter, was quite thick and heavy and measured approximately four square feet. It was never washed. On it were rolled sheets and sheets of pasta, each sheet lightly folded over and cut into noodle strips, or into forms to receive various fillings. I noticed at an early age that neighbors and relatives compared and sized up pasta boards with as much concern and care as they did pasta quality.

Because homemade fresh pasta is made with eggs, the cholesterol count is extremely high. Therefore, in this book, I depend more on the variety of dried pastas available in all food stores and supermarkets because they are not made with eggs. I have included, however, some fresh pastas made at home and those found in refrigerated sections of supermarkets if the nutritional analyses of the prepared dishes were reasonable. Following is a recipe for good fresh homemade pasta with egg whites instead of whole eggs.

Commercial brands of pasta vary in quality, but the best are made from hard wheat of good quality. In the United States, I prefer the American brands of Ronzoni, Buitoni, and San Giorgio. As for the Italian imports, I like Barilla, De Cecco, Delverde, Guido di Napoli, Spiga, and La Molisana. There are many good U.S. and imported Italian pastas in most shops.

Pasta is antiquity itself, and its origins are not known all that well. Let's not fight the battle here of whether Marco Polo brought it to Italy because I believe he didn't. According to food writer Elizabeth David, *macarono* was made from *spelta* (small brown wheat) and first made its appearance before Marco Polo in the reign of the magnanimous Prince Teodoric in Ravenna. By the end of the eighteenth century, pasta was deeply rooted in the tastes of the Italian populace. Some Italians in the north think that pasta as a daily food is unsuitable, but the fact remains that the majority of Italians, in spite of the various rice and polenta dishes in the north, continue to eat *pasta asciutta* (dried pasta) at midday and probably some kind of pasta *in brodo* at night.

Basically, there are two kinds of pasta: homemade pasta, *pasta fatta in casa*, and the factory mass-produced kind, *pasta asciutto*. In this country, factory-made pasta has been the most popular, and it is only recently that pasta shops have opened, making or offering fresh pasta daily.

In ancient times, when the coarsely ground *puls* (flour, somewhat similar to semolina) was combined with water to make pasta to be dried for eventual use, perhaps some of it was consumed right away, and fresh pasta may have been born. No eggs were used at that time; in fact, some fresh pasta in Italy today still omits eggs, notably the "little ears," *orecchiette*, in Puglia in the south of Italy and the flat, string pasta in Genoa called *trenette*, a flat spaghetti that is usually sauced with pesto.

According to the food historian, Giuliano Bugialli, fresh pasta made with eggs is mentioned in the first Italian cookbook from Florence in 1300. This pasta, made with flour, eggs, olive oil, and salt, is still made all over Italy and in most Italian-American homes in the United States where fresh pasta is made. This pasta is always kneaded by hand and rolled out either with a rolling pin or a manually operated machine.

We should note, however, that the fresh pasta marketed in the United States (and in Italy), made with semolina flour but not with eggs, produces a dough of tougher consistency that can be rolled by large industrial machines. In other words, if eggs were added, the dough would be too tender and would break or come apart under the stress of these machines. Commercially made fresh pasta and fresh pasta made at home are two different products.

In Italy, the rules are fairly strict about which sauce goes with which pasta; the general rule being that the thicker, more strongly flavored sauces go with the heavier pastas such as *ziti*, large tubular short pasta. The lighter sauces go with the thinner or smaller shapes. There are hundreds of different shapes of dried pasta because of machine capability, and there are an equal number of different sauces to go with each.

In times past, coarse flour and water were mixed and then dried in the sun to preserve it for travel or later use. Dried flat pasta was made in Roman Sicily and worked its way north. Tubular pasta, made by hand, appeared in the twelfth century. Dried pasta as we know it commercially today didn't appear until the advent of the machine, so it is actually fairly new. When you buy dried pasta, you will see on some packages the words *pasta di pura semola di grano duro;* this means that the pasta is made from the fine flour obtained from the cleaned endosperm or heart of the durum (hard) wheat grain. This is the cream of wheat, and you should select these brands whether they are American or Italian import brands. However, as far as the difference in cooking time is concerned, dried pasta takes about 10 minutes; fresh pasta takes less than 5 minutes.

PASTA SHAPES

Pasta is remarkably versatile. It comes in a variety of shapes and sizes and the imaginative cook can create an infinite number of pasta and sauce combinations. Traditionally, the choice of which pasta to cook was dependent upon the sauce that it was to be topped with. Today, however, such rules no longer apply. Choose pasta for the fun of it and enjoy. Some of the more popular pastas, as shown on the next page, include: (1) Tortellini, (2) Elbows, (3) Little Stars, (4) Orzo, (5) Gnocchi, (6) Conchiglie, (7) Rigatoni, (8) Farfalle, (9) Fusilli, (10) Orichiette, (11) Cavatelli, (12) Mafaldine, (13) Penne, (14) Ziti, (15) Gemelli, (16) Rotelle, and (17) Fettucine.

1
2
3
4
5
6
7
8
9
10
11
12
13
14
15
16
17

HOW TO MAKE PASTA

MAKES 4 SERVINGS

1 1/2 cups all-purpose flour
3 small egg whites
1/2 teaspoon salt
1 teaspoon extra-virgin olive oil
3/4 tablespoon lukewarm water or milk

❶ Measure the flour. Put the flour on a flat surface or in a bowl and form a well deep enough to hold the egg whites.

❷ Put the egg whites into the well. Add the other ingredients. If you are making pasta to stuff, add milk instead of water (it will seal the pasta better). With a small wooden fork or a whisk, beat the egg whites lightly and, in so doing, begin to pick up a little of the flour from inside the well with the fork or whisk. Incorporate the flour into the egg whites until they are no longer runny. A good technique for mixing, if the flour is on a flat surface, is to whisk with one hand, and with the other, hold or support the outside wall of the well. By gently pushing the outer edge of the flour wall with your hand, some of the flour will fall into the well. If the dough is sticky, add a little more flour.

❸ With both hands, bring all the flour from the outside of the well toward the center and make a ball with the dough, including the crumbs of flour caked on the working surface (use a pastry scraper). Put the ball of dough on a flat surface and push down firmly into the center with the heel of your hand. Give the dough a slight turn and push down again. Dust your hands with flour because the dough is likely to stick in the beginning. Knead about 7 minutes. The dough should be smooth and satiny and not tough. Cover with a kitchen towel, 10 to 15 minutes.

Continued on next page

COOKED DRY PASTA

To get this amount of cooked pasta:

1 cup
2 cups
4 cups

Cook this amount of dry pasta:

2/3 cup (2 oz)
1 1/4 cups (4 oz)
2 1/2 cups (8 oz)

❹ Roll out by hand or use a pasta machine. Pasta machines are fitted with smooth rollers that will produce several thicknesses of *sheet*, which is what pasta is called when it has been rolled out by hand or machine. A knob can be turned to widen or narrow the opening between rollers. Most machines have six settings. Cutting rollers, which can be attached to the machine, slice the sheet to the pasta width of your choice. Only one pasta width can be cut at a time.

❺ Before using the machine, cut each ball of dough into six equal pieces. Cover five of them and run the sixth two times through the widest opening. Then run it through a narrower opening. It is not necessary to run the pasta through every opening. For example, on a 6-notch machine, roll the dough through setting 6 (the thickest), 4, 2, and 1 (the thinnest). Lightly, very lightly, flour each strip of dough after it is rolled. After sprinkling the dough with flour, rub the palm of your hand up and down the strip to cover it lightly with flour. Lay the pasta strips on toweling while completing the task.

❻ Fill and form, or shape the pasta (unfilled), as directed in each recipe.

Each serving		**% of calories from fat**	**7**
Calories	194	Total Fat	1.6 g
Protein	7 g	Saturated Fat	0.2 g
Carbohydrates	36 g	Cholesterol	0 mg
Dietary Fiber	1 g	Sodium	332 mg

CRESPELLE, PANCAKES FOR MANICOTTI OR CANNELLONI

MAKES 12 SERVINGS

Most Italian cooks turn these pancakes with their hands. Because the cakes are hot, your fingers will feel burned—hence the name *manicotti*, which means "cooked hands." Classically, manicotti or cannelloni are made from fresh pasta and cut into squares for cannelloni and squares (sometimes circles) for manicotti. This is, in a way, an easier version. After you get the hang of making crespelle, you'll want to do it often. They make great "containers" for a wide variety of fillings.

3 eggs
1 cup water
1 cup all-purpose flour
pinch salt
1 teaspoon butter for greasing the skillet

1. With a whisk, beat the eggs in a bowl. Add the water and whisk again. Add the flour a little at a time, whisking until all is blended. Add only a pinch (1/8 teaspoon) salt. Leave stand at room temperature 45 to 60 minutes.

2. Heat a 7- or 8-inch crepe pan, preferably nonstick. Brush very lightly with butter. Add 3 tablespoons batter and tilt the pan back and forth until the batter covers the bottom. Cook about 1/2 minute on one side, turn over and cook the second side 15 seconds. Slide the shell out of the pan onto a dish.

3. Repeat Step 2 until all the batter is used. Brush the skillet lightly with a little more butter, if it is needed, before pouring more batter into the pan.

Special Note: Crespelle or crepes can be made 1 or 2 days ahead, wrapped in plastic wrap, and refrigerated. They may also be frozen up to 1 month. I usually fill the crespelle before freezing them, so all I have to do is heat them. They can go straight from the freezer into the oven.

Each serving		% of calories from fat 18	
Calories	54	Total Fat	1.2 g
Protein	2 g	Saturated Fat	0.4 g
Carbohydrates	8 g	Cholesterol	47 mg
Dietary Fiber	0.3 g	Sodium	39 mg

PASTA AMOUNTS

One pound of small pasta (small elbows, tubetti, ditalini, and others) will measure about 3 1/2 cups of dried pasta. When small pasta is cooked, it about doubles in amount (1 cup uncooked will be 2 cups cooked).

IMPORTANT PASTA POINTERS

❶ Use a large quantity of water when cooking pasta. When cooking 1/2 pound pasta, use 3 quarts of water; for 1 pound pasta, 6 quarts of water.

❷ Salt is usually added to the boiling water in this book because it adds flavor, but reduce salt in packaged pasta instructions by half.

❸ Do not add oil to boiling water when cooking pasta. Most people think that this keeps pasta from sticking. Stir frequently, instead, and the pasta will not stick.

❹ When draining pasta, always reserve some of the cooking liquid—a cup is usually enough. This liquid can improve your sauce-making. If the sauce is too thick or the pasta too dry, a little added pasta water will thin the sauce or moisten the pasta. Also, if the sauce is too thin, add 1/4 cup of the cooking liquid and simmer the sauce; the starch in the cooking water will thicken the sauce.

❺ Do not rinse pasta by running it under cold water, except in rare instances; cooking directions will suggest rinsing if it is essential to do so. The texture and taste of the pasta depend on the starch clinging to the pasta as it cooks and is drained.

❻ Some pasta lovers use only imported pasta. Imported pastas are usually excellent but so are some American brands. Remember that American companies like Ronzoni were started by Italian immigrants who brought the pasta-making techniques with them to this country.

TOMATOES AND SAUCES

Tomatoes are low in calories and rich in vitamins. A medium-size mature tomato has only 25 calories, 20 milligrams of vitamin C, and 1,400 IUs of vitamin A. Most of the vitamin C is in the jellylike seed packets inside the tomato, which most people squeeze out. I prefer to use plum tomatoes because they have smaller seeds, which do not need to be discarded.

The average half cup of tomato sauce has about 80 to 90 calories versus 25 calories for a half cup of canned tomatoes. A 3 1/2 ounce can of tomato paste has about 80 calories, 50 milligrams of vitamin C, 2,100 IUs of vitamin A, good amounts of B vitamins, and almost 1,000 milligrams of potassium. Always use the reddest tomatoes because they not only have more flavor but also have four times as much vitamin A as green ones.

Diet cannot cure prostate problems, but it has been reported that something in tomatoes plays a role in maintaining the health of this gland. Lycopene, a pigment found in tomatoes (in watermelons, red grapefruit, and berries, too) may help reduce the risk of prostate cancer because it is high in antioxidants and bioflavonoids. As tomatoes cook, they release more lycopene, so tomato-based pasta sauces and soups seem to be beneficial.

VEGETABLES AS NUTRIENTS WITH PASTA

Vegetables are considered to be the cornerstone of a healthy diet; they are replete with nutrients. They provide almost all the minerals and vitamins needed for good health. The starchy vegetables (potatoes, butternut squash, etc.) contain complex carbohydrates, as does pasta, and the complex carbohydrates give us abundant energy. Most provide dietary fiber, and some, like beans, provide important protein. Vegetables, the wonder food, have little or no fat and no cholesterol, and they are low in calories. Throughout this book there are side bars of information about many vegetables but here is a brief summary about their nutrient content. Vegetables are so nutrient-dense that they are joined with pasta in every recipe.

- Roots, bulbs and tubers such as beets: Their tops are especially rich in minerals and vitamins, more so than their bulbs. Carrots have lots of beta carotene, onions (and garlic) may lower blood pressure and cholesterol levels, turnips are fiber sources and rich in vitamin C, and potatoes offer vitamin C and potassium.
- Leafy vegetables such as collards, kale, spinach, radicchio, and salad greens: All leafy vegetables contain vitamin C and are good sources of beta carotene, fiber, and folic acid (a B vitamin). Almost all of them are low-calorie foods.
- Buds, flowers, and stalk vegetables such as asparagus, artichokes, broccoli, cauliflower, and celery: These vegetables are filled with calcium, vitamin C, potassium, and dietary fiber. These vegetables mate well with pasta; you will find combinations of them throughout this book.
- Pods and seeds such as corn, lima beans, green beans, and peas: These vegetables are rich in the B vitamins, calcium, iron, magnesium, potassium, and zinc.

- Fruit vegetables (technically speaking they are fruits but we use them as vegetables) such as eggplant, peppers, summer squashes, and tomatoes: These fruits are favorite pasta partners. They usually have more calories than leafy vegetables but they are rich in vitamin C and fiber, tomatoes especially.

Special note: The cruciferae vegetables include broccoli, cauliflower, collards, and kale as well as cabbage and mustard greens. Brussels sprouts and rutabagas seem to be effective in protecting against certain forms of cancer (stomach and large intestine) and today's research is revealing other anticancer compounds in these vegetables.

OLIVE OIL

Olive oil is essential to Italian cooking and to Italian living. Traditionally, in Italian recipes, olive oil is used in greater amounts than I have chosen to use in this book. I include it because it adds a fruity flavor and because of the fact that it is considered a healthful oil—it is low in saturated fat and does not promote heart disease as has been shown in many studies of Mediterranean people and their eating habits and lifestyles. My main reason for decreasing the amount of olive oil in these recipes is simply this: each tablespoon of olive oil (or any other oil) has 120 calories. Remember to use extra-virgin or first-pressed olive oil because it is the least processed and has the most flavor. Don't be fooled by marketing slogans (such as light or light gold oils) because if it is not extra-virgin, more oil will be needed (meaning more calories) to get any real olive flavor. The first-pressed oils have not been heated and are free from chemical additives. If you choose not to use these olive oils, you may substitute canola oil as I have done in several recipes where the rich taste of olive oil is not necessarily needed. Canola oil is the market name for rapeseed oil which comes from rape seeds. Canola oil is lower in saturated fat than any other oil. It also contains more cholesterol-balancing monounsaturated fat than any oil except olive oil, and Omega-3 fatty acids which studies have found lower both cholesterol and triglycerides.

Important terms to remember in purchasing olive oil include:

- **Extra virgin olive oil:** the cold-pressed result of the first pressing of olives. Extra virgin olive oil is thought to be the finest and fruitiest of the olive oils. It is usually the most expensive.

- ***Fino* olive oil:** *fino* olive oil is the result of blending extra virgin and virgin olive oils.

- **Light olive oil:** "light" refers to the oil's color. It contains the same number of calories as regular olive oil but little of its classic flavor.

- **Olive oil:** once labeled pure olive oil, this oil is a combination of olive oil and virgin or extra virgin olive oils.

- **Virgin olive oil:** a first-pressed oil expressed from olives with a higher level of acidity than extra virgin oil.

GRATING CHEESES

Very hard grating cheeses such as Asiago, Pecorino, sapsago, or Parmesan are important to the fat-conscious cook, because these cheeses, grated finely and used sparingly, can go a long way as a seasoning.

Cheese, as it ages, loses moisture; the cheese becomes more dense in texture and more concentrated in flavor. Most of these grating cheeses come in large heavy wheels and are sold by the piece. The piece of cheese should be freshly grated, so try to avoid the temptation in the supermarkets to buy the already grated cheese in plastic or other containers. Some cognoscenti say it is okay to freeze these grating cheeses, but I don't like to freeze them because I believe they lose some flavor. Instead, wrap the piece of cheese tightly in plastic wrap and refrigerate it, grating it as needed and rewrapping for storage in the refrigerator until it is needed again. Often, shavings are suggested for use with a particular recipe instead of grating. This can be a lovely touch, tasty to be sure, but keep the shavings as thin as possible. The more popular types of these cheeses, most of which are now made in the United States, include:

- Asiago. This cheese is like Parmesan, but it is more granular and pungent in flavor.
- Parmesan. The real Parmesan comes from a restricted area around Parma, Italy, and it is marked Parmigiano-Reggiano. Other cheeses are called granas, which means grainy or granular cheese. Parmesan is made in the United States and other places outside Italy, notably Argentina. Italian Parmesan is straw-colored and has a flaky crystalline texture. The flavor is nutty. American varieties are not as nutty and are saltier.
- Romano. Often called Pecorino Romano, it is usually made from sheep's milk, and it too is made in Italy. Although it is saltier than Parmesan, it can be used in most of the same ways. It is also less expensive than Parmesan and widely available in the United States. I think that it is easier to grate than Parmesan.
- Sapsago. Made in Switzerland from skim milk, Sapsago has less than three grams of fat per ounce. It is flavored with a special kind of clover, so it is greenish in appearance. It is a hard cheese and is grated.

Because most recipes call for a moderate amount of cheese, I usually use Romano and Parmesan more than the other cheeses as a topping.

NUTRITIVE VALUES OF MOST CHEESES USED IN THIS BOOK

1 CUP LOW-FAT (1% MILK) COTTAGE CHEESE			
Calories	164	Total Fat	2 g
Protein	28 g	Saturated Fat	1.5 g
Carbohydrates	6 g	Cholesterol	10 mg
		Sodium	918 mg

Excellent source of calcium and riboflavin and provides thiamin and vitamin A.

1 OUNCE FONTINA			
Calories	110	Total Fat	9 g
Protein	7 g	Saturated Fat	5 g
Carbohydrates	1 g	Cholesterol	33 mg
		Sodium	513 mg

Excellent source of calcium, vitamin A, and some riboflavin.

1 OUNCE GORGONZOLA			
Calories	105	Total Fat	9 g
Protein	6 g	Saturated Fat	5 g
Carbohydrates	negligible	Cholesterol	33 mg
		Sodium	513 mg

Excellent source of calcium, vitamin A, phosphorous, and riboflavin.

1 OUNCE PART-SKIM MOZZARELLA			
Calories	72	Total Fat	5 g
Protein	7 g	Saturated Fat	3 g
Carbohydrates	negligible	Cholesterol	16 mg
		Sodium	132 mg

Excellent source of calcium and phosphorus and also provides vitamin A and riboflavin.

1 OUNCE HARD PARMESAN			
Calories	111	Total Fat	7 g
Protein	10 g	Saturated Fat	5 g
Carbohydrates	1 g	Cholesterol	19 mg
		Sodium	454 mg

Excellent source of calcium and phosphorus and provides riboflavin and vitamin A.

1 OUNCE PROVOLONE			
Calories	100	Total Fat	8 g
Protein	7 g	Saturated Fat	5 g
Carbohydrates	negligible	Cholesterol	35 mg
		Sodium	151 mg

Excellent source of calcium and phosphorus and provides riboflavin and vitamin A.

1 CUP PART-SKIM RICOTTA			
Calories	340	Total Fat	20 g
Protein	28 g	Saturated Fat	12 g
Carbohydrates	13 g	Cholesterol	76 mg
		Sodium	307 mg

Excellent source of calcium, phosphorus, riboflavin, and vitamin A.

1 OUNCE ROMANO			
Calories	110	Total Fat	8 g
Protein	9 g	Saturated Fat	5 g
Carbohydrates	1 g	Cholesterol	29 mg
		Sodium	340 mg

Excellent source of calcium and phosphorus and provides riboflavin and vitamin A.

Note: *1) Cheese does not contain fiber.*
2) One ounce of grated cheese is equal to six tablespoons.

LOW-FAT SUBSTITUTES FOR PASTA DISHES

	SUBSTITUTE	FOR REGULAR
Meat Products		
	Ground turkey or lean ground round	Ground beef
	Turkey bacon	Regular bacon
	Tuna packed in water	Tuna in oil
	Skinless chicken, turkey, etc.	Poultry with skin
Oils		
	Canola oil	Vegetable oil
	Reduced-fat margarine	Margarine
Dairy Products		
	Light cream cheese	Cream cheese
	Nonfat or 1% fat cottage cheese	Creamed cottage cheese
	Nonfat or low-fat sour cream	Sour cream
	Evaporated skim milk	Heavy cream
	Egg whites or egg substitutes	Whole eggs
	Part-skim mozzarella	Whole milk mozzarella
	Skim or 1% milk	Whole or 2%

A GLASS OF WINE

What about a glass of wine with pasta? A 4-ounce glass of red wine has 80 calories; white wine has 75 calories. Many studies show that one or two glasses of wine a day, especially if drunk at mealtimes, may lower the risk of heart disease. A few years ago, the media reported what became known as The French Paradox. This rather large report showed that although the French ate as much fat (and considerably more innards) than Americans, the French rate of heart attacks was only one third as high as that of Americans. The French consume 21 gallons of wine per year per person; Americans drink three gallons per year per person. Several theories are out there about wine's intrinsic health-benefiting properties. It's okay to have a glass or two with pasta, but remember that there is a negative side to consuming more than that amount.

CHAPTER 2
THE NEW LOW-FAT CLASSIC PASTAS

INTRODUCTION

Of the foreign dishes that make up so much of our national cuisine, few are as popular as those of the Italians. Grocery stores and supermarkets are filled with Italian-style products such as California plum tomatoes, Chicago prosciutto, and Wisconsin provolone. And now, most of the stores and markets stock the imported varieties of these foods. When thinking Italian food, the average American will think pasta and, more often than not, think of the classic dishes presented here.

Although there are hundreds of pasta preparations, several have become classics, such as *fettuccine Alfredo, lasagna alla Napoletana, cannelloni ragú Bolognese*, and *pasta primavera*, to mention a few. These classics are usually filled with lots of butter, cream, olive oil, rich cheese, and other high-fat ingredients; the fat culprits are either in the sauce or filling. A source of complex carbohydrates, pasta itself is low in sodium, fat, and calories. By itself, one-half cup of cooked plain pasta has only about 100 calories. In this chapter, where a number of popular classic pasta dishes are presented, the reduction of fat is achieved by either omitting or lowering the amount of butter, cream, and rich cheese; reducing portion size, and increasing the use of herbs and spices whenever possible so that flavor is preserved, and the dishes are tasty.

LINGUINE WITH RED CLAM SAUCE

MAKES 4 SERVINGS

Everyone loves linguine with clam sauce and here is my low-fat version of it. You can also make this with white clam sauce. See recipe for creamy white clam sauce (page 153).

- 1/2 pound linguine
- 1 teaspoon extra-virgin olive oil
- 1/3 cup finely chopped white onion
- 2 cloves garlic, minced
- 1 can (28 ounces) tomato puree
- 2 tablespoons tomato paste
- 1/3 cup dry red wine
- 1/4 teaspoon red pepper flakes
- 2 cans (each 6 1/2 ounces) chopped clams with their juice
- 4 teaspoons finely chopped flat parsley
- 4 tablespoons freshly grated Parmesan cheese, optional

❶ Cook the linguine according to package directions.

❷ While the linguine is cooking, heat oil in a large, nonstick skillet and sauté onions until they become transparent, 3 to 4 minutes. Add garlic and stir for 1 minute.

❸ Add the tomato puree, tomato paste, red wine, and pepper flakes. Bring to a boil, lower the heat and simmer, uncovered, 8 to 10 minutes, stirring several times.

❹ Add the clams and their juice and continue cooking until the clams are heated through, about 5 minutes. Meanwhile, drain the pasta and add to a large bowl. Add one half of the clam sauce, toss the pasta and distribute to four plates. Add more sauce to the top of each serving and garnish with the parsley. Pass the optional cheese.

Each serving		% of calories from fat	8
Calories	416	Total Fat	3.5 g
Protein	24 g	Saturated Fat	0.46 g
Carbohydrates	71 g	Cholesterol	33 mg
Dietary Fiber	9 g	Sodium	228 mg

BALSAMELLA SAUCE (WHITE SAUCE)

THE WONDERS OF GARLIC

When I was growing up, I was told that my grandfather's heavy consumption of garlic spared him from the Spanish flu epidemic of 1918. Several studies document the health benefits of garlic: they claim that it reduces blood pressure, clears bronchitis, and tones up the digestive system because of its inherent antiseptic properties.

Garlic, a member of the lily family, comes in several varieties: white, pink, and mauve. Cultivated since Egyptian times, the best garlic comes from warm climates. Purchase bulbs with firm cloves. Cut off any discoloration on a clove, or it will spoil the taste of your dish.

MAKES 10 SERVINGS OF 1/4 CUP

This sauce, so basic to many Italian dishes, is a cream sauce similar to the French Sauce *béchamel*. Few pasta dishes are quite as luxurious and opulent as a stuffed pasta immersed in a *ragú Bolognese* (see page 38), or a pasta masked with a nutmeg-flavored balsamella and gratinéed with a golden crust of freshly grated Parmesan cheese. The following recipe, however, is not as rich as the original classic, but it is tasty, smooth, and low in total and saturated fat. Compare this recipe to the original, which calls for 3 tablespoons each of butter and flour, 1/2 cup each of heavy cream and whole milk, and so on, to 1 cup of sauce. This sauce is never eaten by itself; when it is combined with other foods in a given dish, the amount of fat calories will be reduced.

3 cups 1% low-fat milk
3 cloves garlic, peeled and crushed
10 black peppercorns
2 small bay leaves
2 1/2 tablespoons margarine
1/3 cup all-purpose flour
pinch salt
freshly grated nutmeg

❶ Put the milk, garlic, peppercorns, and bay leaves in a saucepan over medium heat. Do not boil but let it reach the point where bubbles form around the inside edge of the pan. Cover, remove from the heat, and let stand 15 minutes. Strain and discard the solids.

❷ In a clean saucepan, melt the margarine, add the flour, and whisk for 2 minutes until blended. Do not scorch. Add the strained milk slowly and cook until thick enough to coat a spoon, about 5 minutes. Add salt and nutmeg.

Each serving		% of calories from fat 45	
Calories	73	Total Fat	3.7 g
Protein	3 g	Saturated Fat	1.2 g
Carbohydrates	7 g	Cholesterol	3 mg
Dietary Fiber	0.2 g	Sodium	66 mg

CANNELLONI FILLED WITH TURKEY AND THYME

MAKES 4 SERVINGS

This version omits tomato sauce; however, if you like, you may add 1 cup basic tomato sauce.

- 8 fresh pasta cannelloni, 5 x 5-inch squares, or crespelle (page 13), or packaged, dried cannelloni
- 2 cups balsamella sauce (page 26)
- 3/4 pound ground lean turkey
- 2 tablespoons finely chopped fresh thyme or 2 teaspoons dried
- 2 tablespoons finely chopped flat parsley
- 1/2 cup plus 2 tablespoons freshly grated Parmesan cheese
- 1 egg white, beaten

❶ Cook the fresh pasta, about 1 minute; then, add cold water to the pot to cease the cooking and to make it cold enough to withdraw the pasta by hand. Lay the pasta squares on clean cloth towels and pat them dry. If using packaged, dry cannelloni, cook according to the package directions.

❷ Combine 1 cup balsamella sauce, turkey, thyme, parsley, 1/2 cup Parmesan cheese, and egg white. Stir with a rubber spatula to mix well.

❸ Spoon the filling mixture over each cooked cannelloni or crespelle and fold into a cylinder. Or spoon the filling into the cooked, store-bought dried cannelloni shells. Arrange each one, seam side down, in a spray-oiled baking container about 9 x 13 x 1 or 2 inches. Spoon or pour the remaining balsamella over the pasta (add some tomato sauce here if you wish), topping with 2 tablespoons Parmesan cheese. Cover the dish with foil.

❹ Bake in a preheated 350°F oven 20 minutes. Uncover and bake 10 minutes longer, or until the cannelloni are heated through and bubbling hot.

Each serving		% of calories from fat 40	
Calories	264	Total Fat	11.8 g
Protein	19 g	Saturated Fat	4 g
Carbohydrates	20 g	Cholesterol	110 mg
Dietary Fiber	1 g	Sodium	314 mg

GROUND TURKEY

If the ground turkey has no nutritional analysis on the package, don't buy it. Unfortunately, some meat processors include fat and skin in the ground turkey so that the amount of saturated fat in the package may be greater than that in ground beef. However, if the package shows the nutritional analysis, you may decide it's sufficiently low-fat.

The best procedure to follow, however, is to buy fresh turkey breast, which comes packaged in many ways: tenders, cutlets, medallions, chunks, and so on. You can grind your own with any of these cuts and be assured that the fat grams will be significantly reduced. For example, one pound of ground turkey breast with no skin has less than five grams of fat. Compare that to 25 grams of fat, which I have seen on the nutritional analyses on ground turkey packages.

LOW-FAT TASTY MACARONI AND CHEESE

MAKES 4 TO 6 SERVINGS

2 cups skim milk
1/2 teaspoon hot sauce such as Louisiana or Tabasco
3 tablespoons all-purpose flour
2 cups (8 ounces) coarsely grated low-fat cheddar cheese
1/4 cup freshly grated Parmesan cheese
1/2 cup nonfat sour cream
1 cup thinly sliced fresh mushrooms
2 cloves garlic, minced
1/4 cup finely chopped chives
1/4 teaspoon finely ground fresh nutmeg
2 cups dried small macaroni, such as elbows, ditali, or tubetti, cooked
1/2 cup fresh bread crumbs

1. Put the milk, hot sauce, and flour in a medium saucepan and, over medium heat, whisk constantly to combine the ingredients. Whisk and cook until the sauce is thick enough to coat a spoon, about 5 minutes.

2. Add 1 1/2 cups of the cheddar cheese, Parmesan cheese, sour cream, mushrooms, garlic, chives, and nutmeg. Stir with a rubber spatula until the cheeses melt.

3. Add the cooked and drained pasta, fold with a rubber spatula, and transfer to a lightly oil-sprayed 1-1/2- to 2-quart baking dish.

4. Combine the bread crumbs with the remaining cheddar cheese and set aside.

5. Bake in a preheated 375°F oven for 25 minutes; do not cover. Add the bread crumb and cheese mixture to the top and cook 15 minutes longer to brown the top. Remove dish from the oven and let stand for several minutes before serving.

Each serving		% of calories from fat 14	
Calories	474	Total Fat	7.6 g
Protein	32 g	Saturated Fat	4 g
Carbohydrates	67 g	Cholesterol	19 mg
Dietary Fiber	3 g	Sodium	579 mg

LOW-FAT MARINARA SAUCE WITH ANCHOVIES FOR PASTA

MAKES 4 SERVINGS

This is a wonderful, full, tasty tomato sauce, called marinara because it is considered a fast sauce made by and for sailors (*marinario* in Italian means sailor). There are as many versions of this sauce as there are sailors. My father's family added wine, mushrooms, and anchovy fillets, and this is the way I've presented it here.

- 1 tablespoon extra-virgin olive oil
- 1 cup thinly sliced fresh button mushrooms
- 1 cup finely diced onion
- 1/3 cup finely diced red bell pepper
- 4 garlic cloves, minced
- 1 cup red wine
- 1/3 cup finely chopped flat parsley
- 1 teaspoon sugar
- 1 tablespoon each, chopped fresh basil and oregano or 1 teaspoon each, dried
- freshly ground black pepper
- 1 can (28 ounces) peeled Italian plum tomatoes with liquid, put through a food mill
- 3 flat anchovy fillets, drained, rinsed in cold water, and finely chopped, about 1 teaspoon

❶ In a large pot, heat oil, and sauté mushrooms, onions, and bell pepper until the onions appear translucent, about 5 minutes. Add garlic and sauté 1 minute longer.

❷ Add all the other ingredients except the anchovies, bring to a boil, lower the heat and simmer, covered, 30 minutes. Stir every 10 minutes. Add the anchovies during the last 10 minutes of cooking.

Each serving		% of calories from fat 24	
Calories	149	Total Fat	4 g
Protein	4 g	Saturated Fat	0.6 g
Carbohydrates	16 g	Cholesterol	3 mg
Dietary Fiber	3 g	Sodium	442 mg

PASTA PUTTANESCA

MAKES 4 TO 6 SERVINGS

This classic dish now becomes low fat. It originated in Naples in its red-light district and *puttanesca* means whore. The story goes that, because the sauce takes only 10 minutes to prepare and its ingredients are mostly affordable, it was served hurriedly to gentlemen callers. There is a lot of flavor here, and in or out of the bedroom, it is a sexy and enticing preparation.

1 tablespoon extra-virgin olive oil
3 large cloves garlic, minced
1 can (28 ounces) Italian plum tomatoes put through a food mill
1/4 cup thinly sliced cured green olives
1/4 cup finely chopped flat parsley
2 tablespoons finely chopped fresh oregano or 2 teaspoons dried
2 tablespoons capers, well drained
3 canned anchovies, dried and chopped or 2 teaspoons anchovy paste
1/2 teaspoon red pepper flakes
1/2 pound thin spaghetti

❶ Heat oil in a large skillet, and sauté garlic until lightly browned, 1 to 2 minutes. Add the tomatoes, olives, parsley, oregano, capers, anchovies, and red pepper flakes. Bring to a boil, lower the heat, and cook partially covered until the sauce thickens, about 10 minutes.

❷ Cook the pasta according to package directions. Drain and combine it with half of the sauce. Arrange on four to six plates, and add some of the remaining sauce to each. Garnish with more chopped parsley, oregano, or sliced olives.

Each serving		% of calories from fat	19
Calories	221	Total Fat	3.7 g
Protein	7 g	Saturated Fat	0.4 g
Carbohydrates	36 g	Cholesterol	2 mg
Dietary Fiber	5 g	Sodium	548 mg

THE NEW FETTUCCINE ALFREDO

MAKES 6 SERVINGS

The original dish was named after the founder of Alfredo's in Rome. When another Alfredo (Viazzi) had his Trattoria da Alfredo in New York's Greenwich Village, I used to enjoy tons of *fettuccine all' Alfredo*, which, to serve six, combined 1 1/2 pounds of fettuccine, 6 tablespoons butter, 1/3 pint heavy cream, 3 egg yolks, and 3/4 cup grated Parmesan cheese. It was delicious; but now I am very contented with this new version.

1 1/2 cups balsamella sauce (page 26)
1 1/2 cups freshly grated Parmesan cheese
3/4 pound fettuccine, cooked and drained
1/4 cup finely chopped flat parsley
freshly grated nutmeg and pepper

1. Heat the balsamella sauce in a large skillet but do not boil. Add 1 cup of the Parmesan cheese, and stir slowly and steadily until the cheese melts.

2. Put the cooked pasta in the skillet and, over low heat, toss until the pasta is coated. Arrange pasta on six individual plates, topping with chopped parsley, the remaining Parmesan cheese, and the nutmeg and pepper.

NEW TERMS FOR MILK

The government approved new terms for milk that you should know: Reduced fat milk (2% milk); Light milk (1% milk); Fat-free milk (skim milk). Also, remember that buttermilk is by its nature low-fat. It is made from fat-free milk.

Each serving		% of calories from fat 26	
Calories	410	Total Fat	12 g
Protein	21 g	Saturated Fat	6 g
Carbohydrates	53 g	Cholesterol	23 mg
Dietary Fiber	5 g	Sodium	539 mg

THE NEW CLASSIC NEAPOLITAN LASAGNA

RICOTTA

Some people think ricotta is not cheese because it is made from the whey left over from other cheese, such as mozzarella, Pecorino, and provolone. Ricotta is like cottage cheese, but perhaps more bland. Like cottage cheese, it is white and creamy. In Italy, it is an important ingredient in fillings for ravioli, lasagna, and cannelloni. Ricotta is also used in desserts, such as cannoli. Here, I use ricotta with other ingredients to make a delicious, low-fat lasagna.

MAKES 8 TO 10 SERVINGS

I used to make a lasagna for Mardi Gras, *lasagne di carnevale*, to serve eight to ten people. I used 1/2 cup butter, 1/3 cup olive oil, 1 pound each pork sausage and ground beef, 1/2 pound ground pork, 1 pound whole ricotta, 1 cup each grated Parmesan and Pecorino cheese, and 1/4 pound each mozzarella and fonduta cheese, plus other ingredients. That recipe would defy nutritional analysis. Now I make my lasagna this way and love it. I've allowed the 16 grams of total fat to stand (my general rule is 10 grams of total fat per serving, but this is a party dish to have with a glass of robust red wine).

3/4 pound lasagna (12 sheets)
1/2 pound Italian sausage meat
1 1/2 cups finely chopped onion
4 cloves garlic, minced
1/4 cup dry red wine
1 can (28 ounces) Italian-type plum tomatoes, put through a food mill
2 cups, about 1 1/2 pounds, non- or low-fat ricotta cheese
1 cup freshly grated Parmesan cheese
1 cup low-fat shredded mozzarella
1/3 cup finely chopped flat parsley
freshly ground pepper
2 egg whites
spray oil

❶ Cook the lasagna according to package directions. Remove the pasta, and lay the strips on cloth towels.

❷ Sauté the sausage in a large skillet for 10 minutes or until browned, stirring to break the meat apart. Drain sausage well, and clean the skillet with a paper towel. Return the sausage to the skillet, add the onion and the garlic, and sauté 5 minutes, stirring frequently.

Continued on next page

❸ Add the wine and the tomatoes, cook partially covered 10 minutes, stirring every few minutes.

❹ In a bowl, combine the ricotta, Parmesan cheese, mozzarella, parsley, pepper, and egg whites. Fold ingredients together with a rubber spatula to combine them.

❺ Spray oil on a lasagna baking dish or pan, about 9 x 13 x 2 inches, and spoon a little of the tomato sauce on the bottom of it, spreading the sauce with the back of a spoon. Arrange four sheets of lasagna in the pan (there will be a slight overlap of the strips). Add a third of the tomato sauce and half of the ricotta mixture.

❻ Arrange four more lasagna sheets, add a third of the remaining tomato sauce and the rest of the remaining ricotta mixture. Lay the four remaining pasta sheets on top and spread the remaining sauce over the pasta with the back of a spoon. Cover with foil, and bake in a preheated 350°F oven 20 minutes. Remove the foil, bake 10 minutes longer. Let stand 5 minutes or so before serving.

Each serving		% of calories from fat 38	
Calories	373	Total Fat	16 g
Protein	22 g	Saturated Fat	8 g
Carbohydrates	32 g	Cholesterol	46 mg
Dietary Fiber	2 g	Sodium	632 mg

PASTA E FAGIOLI (PASTA AND BEANS) WITH FIVE HERBS

MAKES 4 SERVINGS

This classic dish is very healthful, made healthier here because of the lower fat, and it is also very tasty. The unusual touch here is the addition of five herbs.

- 1 tablespoon extra-virgin olive oil
- 1 cup finely chopped onions
- 3/4 cup finely chopped carrots
- 5 tablespoons minced fresh herbs including basil, oregano, parsley, thyme, and rosemary; if dried, use 1 teaspoon each
- 3 cups low-sodium defatted chicken or vegetable broth
- 1 can (19 ounces) cannellini beans, drained and rinsed
- 1 cup dry pasta such as tubetti, elbows, etc., cooked and drained
- freshly ground pepper
- 4 tablespoons freshly grated Pecorino or Parmesan cheese
- grated carrot for additional garnish

❶ Heat oil over medium heat in a medium size soup pot. Add onions, carrots, and three fourths of the herbs. Sauté 2 or 3 minutes, stirring all the time.

❷ Add broth and beans, bring to a boil, lower the heat, and simmer, covered, 15 minutes.

❸ Cook the pasta according to the directions on the package. Do not add oil to the water. Drain the pasta and add cooked pasta and pepper to the soup pot. Simmer 5 minutes longer to develop the flavors. Serve in soup bowls and sprinkle the remaining herbs and the grated carrot into each bowl. Pass the cheese or add a tablespoon to each bowl, but do not cover the garnishment with it.

Each serving		% of calories from fat 22	
Calories	307	Total Fat	7.8 g
Protein	14 g	Saturated Fat	2.3 g
Carbohydrates	46 g	Cholesterol	10 mg
Dietary Fiber	8 g	Sodium	438 mg

WHITE KIDNEY BEANS

Grains are a tower of nutrients, and dried beans and other legumes are rich in protein, carbohydrates, potassium, iron, and B vitamins.

To cook dried beans from scratch, first, look over the beans for any foreign matter, put them in a large bowl, and then cover with water by two inches. Soak overnight, and drain before cooking.

To cook them, use three cups of fresh water for each cup of soaked, dried beans. Bring to a boil in a large pot, lower the heat, and simmer about one hour, or until the beans are tender but still hold their shape. Do not add salt; if you must, add a sprinkle after the beans are cooked. Salt toughens the beans if added before the beans are tender. One cup of dried beans will yield about two and one-half cups of cooked beans.

RAGÚ BOLOGNESE

MAKES 6 SERVINGS WITH 3/4 POUND OF PASTA

1 tablespoon extra-virgin olive oil
2 tablespoons finely chopped onions
2 tablespoons finely chopped celery
2 tablespoons finely chopped carrots
1/2 pound very lean ground beef chuck
salt
freshly ground black pepper
1 cup dry white wine
1/2 cup low-fat milk (1 percent)
freshly grated nutmeg or 1/4 teaspoon ground
3 cups canned Italian plum tomatoes with liquid, put through a food mill
1 teaspoon heavy cream
6 teaspoons freshly grated Parmesan cheese

1. In a large skillet, heat oil, and sauté onions for 2 minutes. Add celery and carrots, and cook for 3 minutes.

2. Add ground meat to the skillet, season with salt, if you wish, and a liberal amount of ground pepper. Cook 6 minutes over moderate heat, breaking up meat with a wooden spoon as it cooks. The meat should be a little pink. Add wine, turn up the heat, and cook until wine evaporates, 5 to 10 minutes.

3. Turn down the heat, add milk and nutmeg, and cook until the milk evaporates, about 5 minutes. Add tomatoes and simmer uncovered for 1 1/2 hours. Stir every 15 minutes.

4. Stir in cream, and toss half of the sauce with the cooked pasta. Add 3 teaspoons of the cheese, and toss the pasta to incorporate it. Serve pasta on a large platter or bowl or in individual servings, adding more sauce and topping with the remaining cheese.

Each serving (incl. pasta)		% of calories from fat 20	
Calories	346	Total Fat	7.7 g
Protein	17 g	Saturated Fat	2.5 g
Carbohydrates	43 g	Cholesterol	17 mg
Dietary Fiber	3 g	Sodium	323 mg

RIGATONI IN A CREAM SAUCE WITH SWEET ROASTED GARLIC

MAKES 4 SERVINGS

Serving pasta with roasted garlic is one of the newer classics. Although whole milk is used here, the end result is still low in fat: 5.1 grams of total fat and only 1 gram of saturated fat. This is a tasty dish.

- 1 large garlic bulb
- 1 tablespoon extra-virgin olive oil and a few drops more
- 1/2 cup nonfat sour cream
- 1/3 cup whole milk
- 1/3 cup finely chopped chives
- 2 tablespoons marsala wine
- 8 ounces rigatoni

1. Roast garlic bulb after slicing about 1/2 inch off the top of the bulb. Spoon 2 or 3 drops of oil over the exposed cut. Wrap carefully in foil and bake in a preheated oven at 350°F for 40 minutes. Cool a little, and squeeze each clove to release the tender, roasted pulp into a skillet.

2. Add sour cream, milk, chives, and marsala to the garlic in the skillet, and stir over medium heat until well combined, about 2 minutes.

3. Cook the rigatoni according to package directions. Drain pasta and transfer it to a bowl. Add remaining olive oil and stir well.

4. Add pasta to the skillet and toss over medium heat, uncovered, 1 to 2 minutes. Serve right away.

GARLIC AND EVIL SPIRITS

In India and China, garlic was credited with warding off evil spirits and curing all sorts of ills including broken bones, bronchitis, tuberculosis, and the common cold. Pliny, the Roman writer, praised garlic as a remedy for no less than 60 ailments. In many countries, it is an indispensable cooking ingredient. In the United States, more than 250 million pounds of it is consumed yearly.

Each serving		% of calories from fat	19
Calories	301	Total Fat	5 g
Protein	10 g	Saturated Fat	1 g
Carbohydrates	50 g	Cholesterol	3 mg
Dietary Fiber	2 g	Sodium	35 mg

ROME'S SPAGHETTINI ALLA TRASTEVERE

THE INIMITABLE BLACK PEPPERCORN

There are four mass-produced varieties, with that from the Malabar Coast (off India) having the finest flavor. The others are Lampong, Brazilian, and Sarawak. However, Tellicherry peppercorns are a notch above the Malabar; they are larger and more mature and have a more developed flavor. Tellicherry are not as mass produced as the other four. Of the other four, Malabar has the best taste. Tellicherry is considered the best tasting of the five.

MAKES 6 SERVINGS

The original recipe uses butter in which to cook the bacon or pancetta. It also uses more black pepper than is suggested here.

1 teaspoon extra-virgin olive oil
1/2 pound lean bacon or pancetta, thinly sliced crosswise
1 tablespoon grated black pepper
3/4 pound thin spaghetti, #9 or #10
1/2 cup freshly grated Romano cheese

1. In a large skillet, heat oil, and sauté bacon or pancetta until the pieces are crisp. Add pepper and toss well. Remove about half of the crisped bacon or pancetta to use later.

2. Cook the pasta according to package directions. Drain; add the cooked pasta to the skillet and toss well. Distribute to six individual plates, top each with the remaining bacon, and sprinkle cheese over each dish before serving.

Each serving		% of calories from fat 28	
Calories	353	Total Fat	11 g
Protein	16 g	Saturated Fat	3.7 g
Carbohydrates	46 g	Cholesterol	41 mg
Dietary Fiber	4 g	Sodium	598 mg

QUICK TOMATO PASTE SAUCE

MAKES 4 SERVINGS WITH 1/2 POUND OF PASTA

This is a really quick, tasty sauce and can be enhanced by adding one-third cup of chopped carrots cut in 1/4-inch cubes, adding them at the time you add the garlic.

2 tablespoons extra-virgin olive oil
2 cloves garlic, minced
2 tablespoons tomato paste
2 tablespoons each, chopped basil and parsley
1/2 teaspoon red pepper flakes or a liberal amount of black pepper

1. Heat the oil in a skillet, and sauté the garlic 1 minute. Add tomato paste and stir. Add 1/3 cup warm water and bring to a boil, dissolving tomato paste completely. Set aside.
2. Add basil, parsley, and pepper just before serving.

Each serving (incl. pasta)		% of calories from fat 23	
Calories	294	Total Fat	7.8 g
Protein	8.3 g	Saturated Fat	1 g
Carbohydrates	47 g	Cholesterol	0 mg
Dietary Fiber	5 g	Sodium	8 mg

PASTA PRIMAVERA

MAKES 6 SERVINGS

Pasta primavera is a favorite dish, but it is high in fat when made with butter and cream. You can make a delicious low-fat version (only 5.3 grams total fat and 2.7 grams saturated fat per serving), and here is the recipe for it. This is a wonderful combination of vegetables with pasta.

3 plum tomatoes, diced 1/2 inch
1 small eggplant (less than 1 pound), peeled and diced 1/4 inch, to make about 2 cups
2 small zucchini, 1x 6 inches each, trimmed and thinly sliced
1 small red, orange, or yellow bell pepper, seeded and diced 1/2 inch
1 large onion, peeled and diced 1/2 inch
4 cloves garlic, minced
3/4 cup low-sodium defatted chicken broth
3/4 cup low-sodium tomato juice
1/2 cup frozen peas
1/2 cup finely chopped fresh basil leaves
3/4 pound thin spaghetti
4 tablespoons Half and Half
1/2 cup freshly grated Parmesan cheese
1/2 cup finely chopped fresh parsley

1. Prepare tomatoes, eggplant, zucchini, peppers, onion, and garlic, and put them in a medium saucepan. Add broth and tomato juice. Bring to a boil, lower the heat, cover and simmer 10 minutes.

2. Add peas and basil, and cook 5 minutes, uncovered, to reduce the liquid.

3. While the vegetables are cooking, cook the spaghetti according to package directions. Drain the pasta and add it to the saucepan.

4. Add the Half and Half and the Parmesan cheese and toss well over low heat. Remove the saucepan and serve the pasta hot on individual plates. Garnish with parsley.

Each serving		% of calories from fat 14	
Calories	322	Total Fat	5 g
Protein	14 g	Saturated Fat	2.7 g
Carbohydrates	55 g	Cholesterol	11 mg
Dietary Fiber	7 g	Sodium	199 mg

VERMICELLI WITH FRESH PLUM TOMATOES AND BASIL

MAKES 4 SERVINGS

This sauce is at its best when the tomatoes are really red and ripe. The beauty of fresh basil with fresh tomatoes is most evident in this recipe.

- 2 tablespoons extra-virgin olive oil
- 3 large cloves garlic, minced
- 1 1/2 pounds ripe plum tomatoes, peeled, seeded and diced
- 1/2 pound dried vermicelli
- 1 cup loosely packed finely chopped basil leaves
- 4 tablespoons freshly grated Parmesan cheese
- freshly grated black pepper

❶ Heat oil in a large, nonstick skillet and sauté the garlic 1 minute, stirring most of the time.

❷ Carefully add tomatoes and simmer over medium heat 12 minutes until they thicken a little. Stir often.

❸ While tomatoes are simmering, cook vermicelli according to package directions. Drain the pasta and transfer it to the skillet. Add basil and toss well for 2 minutes to bring the pasta and the sauce together.

❹ Distribute to four plates, top with Parmesan cheese and a liberal amount of pepper, and serve right away.

Each serving		% of calories from fat 27	
Calories	356	Total Fat	10.5 g
Protein	12 g	Saturated Fat	2.4 g
Carbohydrates	54 g	Cholesterol	5 mg
Dietary Fiber	7 g	Sodium	134 mg

CHAPTER 3
JOYFUL AND HEALTHY PASTA SOUPS

INTRODUCTION

Some of the healthiest low-fat pasta foods can be found in soups—the old-fashioned ones, without butter or cream. Most of these soups include lots of vegetables and little or no meat and poultry and are cooked in one vessel that will conserve vitamins and minerals that would be drained otherwise.

Homemade defatted broths or low-sodium defatted store-bought ones form the basis of most of these soups. In fact, water can be used, and when cooked with vegetables, it makes its own extremely low-fat vegetable broth.

The variety of low-fat healthy soups is endless. The addition of pasta (complex carbohydrates) makes these soups a near-perfect food. Vegetables of all kinds, grains and legumes, and some meat and poultry, all add to this infinite variety. These soups can be made ahead and reheated. Because the addition of pasta thickens the soup, add the pasta just before you are ready to serve it. If pasta does thicken the soup too much, simply add more broth or water.

These soups are so good that I make enough of one soup to last at least two days, and I enjoy soup almost every day. It is the perfect lunch or early supper. I add a simple salad and a piece of bread, and I'm quite happy.

ANGEL HAIR PASTA SOUP WITH SPICY VEGETABLES

MAKES 4 TO 6 SERVINGS

This is an easy and lovely soup. Very thin strands of pasta add a lightness to the delicious mélange of vegetables. It is a very low-fat pasta soup.

- 2 tablespoons extra-virgin olive oil
- 2 large onions, peeled and diced
- 3 medium cloves garlic, minced
- 3 cups tomato juice
- 1 cup water
- 4 nests angel hair pasta (4 ounces)
- 1 can (8 ounces) ready-to-use tomatoes with their juice
- 1/2 cup corn kernels, fresh or frozen
- 1 celery heart, thinly sliced
- 1 medium red bell pepper, cored, seeded, ribs removed, and diced
- 1 tablespoon finely chopped fresh oregano or 2 teaspoons dried
- 1/2 teaspoon each, curry and cumin powder and red pepper flakes
- 4 to 6 teaspoons freshly grated Pecorino cheese

❶ In a large soup pot, heat oil, and sauté onions until they appear limp, about 3 minutes. Stir in garlic and cook 1 minute longer.

❷ Add all other ingredients except the Pecorino cheese. Bring to a boil, lower the heat, and simmer, covered, 30 minutes.

❸ Serve in warmed soup bowls with a topping of grated cheese.

Each serving		% of calories from fat 30	
Calories	165	Total Fat	5.7 g
Protein	5 g	Saturated Fat	0.9 g
Carbohydrates	26 g	Cholesterol	1 mg
Dietary Fiber	3 g	Sodium	582 mg

ADDING PASTA TO SOUP

Pasta may be cooked separately and then added to the soup pot. Some recipes call for this procedure. In such cases, it is best to cook the pasta according to package directions and add it to the soup just before serving time.

Often, pasta is added to the soup pot and cooked with the other ingredients; usually, the pasta is one of the last ingredients to add to the soup.

In either case, pasta in soup, if left for any amount of time, will absorb the liquid, and the broth will thicken considerably; it will not resemble soup. It will look more like a stew. If this happens to you, add some water or low-sodium, defatted broth to thin the soup to achieve the consistency you wish.

BEEF BROTH

FLAT-LEAF PARSLEY IS TASTIER THAN CURLY

One of the most common herbs, flat-leaf parsley, sometimes called Italian parsley, only recently has become popular in this country. The curly variety of parsley took center stage mostly because it was used as a garnish.

With the food revolution came the wider use of flat-leaf parsley, considered by food connoisseurs to have more flavor. Its origin is probably Mediterranean because it was used by the Greeks and Romans. Use it as a garnish, but surely use it as a seasoning. One ounce of parsley provides 43 percent of the RDA of vitamin C, and 18 percent of the RDA of iron for men and 12 percent for women.

MAKES ABOUT 2 QUARTS

2 1/2 pounds beef and veal bones
3 quarts water
1 pound lean beef (top round steak from the hind leg or beef shank), cut in 3 pieces
1 large onion, quartered
1 large carrot, cut into 4 pieces
1 large celery rib with leaves, cut into 4 pieces
1 small fresh tomato, cored and cut in half, or 1 canned plum tomato
3 sprigs fresh flat-leaf parsley

1. Put the bones in a very large soup pot with enough warm water to cover. Bring to a boil over high heat, uncovered, and remove the pot from the heat. Discard the water and rinse the bones and the pot. Return the bones to the pot.

2. Add meat pieces and 3 quarts of water. Bring to a boil over high heat. Add the remaining ingredients. When the boil is reached again, lower the heat to get a slow, steady simmer, and cook 3 hours, covered. It is important to keep the broth at a simmer; if it boils, it will become cloudy.

3. Strain broth through a fine sieve or several layers of cheesecloth. Discard all but the broth. Refrigerate the broth overnight and remove and discard the congealed fat on top, or use a fat skimmer. Use immediately, refrigerate for several days, or freeze for several months. If you refrigerate for a few days, be sure to bring the broth to the boil before using.

Each serving		% of calories from fat	0
Calories	147	Total Fat	0 g
Protein	39 g	Saturated Fat	0 g
Carbohydrates	0 g	Cholesterol	0 mg
Dietary Fiber	0 g	Sodium	589 mg

BEEF CONSOMMÉ

MAKES ABOUT 4 CUPS

This is a richer version than the previous beef broth. Use it as a broth for stuffed pasta soups or wherever you wish a stronger broth.

1 piece lean beef (do not cut up), about 2 pounds
1 large carrot, sliced in 3 pieces
1 medium onion, with peel on, cut in 6 pieces
1 large celery rib with leaves, cut into 2 pieces
8 cups water
1 teaspoon salt

❶ Put the piece of beef in a large soup pot and add all other ingredients. Cook over medium heat, uncovered, to the boiling point. Skim off the froth, lower the heat, cover the pot, and cook at a slow, steady simmer until the meat has rendered its goodness, about 5 1/2 hours. Check the water level every hour and, if necessary, add more.

❷ Strain through a fine sieve or two layers of cheesecloth, and let the broth cool long enough to solidify the fat (this usually takes overnight in the refrigerator). Remove and discard the fat.

Each serving		% of calories from fat 32	
Calories	307	Total Fat	11 g
Protein	38 g	Saturated Fat	3 g
Carbohydrates	8 g	Cholesterol	0 mg
Dietary Fiber	0 g	Sodium	576 mg

CANNELLINI, SPINACH, AND PASTA SOUP

MAKES 8 SERVINGS

This robust, healthy soup can be made ahead, even the day before and reheated.

- 3 tablespoons extra-virgin olive oil
- 1 large onion, diced 1/2 inch
- 1 medium red bell pepper, diced 1/2 inch
- 4 large cloves garlic, minced
- 1 tablespoon dried basil
- 1 1/2 pounds fresh spinach, rinsed, large stems removed and sliced 1/2 inch
- 6 cups water
- 1/2 teaspoon hot pepper sauce
- 1 can (16 ounces) cannellini beans, drained
- 1/2 pound small elbow pasta
- 1/2 cup freshly grated Pecorino cheese

❶ Heat oil in a soup pot, and sauté onion and bell pepper 5 minutes, or until lightly browned. Stir in garlic and basil, and cook 1 minute longer.

❷ Add spinach and cook, covered, 5 minutes.

❸ Add water and hot pepper sauce. Bring to a boil, add beans, lower the heat, and simmer 10 minutes or until beans are thoroughly heated.

❹ Meanwhile, cook the pasta according to package directions. Drain pasta and stir it into the soup.

❺ Serve in warmed bowls topped with the cheese.

Each serving		% of calories from fat 27	
Calories	251	Total Fat	7.8 g
Protein	10 g	Saturated Fat	1.8 g
Carbohydrates	36 g	Cholesterol	7 mg
Dietary Fiber	6 g	Sodium	217 mg

BROCCOLI AND PASTA SOUP

MAKES 6 SERVINGS

This is a substantial, rustic tasty soup appreciated by people who live in Rome. It should be somewhat spicy hot; if the half dried chili pepper isn't enough, add a little more or some red pepper flakes. The pasta is cooked separately and the water it cooks in should be reserved, to thin the soup at the end of the preparation. But remember, this is not too liquid a soup.

1 bunch fresh broccoli
1/4 cup finely chopped pancetta or bacon
2 medium cloves garlic, minced
1/2 dried chili pepper (the tip end)
1/2 cup dry white wine
2 cups water
1/2 pound dry small pasta
2 tablespoons extra-virgin olive oil
salt, if needed
6 tablespoons freshly grated Pecorino cheese

❶ Trim the broccoli spears, and cut into 1-inch florets. Peel the edible parts of the stems and thinly slice. Put all in a large bowl, add water to cover, and set aside.

❷ Sauté pancetta or bacon in a large soup pot, and let it crisp over medium heat, about 5 minutes. Add garlic and chili pepper, stir well, and cook 1 minute.

❸ Drain the broccoli pieces, and add them to the soup pot with wine. When wine has evaporated, add water. Cover the pan, lower the heat, and cook broccoli until tender, about 10 minutes.

❹ While broccoli is cooking, cook pasta according to package directions. Drain the pasta, reserving the cooking liquid, and put pasta in a bowl. Stir in olive oil, and spoon the pasta into the soup pot. If the soup seems too thick for your taste, do not add all the pasta. Add some of the reserved cooking liquid, a half cup at a time. Stir well and add more liquid, if needed. Check the salt seasoning, but don't add too much because the soup will be topped with Pecorino cheese.

Each serving		% of calories from fat 31	
Calories	279	Total Fat	10 g
Protein	10 g	Saturated Fat	3 g
Carbohydrates	34 g	Cholesterol	12 mg
Dietary Fiber	2 g	Sodium	174 mg

CHICKPEA, TOMATO, AND PASTA SOUP WITH THYME

MAKES 6 TO 8 SERVINGS

This is a wonderful combination of flavors and a real hearty low-fat soup. We had it for supper one night a week when I was growing up.

- 2 tablespoons extra-virgin olive oil
- 2 medium onions, thinly sliced
- 1/2 teaspoon dried thyme
- 2 large cloves garlic, minced
- 2 cans (1 pound each) plum tomatoes, seeded and chopped
- 4 cups cooked pasta (elbows, small shells, or other small pasta)
- 6 cups homemade beef broth, page 48, or 3 cups low-sodium canned plus 3 cups water
- 2 cans (20 ounces each) chickpeas, drained and rinsed well
- freshly ground black pepper
- 1/2 cup freshly grated Pecorino cheese

1. Heat oil in a large soup pot. Add onions and thyme and sauté until onions soften, about 5 minutes.

2. Add the garlic and tomatoes, and cook, uncovered, over low to medium heat, 15 minutes.

3. Cook the pasta according to package directions, drain, and set aside.

4. Add the broth and the chickpeas to the tomatoes, and cook, partially covered, over medium heat, 15 minutes. Add the pasta and pepper to taste, and cook just to heat the pasta through.

5. Serve with cheese.

Each serving		% of calories from fat 24	
Calories	373	Total Fat	10 g
Protein	18 g	Saturated Fat	2.4 g
Carbohydrates	55 g	Cholesterol	9 mg
Dietary Fiber	7 g	Sodium	398 mg

THYME IS VIBRANT

Thyme is one of the best herbs to cook with. It is especially good with poultry and pork. Thyme is very popular in the south, where it is used in pea soup with ham (not a low-fat dish), as well as other preparations. French thyme has a smoky-green color, and some think that it has a superior flavor.

Other varieties of thyme include lemon, orange, and caraway, all with different flavors. The plant is small and bushy, with dark-green leaves and purple flowers. This is a versatile herb, but use it with discretion. It also is good with fish and vegetables, and it holds a special place in fillings for many stuffed pastas.

PASTA SOUP WITH ESCAROLE AND PEAS

MAKES 6 SERVINGS

This is one of the easiest soups to make. Some people add a dollop of butter just before serving, but that is up to you. You can use young dandelions, curly endive, or spinach instead of the escarole, using one to one and a half pounds of greens.

1 tablespoon extra-virgin olive oil
1 large onion, diced into 1/2-inch pieces
freshly ground black pepper
8 cups homemade chicken broth (page 59) or 4 cups low-sodium canned broth plus 4 cups water
1 large head escarole, trimmed, rinsed well, and shredded
5 ounces frozen green peas, thawed
1 cup uncooked small pasta
6 teaspoons freshly grated Pecorino or Asiago cheese

❶ Heat the oil in a large soup pot and cook the onion until it turns soft, about 4 minutes (do not brown it). Liberally add black pepper.

❷ Add the broth, escarole, and the peas. Bring to a boil. Lower the heat to get a slow, steady simmer, and cook, covered, 15 minutes.

❸ Stir in the pasta and cook, uncovered, until the pasta is tender, 10 to 15 minutes. Serve in warm bowls with cheese.

Each serving		% of calories from fat 29	
Calories	142	Total Fat	4.7 g
Protein	7 g	Saturated Fat	1.4 g
Carbohydrates	20 g	Cholesterol	5 mg
Dietary Fiber	5 g	Sodium	143 mg

CURRIED SPINACH SOUP WITH ALPHABET PASTA

MAKES 4 SERVINGS

I like curried soups, and I know you'll enjoy this one. Curry and ginger are not strangers to Italian cooking, especially in the south. Waverley Root, a food writer, noted that ginger and other spices were used in southern Italian cooking ever since the spice routes to Italy were established hundreds of years ago.

1 tablespoon extra-virgin olive oil
2 tablespoons reduced-fat chicken broth
1 large onion, diced 1/2 inch
3 large cloves garlic, minced
1 teaspoon curry powder
1/4 cup dry white wine
4 cups water
1 tablespoon chicken broth granules
1/2 pound fresh spinach, rinsed well, large stems removed, and coarsely chopped
freshly ground black pepper
1/3 cup alphabet pasta
2 cups 1 percent milk
salt

❶ Heat oil and 2 tablespoons of broth in a soup pot and sauté onion until soft, 3 minutes. Stir in garlic and cook 1 minute. Add the curry and stir 1 minute over medium heat.

❷ Add the wine, water, chicken granules, spinach, and a liberal amount of pepper. Bring to boil, lower the heat, and simmer, covered, 5 minutes. Transfer to the bowl of a processor and puree half of the mixture at a time.

❸ Return the soup to the pan in which it cooked, bring it to a boil, add the pasta, and cook 6 minutes, stirring often. Add the milk, bring to a simmer, test for seasoning and add a pinch of salt if necessary. Serve in warmed bowls.

Each serving		% of calories from fat 25	
Calories	174	Total Fat	5 g
Protein	8 g	Saturated Fat	1.3 g
Carbohydrates	22 g	Cholesterol	5 mg
Dietary Fiber	3 g	Sodium	385 mg

FARFALLE PASTA AND PARMESAN SOUP

MAKES 6 TO 8 SERVINGS

Farfalle is a popular bow-tie shaped pasta available almost anywhere. When they are homemade for soup, they are cut into smaller butterflies. The pasta can be easily homemade for soup or other preparations.

2 1/4 cups all-purpose flour
salt
3 eggs, beaten
1/2 cup freshly grated Parmesan cheese
5 cups each, homemade beef and chicken broths, (pages 48 and 59) or 2 1/2 cups each, low-sodium, defatted beef and chicken broths and 5 cups water

❶ Sift flour with salt onto a flat work surface. Make a well in the center. Add eggs and Parmesan to the well and mix together to form a smooth dough. Flatten the dough either with the palms of your hands or with a rolling pin and roll the dough out to make a thin sheet, about 1/8 inch thick. Using a tooth-edged ravioli cutter, cut the pasta sheet into 1 1/2-inch strips then into 3/4-inch pieces (medium bows). Pinch each piece (3/4 x 1 1/2 inches) in the middle to form a butterfly shape. If you prefer smaller pieces of pasta, cut the strips into 1/2 by 1 inch (small bows), still pinching in the center of each piece. This will give you small, medium, or larger farfalle, but make only 1 size for the soup.

❷ Bring broth to boil in a large soup pot, add pasta, and cook until they rise to the top and are cooked, about 7 minutes.

Each serving		% of calories from fat 18	
Calories	245	Total Fat	5 g
Protein	13 g	Saturated Fat	2 g
Carbohydrates	37 g	Cholesterol	112 mg
Dietary Fiber	2 g	Sodium	186 mg

MALFATTINI IN BROTH, BOLOGNA STYLE

MAKES 8 SERVINGS

This dough is fairly solid, formed into a ball, left to dry, and then made into pasta bits the size of rice grains, and then cooked in broth. It is a famous and popular dish in Romagna—a flat land in Italy where the Po flows. (The area is so flat that the ancient Etruscan town of Marzabotta outside Bologna had street grids even before the Romans.) The cuisine benefits from the richness of the Po valley where durum wheat is grown to make pasta so flavorful and so delicious *in brodo.*

2 1/2 cups flour
3 eggs
8 cups homemade beef broth (see page 48) or 4 cups canned plus 4 cups water
3/4 cup freshly grated Parmesan cheese
1/4 cup finely chopped flat-leaf parsley

❶ Make the dough by mixing the flour and egg, and form a ball. Dust with flour, and leave the dough to dry on a counter top, loosely covered, 2 hours.

❷ Slice the dough ball into 1/2-inch-thick slices and let them dry 1/2 hour longer.

❸ Using either a mezzaluna or a sharp knife, cut the dough pieces to resemble grains of rice. You will need to add small amounts of flour to keep the pasta dry and to ease the cutting. (Toss the pasta pieces with some flour every minute or so of cutting but use as little flour as possible.) Let dry, about 1 hour.

❹ Heat broth in a medium soup pot and bring to a boil. Lower the heat to get a slow, steady simmer.

❺ Add pasta to the broth and cook until tender, about 5 minutes. Sprinkle parsley into each bowl and serve with Parmesan cheese.

Note: This pasta may be made ahead and frozen. Spread the pasta grains on a lightly floured cookie pan with a rim (be sure it fits into your freezer), and cover with freezer wrap.

Each serving		% of calories from fat 26	
Calories	238	Total Fat	7 g
Protein	13 g	Saturated Fat	3.5 g
Carbohydrates	32 g	Cholesterol	92 mg
Dietary Fiber	2 g	Sodium	310 mg

MOM'S CHICKEN BROTH

MAKES ABOUT 2 QUARTS

Good broth always simmered in big pots on stoves in our family kitchens. Any soup bone put into the soup should be cracked, and parsley stems, not parsley leaves, should be used. In addition to chicken parts, my mother always added a cracked veal bone. Here is her recipe.

3 pounds chicken parts (wings, necks, gizzards, backs, and other bones)
1 pound veal marrow bone, cracked
3 quarts water
1 leek, including green part, washed carefully and coarsely chopped
1 large carrot, cut into 1/2-inch slices
6 parsley stems, cut into 1-inch pieces
2 sprigs fresh thyme or 1 teaspoon dried
12 peppercorns
1 teaspoon salt

1. Combine chicken parts, veal bones, and water in a very large soup pot, and bring to a boil over medium high heat, uncovered. Skim off foam, about 10 minutes.

2. Add all other ingredients, and bring broth to a boil again over medium high heat, uncovered.

3. Lower heat, to get a slow, steady simmer. Cook, partially covered, for at least 2 hours. Strain, refrigerate, and defat. Use immediately or store in the refrigerator for up to 3 days or freeze for several months.

CANNED BROTHS

A problem of legitimate health concern has to do with the high amount of sodium in canned broth and more so in bouillon cubes. Grocery shops and supermarkets carry low-sodium broths (and these are the ones you should use), and they may be used full strength. If you do not plan to use low-sodium broth, it is suggested that regular canned broth be combined with water in equal amounts for two reasons: (1) to reduce the amount of sodium and (2) to approximate the gentler quality of Italian broths. Remember, however, that homemade broths are easy to make, freeze well, and are always on hand for soup making.

Fat-free chicken broth: one cup			
Calories	30	Total Fat	0 g
Protein	6 g	Saturated Fat	0 g
Carbohydrates	0 g	Cholesterol	0 mg
Dietary Fiber	0 g	Sodium	170 mg

QUADRUCCI WITH LIMA BEANS IN CHICKEN BROTH

MAKES 8 SERVINGS

Quadrucci are little squares of pasta. You can make your own by cutting strings of freshly made fettuccine (or store-bought fresh in dairy counters) into squares. You can find them as dried pasta in boxes in most supermarket pasta sections.

- 1 tablespoon extra-virgin olive oil
- 1 ounce pancetta, prosciutto, or bacon, finely chopped
- 1 small onion, finely chopped
- 1 small carrot, finely chopped
- 1 medium celery rib, finely chopped
- 1 package (10 ounces) frozen lima beans or 1 can (14 ounces), drained and rinsed
- 2 1/2 quarts homemade chicken broth (page 59), or low-sodium canned broth
- 1/2 pound quadrucci or similar pasta
- 3/4 cup freshly grated Parmesan cheese
- 2 tablespoons finely chopped fresh flat-leaf parsley

1. Heat oil in a large soup pot, and cook the pancetta, onion, carrot, and celery until lightly browned, about 5 minutes. Add lima beans and warmed broth. Bring to a boil, lower the heat to get a slow, steady simmer, and cook, covered, 10 minutes.

2. Turn up the heat, add the pasta, and cook, uncovered, until the pasta is done. Remember that fresh pasta will cook in a couple of minutes; dried pasta may take about 10 minutes.

3. When the pasta is cooked, remove the pan from the heat. Slowly sprinkle the cheese into the soup, a little at a time. Add the parsley, stir well, and serve the soup hot.

Each serving		% of calories from fat 28	
Calories	258	Total Fat	8.3 g
Protein	15 g	Saturated Fat	3.6 g
Carbohydrates	34 g	Cholesterol	15 mg
Dietary Fiber	5 g	Sodium	350 mg

PASTA AND CHICKPEA SOUP

DRIED CHICKPEAS

If you wish to use dried chickpeas, use one-half pound, and soak them overnight in water to cover. Transfer the chickpeas and their water to a large soup pot, and add two peeled garlic cloves tied in a small cheesecloth packet (for easy removal later) and some salt and pepper. Bring to a boil, lower the heat to get a slow, steady simmer, and cook, covered, until they are tender, about one and a half hours. They will absorb water. Drain the chickpeas, reserving the cooking liquid. Combine two quarts of hot water and the cooked chickpeas without the garlic packet.

MAKES 8 SERVINGS

- 1 tablespoon extra-virgin olive oil
- 1/4 cup finely chopped pancetta or bacon
- 3 large cloves garlic, minced
- 2 tablespoons tomato paste
- 6 chopped anchovy fillets, soaked in water for 30 minutes, drained and dried
- 1 large sprig fresh rosemary
- 1 1/2 cans (20 ounces) chickpeas, drained and rinsed well
- 2 quarts almost boiling water
- 1/2 pound small pasta (small elbows, tubetti, etc.)
- salt
- freshly ground black pepper
- 1/2 cup freshly grated Romano cheese, optional

1. Heat oil in a large soup pot and cook pancetta or bacon over medium heat until it crisps, about 5 minutes. Add garlic, stir well, and cook 1 minute.

2. Add tomato paste, anchovies, rosemary, half of the chickpeas, and the almost boiling water (the water should be very h to receive the pasta). Bring to a boil over medium high heat; lower the heat to get a slow, steady simmer.

3. Add the pasta and cook, uncovered, until the pasta is tender, about 10 minutes. While the pasta is cooking, puree th other half of the chickpeas, and add to the soup at any point o cooking except the last few minutes because the pureed chick peas need to be heated through. Taste soup before adding any salt.

4. Remove the rosemary sprig, spoon the soup into warm bowls, and sprinkle liberally with pepper. Add grated cheese, if you wish.

Each serving		% of calories from fat 24	
Calories	234	Total Fat	6.3 g
Protein	9 g	Saturated Fat	1.2 g
Carbohydrates	35 g	Cholesterol	7 mg
Dietary Fiber	5 g	Sodium	348 mg

SPAGHETTINI IN FISH BROTH

MAKES 6 SERVINGS

Pasta is not always cooked in meat and poultry broths. It is also delicious in fish broths. Here's an easy dish and a good-tasting one. The presentation is unusual.

For the broth:

3 pounds haddock or other white fish in the markets, cleaned and rinsed well
1 medium onion, coarsely chopped
1 celery rib, sliced
1 bay leaf
3 quarts water
salt

For the soup:

2 tablespoons extra-virgin olive oil
1 large clove garlic, halved
2 1/2 tablespoons tomato puree
6 cups fish broth
1/2 pound spaghettini, cut in thirds
1 1/2 teaspoons anchovy paste
1/4 cup finely chopped fresh flat-leaf parsley
juice of 1 lemon

❶ To make the broth, put fish, onion, celery, bay leaf, and the water in a large soup pot. Bring to a boil, and lower the heat to get a slow, steady simmer. Add some salt, and cook, covered, 30 minutes. Drain and reserve the broth. Set aside 6 cups and reserve or freeze the remainder for another use. Pick the white meat off the fish, without bones, and place in a bowl. Set aside.

Continued on next page

❷ To make the soup, heat the oil in a large soup pot, add the garlic halves, and cook over medium heat until they turn golden. Remove the garlic and discard. Add the tomato puree and cook 2 minutes. Add the fish broth, turn up the heat, and bring to a boil.

❸ Stir in pasta and cook until tender, about 10 minutes, stirring frequently. Stir in anchovy paste and most of the parsley.

❹ To serve, spoon pasta and broth into warm bowls. Toss the reserved white fish in the lemon juice with the remaining parsley. Spoon some of the fish mixture into the center of each bowl.

Each serving		% of calories from fat 16	
Calories	433	Total Fat	8 g
Protein	55 g	Saturated Fat	1 g
Carbohydrates	34 g	Cholesterol	143 mg
Dietary Fiber	2 g	Sodium	278 mg

SPINACH, FENNEL, AND PASTINA SOUP

MAKES 4 TO 6 SERVINGS

Fresh fennel adds a freshness to this soup and is the secret ingredient. It is a thick and hearty soup and should be served warm.

1 tablespoon extra-virgin olive oil
3 large cloves garlic, minced
1 10-ounce package fresh spinach, stemmed, rinsed, and coarsely sliced
spray oil
1 medium onion, diced 1/2 inch
1 large fresh fennel bulb, trimmed and diced 1/2 inch
2 to 3 cups low-sodium defatted chicken broth
1/2 cup 1 percent milk
1/3 cup nonfat plain yogurt
1/2 cup uncooked pastina, cooked and drained
1 tablespoon fresh lemon juice
freshly ground black pepper
1/4 cup finely chopped chives

❶ Heat oil in a soup pot and sauté garlic 1 minute. Add the spinach, toss well, cover the pan, and steam 5 minutes. Set aside.

❷ Spray oil a large nonstick skillet and put it over medium heat. Add onion and sauté 5 minutes, until onion is soft. Add fennel, and sauté until lightly browned, about 8 minutes. Add 1/2 cup of broth, lower the heat, and cook until the fennel is tender. Transfer to the bowl of a processor adding the spinach at the same time. Pulse until pureed. Transfer to the soup pot.

❸ Add 2 cups of broth, milk, and yogurt. Heat over medium heat. Add the cooked pastina, lemon juice, and a liberal amount of pepper. If you want a thinner soup, add more warmed broth. Serve in warm bowls adding a sprinkle of chopped chives.

Each serving		% of calories from fat 28	
Calories	128	Total Fat	4 g
Protein	6 g	Saturated Fat	1 g
Carbohydrates	19 g	Cholesterol	3 mg
Dietary Fiber	0.4 g	Sodium	105 mg

WINTER SOUP OF PASTA AND LEEKS

MAKES 6 TO 8 SERVINGS

This is a hot, satisfying soup that helps keep us comfortable in winter. Leeks and dried mushrooms make a tasty, heart-warming, and low-fat soup.

2 quarts water
2 medium leeks, carefully rinsed and thinly sliced
2 large cloves garlic, minced
1 cup bread crumbs from stale bread
1 medium onion, diced into 1/2 inch pieces
1/4 cup dried porcini mushrooms, soaked in white wine or warm water, strained, reserving liquid, and finely chopped
1 tablespoon unsalted butter
salt
freshly ground black pepper
1/2 pound uncooked small pasta
1/4 pound fontina cheese cut into small pieces

1. Put the water in a large soup pot and add the leeks, garlic, bread crumbs, onion, mushrooms, and butter. Strain the mushroom liquid through cheesecloth and add it to the soup pot. Bring to a boil, lower the heat to get a slow, steady simmer, and cook, covered, 30 minutes.

2. Add the pasta, and cook, uncovered, until the pasta is tender, about 10 minutes.

3. Just before serving, add the cheese, stir well, and spoon into warm bowls.

Each serving		% of calories from fat 24	
Calories	364	Total Fat	9.8 g
Protein	15 g	Saturated Fat	5 g
Carbohydrates	54 g	Cholesterol	27 mg
Dietary Fiber	4 g	Sodium	315 mg

SWISS CHARD AND PASTA SOUP

RICH, COMPLEX, AROMATIC SOY SAUCE

Soy sauce has become so popular in this country that it can be found in most supermarkets and small groceries. When I buy it, I look for soy sauce that is naturally brewed and aged, to ensure full flavor. Some soy sauces are made with caramel coloring and hydrolyzed vegetable protein, but they are not as flavorful as those that are naturally brewed. Use low-sodium soy sauce because it will have about 50 percent less sodium than the others.

MAKES 4 TO 6 SERVINGS

A healthful cookbook will include Swiss chard, a vegetable that more of us should enjoy.

- 3/4 pound fresh Swiss chard, trimmed and rinsed thoroughly
- 1 tablespoon extra-virgin olive oil
- 2 small zucchini, each 1 x 6 inches, ends removed and diced 1/2 inch
- 3 large cloves garlic, minced
- 6 cups water
- 1 tablespoon low-sodium soy sauce
- 1 tablespoon chicken broth granules
- 1/2 teaspoon red pepper flakes
- 1 cup small elbows or ditalini
- 2 ounces egg substitute
- 4 to 6 teaspoons freshly grated Parmesan cheese

❶ Snip the leaves off the stems of the Swiss chard and thinly slice the stems. Coarsely chop the leaves. Together, you should have about 2 1/2 cups of chard.

❷ Heat oil in a soup pot. Sauté chard and zucchini 4 minutes, stirring frequently. Stir in garlic and cook 1 minute longer.

❸ Add water, soy sauce, chicken granules, and red pepper flakes. Bring to boil, lower the heat, and simmer 5 minutes.

❹ Add pasta and cook according to package directions. Add the egg substitute to the hot soup, stirring all the time. It will solidify and form ribbons as soon as it is in the soup. Remove from the heat.

❺ Serve in warmed bowls, and add some Parmesan cheese to each.

Each serving		% of calories from fat 25	
Calories	124	Total Fat	3.6 g
Protein	6 g	Saturated Fat	0.7 g
Carbohydrates	17 g	Cholesterol	1 mg
Dietary Fiber	2 g	Sodium	439 mg

TURKEY SOUP WITH ORECCHIETTE "LITTLE EARS" AND FRESH SPINACH

MAKES 6 TO 8 SERVINGS

This is a good soup with lots of healthful things in it. It is thick and may be served as a main course.

2 tablespoons extra-virgin olive oil
1 large onion, peeled and chopped
2 large cloves garlic, minced
2 medium celery ribs, rinsed and thinly sliced
2 medium carrots, pared and thinly sliced
1 large green pepper, cored, seeded, ribs removed and diced 1/2 inch
1/4 cup finely chopped flat parsley
2 quarts low-sodium, defatted chicken broth
2 cups orecchiette ("little ears") pasta
2 cups diced cooked turkey
2 tablespoons orange zest
1 package (10 ounces) fresh spinach, stems removed and discarded and leaves thinly sliced
2 to 3 tablespoons freshly grated Parmesan cheese

❶ In a soup pot, heat oil, and sauté onion 2 to 3 minutes until it appears limp. Stir in garlic and sauté 1 minute longer.

❷ Add celery, carrots, green pepper, and parsley, and cook until the vegetables take on some color, about 5 minutes.

❸ Add the broth, bring to a boil, lower the heat, and simmer, partially covered, 15 minutes.

❹ Add pasta to the soup pot and cook according to package directions.

❺ Add diced turkey and orange zest, and heat thoroughly, about 3 minutes. Add the sliced spinach, stir well, and remove from the heat.

❻ Serve in warmed individual bowls and top each with Parmesan cheese.

Each serving		% of calories from fat	28
Calories	224	Total Fat	7 g
Protein	19 g	Saturated Fat	2 g
Carbohydrates	24 g	Cholesterol	36 mg
Dietary Fiber	3 g	Sodium	196 mg

A ROMAN PASTA SOUP (WITH POTATOES)

MAKES 8 SERVINGS

It is best to use small pasta such as small shells or ditalini. This combination of simple ingredients is very tasty, economical, healthful, and low fat. Make it ahead, and enjoy it later. If you make it a day before, cook everything except the pasta, which should be added just before serving.

1 tablespoon extra-virgin olive oil
1 bacon slice, diced into 1/2-inch pieces
1 small onion, diced into 1/2-inch pieces
1/4 cup finely chopped flat-leaf parsley
8 cups homemade mixed broth of beef (4 cups, page 48) and chicken (page 59) or low-sodium canned broths
4 medium potatoes, peeled and cut into 1/2-inch cubes
freshly ground black pepper
1/2 pound small pasta
3/4 cup freshly grated Pecorino cheese

1. Heat oil in a large soup pot, and cook bacon, onion, and parsley until bacon crisps, about 5 minutes.

2. Add broth and potatoes. Bring to a boil, lower the heat to get a slow, steady simmer, and cook, covered, until potatoes are almost done, about 15 minutes. Add a liberal amount of pepper.

3. Add the pasta and cook according to package directions.

4. Serve in warm bowls with a tablespoon of cheese on top.

Each serving		% of calories from fat 24	
Calories	262	Total Fat	7 g
Protein	13 g	Saturated Fat	2.9 g
Carbohydrates	38 g	Cholesterol	14 mg
Dietary Fiber	2 g	Sodium	248 mg

VEGETABLE BROTH

MAKES ABOUT 2 QUARTS

If you prefer a broth made without meat or poultry, use this one. I think it is most tasty.

15 cups water
1 pound mushrooms, wiped clean and coarsely chopped
4 large carrots, cut into 1/2-inch slices
4 large celery ribs with leaves, cut into 1/2-inch slices
2 medium boiling potatoes, unpeeled, washed well and cut into 1-inch pieces
1 leek, including green part, washed carefully and cut into 1/2-inch slices
6 cloves garlic, unpeeled, cut in halves
12 peppercorns
6 parsley stems, cut into 1-inch pieces

❶ Combine all of the ingredients in a very large soup pot and bring to a boil over high heat. Lower the heat to get a slow, steady simmer, and cook, uncovered, 1 1/4 hours.

❷ Strain and discard vegetables, or reserve them for another use. Use the broth immediately, refrigerate up to 3 days, or freeze up to 1 month.

Each serving		% of calories from fat 20	
Calories	160	Total Fat	3.7 g
Protein	16 g	Saturated Fat	0 g
Carbohydrates	24 g	Cholesterol	0 mg
Dietary Fiber	0 g	Sodium	405 mg

CHAPTER 4
TASTY, TASTY TOMATO PASTA DISHES

INTRODUCTION

If you like pasta, but dislike what it does to your waistline, this chapter is for you. Pasta, the heart of Italian cooking, by itself, is almost fat free and is relatively low in calories. Dry packaged pasta is second only to chicken as the favorite meal in America, and last year, according to the National Pasta Association, more than one and a half billion (yes, billion) pounds were sold. The newest innovation in cooking and serving pasta is preparing sauces in a new low-fat manner. Roasted garlic in pasta, for example, is almost as popular as tomatoes and basil. Many different food cultures are crisscrossing, and this can be seen clearly in the newly evolving pasta dishes.

Who doesn't love pasta with its tomato, cream, meat, and other sauces? We all do. Even though pasta by itself may be low in fat, the high-fat culprit in pasta preparations is the sauce or ingredients that top it. Butter and cream sauces such as "Alfredo" are overly high in fat and calories. See the new low-fat version on page 33. Our favorite pastas are loaded with unnecessary fat, high-fat cheeses, unnecessary butter and cream, overly rich sausages, bacon and other fat meats, and too much olive oil. But, in this chapter, these fats are reduced.

The results are certainly not in on artificial fat substitutes, and an extra dose of salt is often used to make up for the loss of flavor due to the reduction of fatty ingredients. Some recipes in other books use overly processed foods, thick with chemicals. All of these attempts to make low-fat foods taste good compromise nutrition and may, in the end, cause harm. I rely on a minimum of such foods, emphasizing greater use of vegetables (especially dark, leafy greens), herbs and spices—in other words, the healthier foods. Because pasta itself is a simple food, it can be easily enhanced by such naturally low- or no-fat ingredients as herbs and spices.

Tomato sauces are the most popular sauces for pasta in the United States. They are usually combined with pork sausages, ground beef, or lamb, and these meats are simply too high in fat. In this chapter, tomato sauces are lower in fat, yet they are very tasty because they are cooked with vegetables, herbs, and wines. See Chapter 1 (pages 15–16) for nutrient information.

FRESH TOMATO SAUCE WITH CILANTRO AND LIME JUICE

MAKES 4 SERVINGS WITH 1/2 POUND OF PASTA

This is a fiery sauce, and I suggest that you have a loaf of Italian bread to eat along with this pasta. If you're out of fresh cilantro, use fresh flat-leaf parsley instead.

2 tablespoons extra-virgin olive oil
4 medium cloves garlic, minced
2 1/2 pounds fresh plum tomatoes, skinned, seeded and diced 1/2 inch
1/2 cup loosely packed, finely chopped fresh cilantro
1/2 cup finely chopped onion
3 tablespoons fresh lime juice
1 tablespoon tomato paste
2 jalapeño chilies, minced
2 teaspoons chili powder
1/2 pound of pasta

1. Heat oil in a small skillet and sauté garlic 1 minute. Remove from the heat.

2. Put tomatoes in a large bowl, add oil and garlic, and toss well.

3. Add all other ingredients, stir well, and leave at room temperature for an hour or so to allow the flavors to develop.

4. Add drained cooked pasta.

THE HEAT OF THE JALAPEÑO

The jalapeño pepper is the overnight star of the culinary world. Its flavor differs from hot red pepper. Dried, ground jalapeño pepper is stronger than cayenne, but the heat disappears sooner. It should be added toward the end of cooking because its hotness disappears rather quickly. Crushed red pepper flakes are used in many recipes in this book; the powdered form can be substituted but crushed pepper is preferable.

It has been said that eating hot peppers increases the metabolism, reducing the calories retained from a meal by about 10 percent.

Each serving (incl. pasta)		% of calories from fat 21	
Calories	375	Total Fat	9 g
Protein	11 g	Saturated Fat	1 g
Carbohydrates	63 g	Cholesterol	0 mg
Dietary Fiber	8 g	Sodium	43 mg

BASIC TOMATO SAUCE

HOW TO PEEL, SEED, AND DICE TOMATOES

The tomatoes should be ripe. The reason for peeling and seeding is to remove the tough skins and the bitter seeds.

Cut a very shallow X through the bottom skin of each tomato. Bring a large pot of water to boil and place two or three tomatoes at a time in it. Count to twelve. With a slotted spoon, remove the tomatoes to a bowl of cold water to cease cooking them.

Peel the tomatoes beginning at the X edges, which will have begun to curl. Core each tomato and cut it in half. Gently squeeze each half over the sink to remove the seeds. Dice the tomatoes.

MAKES 4 SERVINGS WITH 1/2 POUND OF PASTA

This is as simple and as tasty as a tomato sauce can be. It stores well for several days in the refrigerator and freezes well for several months. The recipe does not need salt because the canned tomatoes have enough of it. The trick here is to sauté the vegetables in broth instead of oil; the oil, however, is added at the end and the one tablespoon delivers considerable flavor. This sauce is excellent with pasta, and it may also be used as a sauce with the meatballs in Chapter 9. Combine the meatballs and the sauce in a covered skillet, and cook over moderate heat until the meat and sauce are thoroughly heated.

- 2 tablespoons low-sodium, defatted vegetable or chicken broth
- 2 medium cloves garlic, minced
- 1 medium onion, finely diced
- 1 can (28 ounces) plum tomatoes with basil, put through a food mill including liquid
- 2 teaspoons sugar
- 1/2 teaspoon dried thyme
- freshly ground pepper
- 1 tablespoon extra-virgin olive oil

❶ In a large skillet, add broth, garlic, and onion, and sauté them until the liquid almost disappears, 2 or 3 minutes.

❷ Add all other ingredients except the olive oil; be liberal with the pepper. Bring to a boil, lower the heat, cover the pan, and simmer 15 minutes. Add olive oil and stir well. Remove from heat and serve over fresh pasta.

Each serving (incl. pasta)		% of calories from fat 24	
Calories	166	Total Fat	4.5 g
Protein	5 g	Saturated Fat	0.6 g
Carbohydrates	28 g	Cholesterol	18 mg
Dietary Fiber	3 g	Sodium	333 mg

FILETTO SAUCE

MAKES 6 TO 8 SERVINGS WITH 1 POUND OF SHELLS OR OTHER SUBSTANTIAL PASTA

This is a light tomato sauce, and it should not be overcooked. It's a popular sauce in Italy. If you see the restaurant staff eating pasta in the back of the restaurant or trattoria, the chances are good that this sauce is on their pasta. It's flavorful because of the combination of the garlic, onion, oregano, and basil. Tomato paste or tomato puree should not be substituted. It is easy to double or triple this recipe for freezing or later use.

- 2 tablespoons extra-virgin olive oil
- 2 medium cloves garlic, minced
- 2 medium onions, chopped fine
- 1/2 teaspoon salt
- 1 tablespoon finely chopped fresh oregano or 1/2 teaspoon dried
- 2 tablespoons finely chopped fresh basil or 2 teaspoons dried
- 1/4 teaspoon red pepper flakes
- 2 pounds ripe plum tomatoes, peeled, seeded, and chopped or 1 can (28 ounces) Italian plum tomatoes, put through a food mill
- 1 teaspoon sugar
- freshly ground black pepper

❶ In a large saucepan, heat oil, add garlic, and sauté 1 minute until garlic begins to change color. Add onions and sauté them until they become translucent. Add salt, oregano, basil, and red pepper flakes. Stir well.

❷ Add tomatoes and sugar, bring to a boil, lower the heat, and simmer, partially covered, 30 minutes. Stir about every 5 minutes. Adjust seasoning and add freshly ground pepper.

Each serving (incl. pasta)		% of calories from fat 15	
Calories	297	Total Fat	4.9 g
Protein	9 g	Saturated Fat	0.7 g
Carbohydrates	55 g	Cholesterol	0 mg
Dietary Fiber	4 g	Sodium	146 mg

FILETTO SAUCE

Filetto sauce is basic to Italian cooking and has the advantage of being extended for use as another sauce. For example, its versatility is adapted to the quick ragú Bolognese sauce on page 38.

For most dishes, about 2 cups of sauce are adequate for one-half to three-quarters pound of pasta. Use less if you want your pasta more thinly sauced.

These sauces can easily be doubled and tripled; they freeze well and will keep in the refrigerator for about five days.

FILETTO SAUCE FOR ZITI

MAKES 6 TO 8 SERVINGS WITH 1 POUND OF ZITI

This is a somewhat stronger version of the filetto sauce on page 77. It is better suited for a heavier pasta, such as ziti. More garlic and two kinds of wine in the sauce make the change.

2 tablespoons extra-virgin olive oil
4 medium cloves garlic, minced
1/4 cup finely chopped fresh basil or 2 teaspoons dried
2 cups tomato sauce (page 76)
1/2 cup red wine
1/4 cup marsala wine
1/2 cup Pecorino cheese
1 pound of ziti

❶ Heat oil in a large skillet and sauté garlic 1 minute. Add basil, tomato sauce, and red and marsala wines, and cook over low heat at a simmer for 10 minutes until the sauce is thoroughly heated.

❷ Cook the ziti, drain, and return to the pot in which they cooked. Add half of the sauce and half of the cheese. Toss well. Transfer the pasta to a serving platter or to individual dishes. Spoon the remaining sauce and cheese over the pasta.

Each serving (incl. pasta)		% of calories from fat 19	
Calories	279	Total Fat	6 g
Protein	9 g	Saturated Fat	1.7 g
Carbohydrates	43 g	Cholesterol	7 mg
Dietary Fiber	3 g	Sodium	92 mg

QUICK TOMATO SAUCE WITH MARSALA

MAKES 4 SERVINGS WITH 1/2 POUND OF PASTA

Marsala wine adds a flavor here that is distinctive. If you don't have Marsala, use a tawny port or a strong, dry red wine.

2 cups fresh peeled, seeded, and diced plum tomatoes, or canned Italian plum tomatoes with juice
1 tablespoon extra-virgin olive oil
2 small onions, chopped fine
1 large clove garlic, minced
4 slices bacon, cooked crisp, patted dry in paper towels, and crumbled
salt
freshly ground black pepper
1/2 cup marsala wine
1/2 teaspoon dried oregano
1/2 pound of pasta

❶ Put tomatoes through a food mill. Do not use a blender. A food mill will puree the pulp and get rid of the seeds; a blender chops the seeds along with the tomatoes and makes the sauce bitter.

❷ In a large skillet or medium saucepan, heat oil and cook onions until soft, about 5 minutes. Add garlic and cook 1 minute longer. Add the tomato puree and the crumbled bacon. Season with salt and pepper. Boil this sauce hard for 3 minutes.

❸ Add marsala wine and oregano, and simmer another 5 minutes, uncovered. Serve over hot cooked pasta.

Each serving (incl. pasta)		% of calories from fat 28	
Calories	440	Total Fat	13.9 g
Protein	15 g	Saturated Fat	3.9 g
Carbohydrates	53 g	Cholesterol	16 mg
Dietary Fiber	4 g	Sodium	529 mg

FRESH, UNCOOKED TOMATO SAUCE

MAKES 6 SERVINGS WITH 3/4 POUND OF PASTA

This sauce can be prepared ahead of time and may be held at room temperature for as long as half a day. If made the day before, refrigerate the sauce but bring it to room temperature before adding it to hot pasta.

3 large ripe tomatoes, peeled, seeded, and cut into 1/2-inch pieces
1 large clove garlic, minced
1 small onion, chopped fine
8 large basil leaves, chopped fine or 1 teaspoon dried
1 tablespoon finely chopped fresh oregano or 1/2 teaspoon dried
1 teaspoon finely chopped fresh rosemary or 1/2 teaspoon dried
salt
freshly ground pepper
2 tablespoons extra-virgin olive oil
juice from 1 1/2 lemons, about 4 tablespoons

1. Place the tomatoes in a bowl. Add all other ingredients and toss well. Be liberal with the pepper.

2. Cook, drain, and sauce the pasta with half of the tomatoes. Serve the pasta on a large platter or in individual bowls, adding the remaining sauce to the top.

OLIVE OIL

In this book, olive oil has been used sparingly because one tablespoon contains 115 calories and about 12 grams of fat. Olive oil is great tasting, so it is used in recipes where flavor is of primary concern. Also, olive oil contains no cholesterol and is very digestible. Tests conducted by the American Heart Association's Nutrition Committee showed that using oil in place of saturated fats in the diet reduces blood cholesterol, but it's still wise to cut consumption of all fats.

Each serving (incl. pasta)		% of calories from fat 18	
Calories	290	Total Fat	5.9 g
Protein	9 g	Saturated Fat	0.8 g
Carbohydrates	51 g	Cholesterol	0 mg
Dietary Fiber	4 g	Sodium	10 mg

ROASTED TOMATO AND ONION SAUCE

MAKES 4 SERVINGS WITH 1/2 POUND OF PASTA

This sauce is one of my favorites because the roasted tomatoes have an extra bounce of taste. Baked tomatoes develop a wonderful taste as their natural sugar begins to carmelize, although the taste is not sweet.

4 tablespoons extra-virgin olive oil
2 large onions, diced
2 pounds large ripe plum tomatoes, about 12 to 14, stem end removed and halved lengthwise
4 medium cloves garlic, minced
1/2 cup basil and parsley finely chopped together
1 teaspoon sugar
salt
freshly ground black pepper

❶ Combine all ingredients in a large roasting pan. Toss well.

❷ Preheat oven to 250°F; bake 2 to 3 hours until tomatoes begin to appear dried out but are actually still moist. Stir the tomato mixture several times during the "roasting" period. The sauce should be chunky.

Each serving (incl. pasta)		% of calories from fat 32	
Calories	430	Total Fat	15.5 g
Protein	11 g	Saturated Fat	2 g
Carbohydrates	64 g	Cholesterol	0 mg
Dietary Fiber	6 g	Sodium	28 mg

SPICY TOMATO, BACON, AND VODKA SAUCE

MAKES 4 SERVINGS WITH 1/2 POUND OF PASTA

This sauce is very tasty and easy to make. It is spicy, so if you like less spice (heat), add fewer pepper flakes.

1 tablespoon extra-virgin olive oil
1/3 cup finely diced Canadian bacon (1 slice)
2 large cloves garlic, minced
2 cups tomato sauce, page 76
1/4 cup vodka
1/2 teaspoon red pepper flakes
1/4 cup finely chopped fresh parsley

1. Heat oil in a large skillet and sauté bacon until it begins to crisp, 2 to 3 minutes. Add garlic, stir, and cook 1 minute longer.

2. Add tomato sauce, vodka, and pepper flakes, and bring to a boil. Lower the heat and simmer until the sauce is thoroughly heated, about 5 minutes.

3. Serve the sauce over cooked and drained pasta or add the pasta to the skillet, toss, and garnish with parsley before serving.

Each serving (incl. pasta)		% of calories from fat 13	
Calories	337	Total Fat	5 g
Protein	11 g	Saturated Fat	0.8 g
Carbohydrates	54 g	Cholesterol	4 mg
Dietary Fiber	4 g	Sodium	132 mg

GARLICKY TOMATO SAUCE WITH VEGETABLES

MAKES 4 SERVINGS WITH 1/2 POUND OF PASTA

This sauce is one of the lowest-fat pasta sauces in this book, and it is one of the tastiest. You may want to add half the amount of red pepper flakes; taste it and add more if you want.

- spray oil
- 1 medium onion, finely diced
- 1/4 cup finely diced carrot
- 1/2 cup finely diced celery
- 1/4 cup finely diced green pepper
- 8 medium cloves garlic, minced
- 1/2 cup red wine
- 1 tablespoon dried oregano
- 1/2 teaspoon red pepper flakes
- 4 cups canned plum tomatoes and their juices put through a food mill
- 1 tablespoon chicken bouillon granules
- 1 tablespoon tomato paste
- 1 tablespoon balsamic vinegar
- 1 teaspoon sugar

❶ Spray oil on a large, nonstick skillet, and place it over medium heat. Add onion, carrot, celery, green pepper, and garlic, and sauté 2 to 3 minutes to soften the vegetables.

❷ Add wine, oregano, and pepper flakes, and cook 5 minutes to let the wine cook down. Stir frequently.

❸ Add tomatoes, chicken bouillon, tomato paste, balsamic vinegar, and sugar. Bring to a boil, lower the heat, and simmer, uncovered, 40 minutes. Stir every 5 minutes or so.

Each serving (incl. pasta)		% of calories from fat	5
Calories	339	Total Fat	2 g
Protein	11 g	Saturated Fat	0.3 g
Carbohydrates	66 g	Cholesterol	0 mg
Dietary Fiber	8 g	Sodium	657 mg

THIN SPAGHETTI WITH WINE AND TOMATO SAUCE

MAKES 6 SERVINGS

Oregano is mated to fresh tomatoes in this robust sauce enriched with onions, garlic, and red wine.

4 tablespoons extra-virgin olive oil
1 large onion, finely chopped
2 large cloves garlic, minced
3 pounds fresh tomatoes, peeled, seeded, and cut into 1/2-inch pieces
1/3 cup tomato paste
2 cups Cabernet Sauvignon wine
1 tablespoon finely chopped fresh oregano or 1 teaspoon dried
1/2 teaspoon salt
freshly ground pepper
3/4 pound thin spaghetti

❶ Heat oil in a large skillet and sauté onion until translucent, about 4 minutes. Stir in garlic and sauté 1 minute longer.

❷ Add tomatoes, tomato paste, wine, oregano, salt, and pepper. Bring to a boil, lower the heat, and simmer 20 minutes, uncovered.

❸ While the sauce is cooking, cook the pasta, drain it, and add it to the sauce. Toss well and serve right away.

Each serving		% of calories from fat 23	
Calories	428	Total Fat	10.8 g
Protein	11 g	Saturated Fat	1.4 g
Carbohydrates	61 g	Cholesterol	0 mg
Dietary Fiber	8 g	Sodium	229 mg

TOMATO, CHEESE, AND HERB SAUCE

MAKES 4 SERVINGS WITH 1/2 POUND OF PASTA

Fresh fennel is available in produce sections of most supermarkets. If you can't find it fresh, use celery instead. But go for the fresh fennel because it is a delight to savor.

4 large ripe globe tomatoes, skinned, seeded, and chopped 1/2 inch
1/2 cup thickly grated Pecorino cheese
1/2 cup finely chopped fresh fennel
1/4 cup finely chopped fresh basil
1/4 cup finely chopped fresh oregano
2 tablespoons extra-virgin olive oil
3 medium cloves garlic, minced
pinch red pepper flakes
1/2 pound of pasta

❶ Prepare tomatoes, cheese, fennel, and herbs, and set aside.

❷ Heat oil in a large skillet and sauté garlic until it begins to change color, about 1 minute. Remove the skillet from the heat.

❸ Add tomatoes, cheese, fennel, herbs, red pepper, and cooked pasta to the skillet, toss, and serve.

Each serving (incl. pasta)		% of calories from fat 28	
Calories	376	Total Fat	11.8 g
Protein	13 g	Saturated Fat	3 g
Carbohydrates	55 g	Cholesterol	13 mg
Dietary Fiber	6 g	Sodium	167 mg

"LITTLE EARS" ORECCHIETTE WITH OLIVES, OREGANO, AND FRESH TOMATOES

MAKES 6 SERVINGS

These green olives are tart and tasty. The dish is spicy because of the red pepper flakes. If you can't find little ears pasta, use another small pasta such as penne or rotelle.

6 large tomatoes, peeled, seeded, and chopped 1/2 inch
3/4 cup sliced, pitted, green olives, such as Kalamata or green Sicilian
1/4 cup finely chopped fresh flat parsley
1/4 cup extra-virgin olive oil
3 medium cloves garlic, minced
1 tablespoon finely chopped fresh oregano or 1 teaspoon dried
1/2 teaspoon red pepper flakes
3/4 pound little ears pasta (orecchiette)

❶ In a large bowl, put tomatoes, olives, parsley, olive oil, garlic, oregano, and the pepper flakes. Toss mixture well and leave at room temperature about 2 hours.

❷ Cook the pasta, drain it, reserving about 1 cup of the cooking liquid, and add the pasta to the bowl. Toss well. If the pasta is too dry, add 2 or 3 tablespoons or more of the pasta cooking liquid.

Each serving		% of calories from fat 30	
Calories	371	Total Fat	12.5 g
Protein	10 g	Saturated Fat	1.7 g
Carbohydrates	56 g	Cholesterol	0 mg
Dietary Fiber	5 g	Sodium	166 mg

TOMATO SAUCE WITH COGNAC

MAKES 4 TO 6 SERVINGS WITH 1/2 POUND OF PASTA

The alcohol in the cognac will cook away, but the flavor remains.

2 tablespoons extra-virgin olive oil
3 large cloves garlic, minced
1 can (28 ounces) plum Italian-style tomatoes with their juices, put through a food mill
1/2 cup cognac
salt
freshly ground pepper
3/4 pound of pasta
1/4 cup finely chopped chives

❶ Heat oil in a large, nonstick skillet and sauté garlic 1 minute, stirring most of the time.

❷ Carefully add tomatoes, cognac, salt, and pepper. Bring to a boil, lower the heat, and simmer 15 minutes. If the tomatoes thicken too much, add 1 or more tablespoons of the pasta cooking liquid.

❸ To serve, combine sauce with pasta and distribute among four to six individual plates. Garnish with chives and serve right away.

Each serving (incl. pasta)		% of calories from fat 15	
Calories	338	Total Fat	5.7 g
Protein	9 g	Saturated Fat	0.8 g
Carbohydrates	49 g	Cholesterol	0 mg
Dietary Fiber	5 g	Sodium	243 mg

TOMATO SAUCE WITH DRIED HERBS

MAKES 5 SERVINGS WITH 1 POUND OF SPAGHETTI

This basic tomato sauce places its emphasis on herbs. It can be used in place of the basic tomato sauce on page 76.

2 tablespoons extra-virgin olive oil
1/2 cup finely chopped onion
2 large cloves garlic, minced
2 1/2 cups Italian-style tomatoes, put through a food mill
1 can (6 ounces) tomato paste
1 1/2 cups water
freshly ground pepper
1 teaspoon dried basil, crumbled
1 teaspoon dried oregano, crumbled
1/2 teaspoon dried thyme, crumbled
1 pound of spaghetti
grated Parmesan cheese

❶ Heat oil in a large skillet and sauté onion until it becomes opaque, about 4 minutes. Add garlic and cook 1 minute longer.

❷ Add tomatoes, tomato paste, water, a liberal amount of pepper, and the herbs. Bring to a boil, lower the heat, and simmer 30 minutes, uncovered.

❸ Serve with 1 pound of cooked thin spaghetti or other pasta of your choice. Add Parmesan cheese, if you wish.

Each serving (incl. pasta)		% of calories from fat 24	
Calories	239	Total Fat	6.4 g
Protein	7 g	Saturated Fat	0.9 g
Carbohydrates	38 g	Cholesterol	0 mg
Dietary Fiber	4 g	Sodium	491 mg

TOMATO, BASIL, AND MOZZARELLA WITH TAGLIOLINI

MAKES 6 SERVINGS

This is a lovely dish because it is sauced so simply. The sauce is fresh and is delicious with the hot pasta. If you find the pasta too dry, add a little more tomato juice.

6 tomatoes, peeled, seeded, and chopped in 1/2-inch pieces
1/2 cup bottled low-sodium tomato juice
1/2 pound skim milk mozzarella, shredded
1/3 cup finely chopped basil leaves
2 tablespoons extra-virgin olive oil
2 cloves garlic, minced
2 tablespoons finely chopped flat parsley
1 teaspoon sugar
freshly ground pepper
3/4 pound tagliolini, cooked and drained

❶ All ingredients except the pasta should be at room temperature. The pasta should be freshly cooked and drained.

❷ In a bowl, add all the ingredients. Check for salt seasoning; if needed, add a pinch. Toss well and serve.

Each serving		% of calories from fat 27	
Calories	393	Total Fat	12 g
Protein	18 g	Saturated Fat	4.6 g
Carbohydrates	53 g	Cholesterol	22 mg
Dietary Fiber	6 g	Sodium	192 mg

TOMATO SAUCE WITH FRESH AND DRIED FENNEL

MAKES 4 SERVINGS WITH 1/2 POUND OF PASTA

Florentine fennel, also called finocchio, is used fresh in many ways. The bulb can be chopped and used in pasta as a vegetable, and it is truly delicious. The fennel seed, like the vegetable it comes from, has a delicate anise flavor. It should be used sparingly, but is a delight with many pastas.

1 teaspoon extra-virgin olive oil
1 teaspoon dried fennel seeds
1 1/2 cups fresh fennel, diced 1/2 inch
2 cups tomato sauce (page 76)
salt
freshly ground black pepper

❶ Heat oil in a large skillet and toast the dried seeds 30 seconds. Add fresh fennel, toss, and sauté 2 minutes.

❷ Add tomato sauce and heat thoroughly. Add salt, if needed, and a liberal spray of pepper.

Each serving (incl. pasta)		% of calories from fat	8
Calories	281	Total Fat	2.5 g
Protein	10 g	Saturated Fat	0.3 g
Carbohydrates	56 g	Cholesterol	0 mg
Dietary Fiber	6 g	Sodium	48 mg

TOMATO SAUCE WITH TUNA, CAPERS, AND LEMON

MAKES 4 SERVINGS WITH 1/2 POUND OF PASTA

Tuna in a tomato sauce for pasta is one of my favorites. It's easy to make.

- 1 tablespoon extra-virgin olive oil
- 1/2 cup chopped onion
- 1/4 cup finely chopped flat parsley
- 2 tablespoons capers, rinsed
- 2 tablespoons finely minced lemon zest
- 1 can (6 ounces) tuna, packed in water, drained and flaked
- 2 cups tomato sauce, page 76
- freshly ground pepper
- 1/2 pound of pasta
- grated Parmesan cheese

1. Heat oil in a large skillet and sauté onions until translucent, 3 to 4 minutes.
2. Add parsley, capers, and lemon zest, and sauté 1 minute.
3. Add tuna and tomato sauce, and heat thoroughly, 3 to 4 minutes. Add a liberal amount of freshly ground pepper.
4. Add the cooked and drained pasta to the skillet, toss well over medium heat, and serve warm. Some people like to add a topping of Parmesan cheese.

CAPERS

Used for hundreds of years as a condiment, capers are the flower buds of crooked, climbing shrubs found in the Mediterranean region. The capers are salted and preserved in brine. They should be green and firm. They are available in all grocery stores and supermarkets. After you have opened them, capers will keep for months refrigerated. I've seen them growing in Sicily, and they looked quite wild to me. They grow in Greece and farther east, as well as in North Africa. There are many ways to use capers, even as a garnish, and they are so tasty in certain pasta dishes.

Each serving (incl. pasta)		% of calories from fat	13
Calories	347	Total Fat	5 g
Protein	20 g	Saturated Fat	0.7 g
Carbohydrates	56 g	Cholesterol	13 mg
Dietary Fiber	5 g	Sodium	334 mg

TOMATO, TARRAGON, AND CAPER SAUCE

MAKES 6 TO 8 SERVINGS WITH 1 POUND OF SPAGHETTI

This very low-fat sauce capitalizes on tarragon and capers for its extra taste boost. It's easy to prepare, and although I enjoy it with thin spaghetti, you could use almost any type of pasta.

1 tablespoon extra-virgin olive oil
1 small onion, peeled and finely diced
3 large cloves garlic, minced
1 can (28 ounces) Italian-style plum tomatoes with their juices, put through a food mill
1/4 cup tomato paste
1/4 cup finely chopped fresh tarragon leaves or 1 teaspoon dried
1/4 cup drained capers, rinsed and drained again
1 pound thin spaghetti
6 to 8 tablespoons freshly grated Parmesan cheese
freshly ground pepper

❶ Heat oil in a large, nonstick skillet and sauté onions 4 minutes, until limp. Add garlic and sauté 1 minute longer.

❷ Add tomatoes, tomato paste, tarragon, and capers, and simmer over medium heat, uncovered, 15 minutes.

❸ Serve on cooked thin spaghetti, adding cheese and freshly ground black pepper.

Each serving (incl. pasta)		% of calories from fat 11	
Calories	291	Total Fat	3.5 g
Protein	12 g	Saturated Fat	1.4 g
Carbohydrates	51 g	Cholesterol	4.92 mg
Dietary Fiber	5 g	Sodium	462 mg

TOMATO VEGETABLE SAUCE

MAKES 4 SERVINGS WITH 1/2 POUND OF PASTA

The vegetables in this sauce add all the flavor. It will keep refrigerated for two to three days and may be frozen up to a month. This is delicious!

2 pounds ripe plum tomatoes or 2 cups canned Italian plum tomatoes
2/3 cup onions, diced 1/2 inch
2/3 cup carrots, diced 1/2 inch
2/3 cup celery, including light green leaves, diced 1/2 inch
2 tablespoons finely chopped parsley
1 teaspoon sugar
salt
freshly ground black pepper
2 tablespoons extra-virgin olive oil
1/2 pound of pasta

❶ If using fresh tomatoes, wash them well, cut each in half, and cook over low heat in a covered pan for 15 minutes. Put them through a food mill and make a fine puree. If using canned tomatoes, measure 2 cups into a food mill along with 1/2 cup of juice from the can and puree.

❷ In a medium saucepan, combine tomatoes with onions, carrots, celery, and parsley. Add the sugar, salt, and pepper, and simmer, covered, over low heat, 30 minutes.

❸ Transfer the tomato and vegetable mixture to a food mill and return the puree to the pan in which it cooked. Add the olive oil and simmer for 10 minutes over low heat. The pan should be partially covered. Stir several times with a wooden spoon or rubber spatula to clean the sides of the pan.

❹ Add cooked and drained pasta to the skillet, and toss on medium heat 2 minutes. Serve warm.

Each serving (incl. pasta)		% of calories from fat 22	
Calories	355	Total Fat	8.7 g
Protein	10 g	Saturated Fat	6 g
Carbohydrates	61 g	Cholesterol	0 mg
Dietary Fiber	6 g	Sodium	47 mg

SPAGHETTINI WITH FRESH PLUM TOMATO, BASIL, AND CAPER SAUCE

MAKES 8 SERVINGS AS APPETIZER, 6 AS MAIN DISH

This simple, elegant pasta has lots of flavor. The tomatoes must be fully red and ripe, and the basil must be fresh and green. It's an excellent first course because it can be made and left to stand before serving.

- 2 pounds fresh plum tomatoes, peeled, seeded, and chopped into 1/2 inch pieces
- 1 cup chopped fresh basil and 1/4 cup thinly sliced basil, kept separate
- 1/3 cup drained capers, rinsed and dried
- 1/4 cup sherry wine vinegar
- 1/4 cup extra-virgin olive oil
- salt
- freshly ground pepper
- 1 pound spaghettini, cooked and drained

❶ Combine the tomatoes and chopped basil in a large bowl and leave at room temperature for about 1 hour. Or refrigerate, but bring to room temperature before the next step.

❷ Add capers, vinegar, oil, salt, and pepper, and mix well.

❸ Add the cooked pasta, toss well, and let stand 5 to 10 minutes before serving. Transfer to a large platter, garnish with sliced basil, and serve.

Each serving		% of calories from fat 23	
Calories	310	Total Fat	8.2 g
Protein	9 g	Saturated Fat	1.1 g
Carbohydrates	50 g	Cholesterol	0 mg
Dietary Fiber	4 g	Sodium	220 mg

TOMATOES, OLIVES, AND OREGANO SAUCE

MAKES 4 SERVINGS WITH 1/2 POUND OF PASTA

This sauce is extra tasty because of the wine and olives. The olives should be cured. Most supermarkets carry them in their deli sections, but you may find them in jars on the shelves.

1 tablespoon extra-virgin olive oil
2 large cloves garlic, minced
1/4 cup chopped, cured black olives
1 tablespoon finely chopped fresh oregano or 1 teaspoon dried
2 cups tomato sauce (page 76)
1/4 cup red wine
1/2 pound of pasta
2 tablespoons freshly grated Parmesan cheese

❶ Heat oil in a large skillet and sauté garlic for 1 minute. Add olives and oregano, and stir over heat for 1 more minute.

❷ Add the tomatoes and wine, bring to a slow boil, lower the heat, and simmer until the sauce is heated through, 3 or 4 minutes.

❸ Add the cooked, drained pasta to the skillet, toss well, and serve, topped with cheese.

Each serving (incl. pasta)		% of calories from fat 18	
Calories	326	Total Fat	6.5 g
Protein	11 g	Saturated Fat	1.3 g
Carbohydrates	55 g	Cholesterol	2 mg
Dietary Fiber	4 g	Sodium	163 mg

UNCOOKED SUN-DRIED TOMATO SAUCE

MAKES 4 TO 6 SERVINGS WITH 1/2 POUND OF PASTA

Sun-dried tomatoes sometimes seem to be overworked, but I like them in this recipe where they are pureed to make a sauce with quite a punch. It is very good with artichoke pasta.

- 4 ounces sun-dried tomatoes, coarsely chopped
- 3 medium cloves garlic, coarsely chopped
- juice of 1 lemon, about 3 tablespoons
- 1/4 cup grapeseed oil
- 1/2 cup low-sodium, defatted chicken broth
- freshly grated pepper
- 1/4 cup finely chopped scallions
- 1/2 pound artichoke pasta

❶ Put tomatoes and garlic in the bowl of a processor and pulse. Add lemon juice, oil, chicken broth, and scallions, and pulse to make a sauce. Taste for seasoning and add pepper and a bit of salt, if needed.

❷ Cook pasta according to package directions, drain it, and transfer it to a bowl. Add the sauce, toss well, and serve.

Each serving (incl. pasta)		% of calories from fat 20	
Calories	492	Total Fat	11 g
Protein	15 g	Saturated Fat	1.3 g
Carbohydrates	83 g	Cholesterol	0.4 mg
Dietary Fiber	2 g	Sodium	409 mg

TOMATOES, MUSHROOMS, AND BASIL SAUCE

MAKES 6 SERVINGS WITH 3/4 POUND OF PASTA

This sauce should be served warm over freshly cooked pasta. The mushrooms and thyme are the special flavors.

- 3 tablespoons extra-virgin olive oil
- 1 medium onion, diced
- 6 medium cloves garlic, minced
- 3/4 pound mushrooms, sliced
- 1/3 cup slivered basil leaves
- 2 teaspoons finely chopped fresh thyme or 1 teaspoon dried
- 1 cup white wine
- 1 can (15 ounces) diced tomatoes
- 3/4 cup low-sodium, defatted chicken broth
- 3/4 pound of pasta

❶ Heat oil in a large skillet and cook onions until they become translucent, 3 to 4 minutes. Add garlic and sauté 1 minute.

❷ Add mushrooms, basil, and thyme. Cook 5 minutes. Add the wine and cook 5 minutes more or until most of the wine evaporates.

❸ Add tomatoes, including the liquid, and broth, stir well, and simmer 5 minutes, uncovered. Serve over hot pasta.

Each serving (incl. pasta)		% of calories from fat 21	
Calories	359	Total Fat	8.5 g
Protein	10 g	Saturated Fat	1.25 g
Carbohydrates	53 g	Cholesterol	1 mg
Dietary Fiber	5 g	Sodium	137 mg

VERMICELLI WITH A LIGHT TOMATO BASIL SAUCE

MAKES 6 SERVINGS

Sweet basil is the essence of this delicious sauce. The recipe will make more sauce than you need; refrigerate or freeze any leftover sauce. It is excellent served over a baked potato, grilled eggplant, or zucchini slices and can always be served over some more pasta.

- 2 cans (28 ounces each) Italian-style plum tomatoes with basil, put through a food mill
- 1 cup finely chopped fresh basil
- 1 teaspoon dried basil
- 4 medium cloves garlic, minced
- 2 teaspoons sugar
- salt
- freshly ground pepper
- 3/4 pound vermicelli
- 1/4 cup toasted pine nuts

❶ Put tomatoes, basil, garlic, sugar, a little salt, and a liberal amount of pepper in a large skillet. Bring to a boil, lower the heat, and simmer, uncovered, 30 minutes, stirring frequently. Remove half of the sauce and set it aside. Leave the other half of the sauce in the skillet, but turn off the heat.

❷ Cook the pasta according to package directions. Drain the pasta and transfer it to the skillet. Toss well over low heat. Divide the pasta among six plates or put all of it on a platter. Add a tablespoon of the remaining sauce, or more if you wish, over the pasta and top with the toasted pine nuts.

Each serving		% of calories from fat 11	
Calories	320	Total Fat	3.9 g
Protein	11 g	Saturated Fat	0.6 g
Carbohydrates	57 g	Cholesterol	0 mg
Dietary Fiber	7 g	Sodium	440 mg

CHAPTER 5
THE MAGIC OF HERBS AND SPICES WITH PASTA

INTRODUCTION

One of the most effective ways to enhance the flavor of food, especially when cutting back on fat, is to use herbs creatively. Recognizing this fact, supermarkets have shelves and bins full of fresh herbs, so there is little or no reason to bypass their use.

As soothing, pleasing, and tasty as the plants themselves, the history of herbs stretches far back into time. Egyptians put bunches of herbs in the hands of mummies, and ancient Persians lovingly planted them in their gardens. The Greeks enjoyed them and, to this day, add herbs to most of their dishes. And herbs are essential to Italian cooking, especially in pasta dishes. The Great Herbal, published in 1526, stated basil taketh away melancholy and maketh men merry and glad. What a wonderful thought!

Let's look at the herbs used most often in this book.

• *Basil* is essential to Italian cooking, and this herb blends well with tomatoes, garlic, and pasta. It has a mild sweetness, and I use it frequently as a flavorful pasta ingredient.

• Like the vegetable it comes from, *fennel seed* has a mild licorice flavor, much milder than anise. I use it a lot in Italian pasta dishes and sauces.

• Like basil, *oregano* is considered a quintessential Italian herb and, therefore, a basic herb in pasta and pasta sauce cooking. It is simply wonderful in tomato sauces and soups such as minestrone.

• Its sister herb, *marjoram,* has a more delicate flavor and can be used in place of oregano.

• *Parsley* is the most widely available of all fresh herbs and comes in flat-leaf and curly-leaf forms. I prefer the flat leaf variety because I think it's tastier.

• *Rosemary,* another basic Italian herb, looks like an evergreen, and it is just as fragrant. Its flavor is assertive, so use it sparingly, especially in pasta dishes.

• *Thyme* is also quite strong, but it is wonderful in tomato sauces, soups, and fish/pasta dishes.

Fresh herbs stay fresh longer if you wrap them up in damp paper towels, put them in plastic wrap or bags, and store them in the refrigerator. Although fresh herbs are preferred over dried, it is not always possible to grow them or find the particular one you need at the moment. In this case, use commercially dried herbs, but keep in mind that they are stronger than fresh. When you substitute dried herbs for fresh, use one-half to one teaspoon of crushed herbs and one-fourth to one-half teaspoon of ground herbs for every tablespoon of fresh. Buy dried herbs in smaller packages because, if kept too long, they will lose their flavor, as their volatile oils evaporate.

LITTLE STARS WITH SESAME FLAVORS WITH STEAMED BROCCOLI RABE

MAKES 4 TO 6 SERVINGS

For the broccoli rabe:

2 bunches fresh broccoli rabe, stems trimmed
2 tablespoons extra-virgin olive oil
2 large cloves garlic, minced

For the pasta:

2 cups small pasta, such as little stars (stellette), small shells, and small elbows
1/2 cup thinly sliced scallions
1/4 cup toasted sesame seeds
1/4 cup finely chopped red bell pepper
1/4 cup finely chopped fresh flat parsley
2 teaspoons sesame oil mixed with 1/2 teaspoon Tabasco sauce

Note: To toast the sesame seeds, add them to a hot skillet and stir over medium heat until they lightly brown, about 1 to 2 minutes. Do not let them scorch.

1. Trim the broccoli rabe, rinse well, drain, and cut into 2-inch lengths. Cook in a steamer until it is bright green and tender, about 3 minutes. Set aside.

2. In a skillet, heat oil and sauté garlic 1 minute just to brown it lightly. Add steamed broccoli, toss well, and keep warm.

3. Cook the pasta according to package directions. Drain the pasta well and transfer it to a large bowl. Add the remaining pasta ingredients and toss well.

4. To serve, apportion the broccoli rabe to four to six individual plates. Make a circle of it on each plate, the center of which is empty (like a wreath). Spoon the pasta into the broccoli nest and serve right away.

Each serving		% of calories from fat 39	
Calories	320	Total Fat	14 g
Protein	9 g	Saturated Fat	2 g
Carbohydrates	41 g	Cholesterol	0 g
Dietary Fiber	4 g	Sodium	27 mg

SESAME SEEDS AND OILS

Sesame seeds come from a very fragrant annual herb.They have a nutty, slightly sweet flavor.

Three of my favorite oils to cook with are all sesame oils. One is dark, with a nutty, somewhat strong flavor. It is made from roasted sesame seeds and is available in stores where Chinese and Japanese ingredients are sold. This oil can be used for flavoring and sautéing, but a little bit goes a long way. The second is paler and not quite as strong in taste as the roasted sesame oil. This oil can be used in wok cooking. It, too, is available in markets selling Asian foods. The third type is a sesame chili oil. Sesame oil and chili oil are combined with a fiery result; it should be used with discretion.

BASIL, CHIVE, AND GARLIC SAUCE

MAKES 4 SERVINGS WITH 1/2 POUND OF PASTA

Basil, chives, parsley, and garlic combine here to make a "green" sauce. It is not a pesto sauce because it does not contain nuts, but it does add chives. It is a delicious way to sauce pasta quickly.

2 tablespoons extra-virgin olive oil
4 medium cloves garlic, minced
1/4 cup finely chopped basil leaves
2 tablespoons finely chopped flat parsley
2 tablespoons finely chopped chives
1/2 pound of pasta
4 tablespoons freshly grated Parmesan cheese

❶ Heat oil in a skillet and sauté garlic until it begins to turn color, about 2 minutes. Stir in basil, parsley, and chives, and remove from the heat.

❷ When the pasta is cooked according to package directions, add it to the skillet and toss all ingredients together over medium heat. Serve right away with the Parmesan cheese.

Each serving (incl. pasta)		% of calories from fat 27	
Calories	317	Total Fat	9.8 g
Protein	11 g	Saturated Fat	2 g
Carbohydrates	46 g	Cholesterol	5 mg
Dietary Fiber	5 g	Sodium	120 mg

BASIL PESTO

MAKES 6 SERVINGS WITH 1/2 POUND OF PASTA

Most Italians insist that pesto be made with fresh basil. Some, however, think that it can be made with fresh basil *and* flat parsley (half and half). I have tried both and like both.

1 1/2 cups loosely packed fresh basil leaves
1/4 cup pine nuts (1 1/3 ounces)
2 small cloves garlic, minced
pinch of salt
1 1/2 tablespoons freshly grated Parmesan or Pecorino cheese
2 tablespoons extra-virgin olive oil
1/2 pound of pasta

❶ Classically, these ingredients are ground to a paste in a mortar and pestle, but it is easier to do it in a mini food processor. Add the basil, pine nuts, garlic, and salt. Pulse several times until a thickish paste forms (don't overdo this). Add cheese and pulse one or two times.

❷ Dribble the oil through the opening of the bowl top and pulse two or three times. Use immediately or refrigerate in a covered container for up to 4 days. Some people freeze pesto, but I don't because it is so easy to make it fresh. I also substitute walnuts instead of pine nuts for a variation.

❸ Combine pasta, prepared according to package directions, and the sauce. Serve hot, lukewarm, or at room temperature.

GREEN SAUCES

In Milan, green sauce is made with garlic, bread crumbs, chopped boiled egg, anchovy fillets, finely chopped capers, chopped parsley, olive oil, and salt. The green sauce of Sicily is made largely of olive oil and fresh lemon juice with chopped fresh parsley and fresh oregano, hot water, and salt. *Pesto alla Genoese* may also be called a green sauce. It is made with a lot of patience by putting basil leaves and garlic together in a mortar to make a delicious paste. Garlic, more basil, coarse salt, and toasted pine nuts are also added and ground too. Later, Parmesan or Pecorino cheese is added, followed by olive oil.

Each serving (incl. pasta)		% of calories from fat 24	
Calories	335	Total Fat	9 g
Protein	12 g	Saturated Fat	1.5 g
Carbohydrates	50 g	Cholesterol	1 mg
Dietary Fiber	8 g	Sodium	35 mg

FARFALLE, WATERCRESS, AND RADISHES WITH A FRESH HERB BALSAMIC VINAIGRETTE

THE BALSAMIC WAVE

Balsamic vinegar, a trendy item these days in the United States, has been on the scene in Italy for generations. There it is considered a staple. Good balsamic vinegar is aged at least three years. In Modena, Italy, where the ancient casks are handed down from one generation to the next, balsamic vinegar has been made and packaged for hundreds of years. The vinegar's distinct flavor enhances pasta and pasta salad dressings; the flavor is deep, rich, slightly sweet, yet tart, with a hint of burnt caramel.

MAKES 4 TO 6 SERVINGS

This is a tasty and refreshing pasta dish. If you can, use fresh herbs because they will taste best.

- 2 tablespoons extra-virgin olive oil
- 1/4 cup balsamic vinegar
- 3/4 cup low-salt, defatted vegetable or chicken broth
- 3 large cloves garlic, minced
- 1/4 cup (or 1 teaspoon dried) each of 4 chopped fresh herbs such as chives, basil, oregano, thyme, tarragon, savory, marjoram, or cilantro
- 3/4 pound farfalle, cooked and drained
- 1 bunch watercress, trimmed, washed, and spun dry
- 12 radishes, trimmed and thinly sliced in circles, reserving about 12 slices for garnish
- freshly ground black pepper

❶ Pour oil and vinegar in the bowl of a food processor and pulse until emulsified. With a rubber spatula, transfer the mixture to a large bowl.

❷ Add the broth, garlic, and herbs and stir well.

❸ Add cooked pasta, watercress, radishes, and lots of freshly ground pepper and toss mixture well. Before serving, add a garnish of sliced radishes.

Each serving		% of calories from fat 27	
Calories	266	Total Fat	5.9 g
Protein	8 g	Saturated Fat	.8 g
Carbohydrates	45 g	Cholesterol	0 mg
Dietary Fiber	2 g	Sodium	21 mg

FARFALLONI WITH BASIL, LEMON, AND OREGANO

MAKES 4 SERVINGS

This wonderful pasta combination is one of the easiest to make. Farfalloni are big butterflies, larger than the regular pasta butterflies called farfalle, which can be used if your market doesn't carry the larger ones. The uncooked onions, parsley, and other ingredients are very pleasant with the warm cooked pasta.

- 1/4 finely chopped red onion
- 1/4 cup finely chopped flat parsley
- 4 medium cloves garlic, minced
- 2 tablespoons extra-virgin olive oil
- 2 tablespoons finely chopped fresh basil or 1 teaspoon dried
- 2 tablespoons finely chopped fresh oregano or 1 teaspoon dried
- juice of 1 lemon, about 3 tablespoons
- 3/4 pound farfalloni, cooked according to package directions, and loosely drained (i.e., a bit moist)
- salt
- freshly ground black pepper
- grated Parmesan cheese

Combine all ingredients and toss well. Add a teaspoonful or more of freshly grated Parmesan cheese to each serving if you like cheese on your pasta.

Each serving		% of calories from fat 20	
Calories	350	Total Fat	8 g
Protein	10 g	Saturated Fat	1 g
Carbohydrates	59 g	Cholesterol	0 mg
Dietary Fiber	3 g	Sodium	5 mg

BASIL, QUEEN OF THE HERBS

In the *Great Herbal*, published in 1526, it was written that "basil taketh away melancholy and maketh merry and glad." In spite of this, basil was largely unpopular in the United States until the past three decades, when the pizza-and-pesto craze helped it become a household word. In Italy, it has been the queen of the herb world for centuries.

There are at least fifty varieties of basil, but sweet basil is best because of its fabulous affinity for garlic and tomatoes.

Basil grows easily and profusely. It looks good, smells beautiful, and freezes superbly.

PENNE WITH A SPICY SALSA VERDE

MAKES 4 SERVINGS

Salsa verde in Italian means green sauce. It is a classic sauce for certain meats and some fish, although it is made differently in most regions of Italy. (See page 109.) Here, I have adapted green sauce to go with pasta. I'm sure you'll enjoy this simple pasta preparation. It may seem similar to pesto, but it is not the same thing.

1 cup packed fresh basil leaves
1 cup packed flat parsley leaves
1/2 cup coarsely chopped celery hearts
1/4 cup coarsely chopped shallots
3 large cloves garlic, minced
2 tablespoons extra-virgin olive oil
juice of 1 lemon (about 3 tablespoons)
1 teaspoon beef bouillon granules
1/2 teaspoon red pepper flakes
1/2 pound penne, cooked and drained

❶ Put everything but the pasta in the bowl of a food processor and pulse four or five times to make a textured sauce.

❷ Put the cooked penne in a large bowl, add the green sauce, and toss until the pasta is well coated. If needed, add a tablespoon or two of the pasta cooking liquid to thin the sauce.

SHALLOTS

A member of the onion family, shallots have a mild taste and a thin, golden skin, the color of Spanish onions. They are divided into cloves, usually two to four cloves to one shallot. They keep well for several weeks in the refrigerator, either in the vegetable drawer or in a covered jar. Shallots are imported from France, but they also are grown domestically, mostly in New York and New Jersey.

Each serving		% of calories from fat 21	
Calories	359	Total Fat	8.6 g
Protein	13 g	Saturated Fat	1 g
Carbohydrates	58 g	Cholesterol	0 mg
Dietary Fiber	9 g	Sodium	215 mg

ITALIAN PASTA WITH IMPERIAL ACCENTS

SOY SAUCE, AN AMERICAN STAPLE

Soy sauce has become an American kitchen staple and is a common ingredient in most dishes with oriental flavors.

The soybean, native to Southeast Asia, was cultivated in China as early as 3000 B.C. Considered to be the single most important crop for many countries, soybeans are grown all over the world, including the midwestern United States. Soybeans are rich in protein and oil. Soy sauce is made from a mixture of cooked soybeans and wheat or barley flour, which is salted and fermented. The liquid is dark brown and salty; it tastes somewhat like bouillon. Recipes in this book call for the low-sodium variety and do not need the addition of salt.

MAKES 4 SERVINGS

Use a thin string pasta such as vermicelli or capellini. Serve it with grilled chicken or turkey burgers. If you prefer spicy food, add a good pinch of red pepper flakes to the ingredients.

1/2 pound thin pasta
1/4 cup finely sliced scallions
2 tablespoons low-sodium soy sauce
1 1/2 tablespoons rice wine vinegar
1 1/2 tablespoons creamy peanut butter mixed with 2 tablespoons water
1 tablespoon finely minced fresh ginger root
1 tablespoon sesame oil
1 teaspoon chili oil
1 teaspoon sugar
2 small cloves garlic, minced
1/4 cup finely chopped parsley

1. Bring to boil 4 to 5 quarts of lightly salted water in which to cook the noodles.

2. In a large bowl, combine all other ingredients except noodles and parsley and let stand for 5 to 10 minutes to blend the flavors.

3. Cook the noodles al dente. Drain and run cold water over the pasta. (This is a rare time that pasta is rinsed, but it is important here to stop the cooking.) Drain well and transfer to a bowl.

4. Toss well, transfer to a serving platter, and garnish with the chopped parsley. It is best to eat this pasta at room temperature.

Each serving		% of calories from fat 32	
Calories	280	Total Fat	10 g
Protein	9 g	Saturated Fat	1.7 g
Carbohydrates	39 g	Cholesterol	46 mg
Dietary Fiber	2 g	Sodium	699 mg

OREGANO AND RED WINE TOMATO SAUCE

MAKES 4 TO 6 SERVINGS WITH 1/2 POUND OF PASTA

Sometimes tomatoes are quite acidic, and a scant teaspoon of sugar will bring them around. One day I was out of sugar and substituted honey. I liked it, and here's the result.

1 tablespoon extra-virgin olive oil
1 cup finely chopped white onion
4 medium cloves garlic, minced
1 cup dry red wine
2 tablespoons honey
1/4 cup finely chopped fresh oregano or 2 teaspoons dried
1/4 teaspoon red pepper flakes
pinch of salt
1 can (28 ounces) Italian plum tomatoes, put through a food mill
1 can (6 ounces) no-salt tomato paste
1/2 pound of pasta

❶ Heat oil in a large skillet and sauté onions until they are limp, 3 to 4 minutes. Add the garlic and sauté 1 minute longer.

❷ Add wine and all other remaining ingredients. Bring to a boil, lower the heat, and simmer partially covered, 20 minutes. The sauce will thicken. If it becomes too thick, thin with several tablespoons of water.

Each serving (incl. pasta)		% of calories from fat 10	
Calories	285	Total Fat	3.3 g
Protein	8 g	Saturated Fat	0.4 g
Carbohydrates	49 g	Cholesterol	0 mg
Dietary Fiber	6 g	Sodium	270 mg

ROTELLE WITH FENNEL, OLIVES, AND HERBS

THE POWER OF HOT RED PEPPER FLAKES

The use of red pepper flakes is emphasized in this book because it is an effective way to add spice to a dish.

If a recipe asks for chili oil, you can buy it or make it yourself. Heat two tablespoons of peanut or sesame oil in a small saucepan. When the oil is hot, add ten small, whole chili peppers and fry until the peppers turn brown, about three to five minutes. Remove the pan and add one-half cup of peanut or sesame oil. When cool, store in a glass container with a tight-fitting lid and keep it in the refrigerator. Use as needed. It is not necessary to remove the chili peppers from the oil before storing.

MAKES 6 SERVINGS

Fennel is a wonderful companion to pasta. In this recipe, its crisp freshness and unique taste stand out.

- 2 tablespoons extra-virgin olive oil
- 2 cups chopped onion
- 1 cup diced fresh fennel with 1/2 cup chopped fennel ferns for garnish
- 1 cup diced carrot
- 4 medium garlic cloves, minced
- 1 tablespoon finely chopped fresh oregano or 1 teaspoon dried
- 1/2 teaspoon red pepper flakes
- 1 1/4 cups low-sodium, defatted chicken broth
- 1/4 cup pitted, chopped cured olives (about 10 olives)
- 3 tablespoons capers, drained and rinsed
- 3 tablespoons balsamic vinegar
- 2 cups basic low-fat tomato sauce (page 76)
- 3/4 pound rotelle

❶ In a large pot, heat oil and sauté onion, fennel, and carrot for 10 minutes, until onion appears translucent. Stir in garlic and sauté 1 minute.

❷ Add oregano, red pepper, broth, olives, capers, vinegar, and basic tomato sauce. Bring to a boil, lower the heat, and simmer 5 minutes, partially covered.

❸ Cook the rotelle according to package directions. Drain well and add the pasta and 1/4 cup of the chopped fennel fern to the sauce. Toss over high heat for 1 to 2 minutes and serve after dotting the top of the pasta with the remaining chopped fresh fennel fern.

Each serving		% of calories from fat 18	
Calories	325	Total Fat	6.6 g
Protein	10 g	Saturated Fat	0.9 g
Carbohydrates	5 g	Cholesterol	0 mg
Dietary Fiber	5 g	Sodium	307 mg

TUBETTINI WITH HERBS AND LEMON

MAKES 6 SERVINGS

Tubettini are like tubetti, which are small hollow tubes, only smaller. This recipe uses chicken broth lavishly, which makes the dish unusually good.

1 cup finely chopped fresh herbs such as parsley, tarragon, and basil (about 1/3 cup each)
2 quarts low-sodium, defatted chicken broth
2 cups uncooked tubettini
juice of 1 1/2 lemons, 4 to 5 tablespoons
freshly ground black pepper
6 tablespoons freshly grated Parmesan cheese

1. Prepare herbs and set them aside.

2. In a medium saucepan, bring broth to a boil. Add the pasta and cook according to package directions. Drain the pasta and transfer it to a bowl or platter.

3. Add herbs, lemon juice, and pepper. Toss well. Serve in individual portions or put all of it on a large platter. In either case, top the pasta with Parmesan cheese.

TARRAGON, THE ESSENTIAL HERB

Tarragon has the delicate, fragrant taste of anise or licorice. It is excellent, if used with discretion, in many pasta and fish dishes, including shellfish. Tarragon also enhances the taste of vegetables and salad dressings. Sprinkle some on tomatoes, potatoes, asparagus, mushrooms, or peas or add it to your vinaigrette dressing.

French tarragon can be grown in most gardens in northern climates or in a pot on a windowsill.

Each serving		% of calories from fat 20	
Calories	218	Total Fat	5 g
Protein	12 g	Saturated Fat	3 g
Carbohydrates	33 g	Cholesterol	12 mg
Dietary Fiber	2 g	Sodium	270 mg

CHAPTER 6
ARTICHOKES TO ZUCCHINI: WONDERFUL VEGETABLES WITH PA

INTRODUCTION

If I had to choose one family of food to live with the rest of my life, I would pick vegetables. They can be prepared in an endless variety of ways. Vegetables contain all the essentials of good nutrition: protein, carbohydrates, fats (but only a little), minerals, and vitamins. These elements vary from one vegetable to the next, but no other food group provides more complete nourishment. An added bonus: vegetables are low in calories.

People today want wholesome diets that are low in fat and high in fiber. There is good news for those who concentrate on eating more fresh vegetables, fruits, and whole grains and who lower their intake of caffeine, sugar, and salt; they're taking positive steps to improving their health. Adding vegetables to pasta opens the door to this garden path to health improvement, but, just as importantly, it adds meaningfully to the enjoyment of food.

Being a vegetarian in a mostly carnivorous society often meant second-class gastronomic citizenship. Today, however, more hosts than ever before are serving meatless meals. A few years ago, vegetables meant overcooked carrots, peas, and green beans or an oily salad of bland iceberg lettuce. Even vegetarian restaurants offered little more than sticky rice. These days vegetables occupy a higher rung on the ladder of culinary expertise. Part of the reason is probably the increased awareness of better health. Not too long ago, kitchen stoves were piled high with greasy chicken wings on top of pasta, but there has been a big change of focus, especially in combining vegetables with other foods, in particular, pasta.

Vegetables are abundant, and they should be more prominent in your pasta preparations. They offer more color than any other food, as well as add variety and flavor to your plate. Combining vegetables with pasta gives a new dimension to dining. If you are lucky enough to have a garden and the fresh produce that comes from it, combine freshly picked vegetables with pasta as suggested in these recipes, and ambrosia is only a few minutes away. If you don't have a vegetable garden, don't fret, for supermarkets now offer a wide assortment of fresh vegetables; the trend of shrink-wrapping is disappearing quickly. You can pick and choose as did our grandparents in the open fresh food markets. Pasta with vegetables is not only healthful, it's satisfying. Try pasta with artichokes to zucchini and everything in between; you'll love them.

See pages 15 and 16 for general information on vegetable nutrients.

ARTICHOKE SAUCE WITH ARTICHOKE PASTA

MAKES 4 SERVINGS

Artichoke pasta is very low in fat, and many consider it to be a gourmet item. In this recipe, the flavor of artichokes is enhanced by adding artichoke hearts to the sauce.

3 tablespoons canola oil

2 medium cloves garlic, minced

2 cups canned artichoke hearts, drained, rinsed, and dried, cut into 1/2-inch-wide slices

1/2 pound artichoke string pasta

1. In a large skillet, heat oil and sauté garlic for 1 to 2 minutes. Add artichoke pieces and sauté until lightly brown.

2. Cook pasta according to package directions, drain it well, and add it to the skillet with the artichoke pieces. Over medium heat, toss well for about 1 minute. Serve right away.

Each serving		% of calories from fat 30	
Calories	320	Total Fat	11 g
Protein	9 g	Saturated Fat	1 g
Carbohydrates	45 g	Cholesterol	0 mg
Dietary Fiber	8 g	Sodium	55 mg

BABY ARTICHOKES AND GOAT CHEESE PASTA

MAKES 4 SERVINGS

This is best when made with fresh, small artichokes, but it can be made with canned artichoke hearts. A one-pound can will do if you slice the hearts. Drain and dry them, add them to the oil, sauté them for four or five minutes, and continue with the recipe.

- juice of 2 lemons, about 6 tablespoons
- 16 baby artichokes
- 2 tablespoons extra-virgin olive oil
- 2 very thin slices of salami, cut in thin strips
- 2 medium cloves garlic, minced
- 1/2 pound fusilli, cooked and drained
- 1/2 cup finely chopped flat parsley
- 3 tablespoons crumbled goat cheese
- 4 tablespoons freshly grated Parmesan cheese

1. Put lemon juice in a large bowl.

2. Trim artichokes so that only the tender, soft green leaves remain. Slice each artichoke lengthwise in four and place in the bowl with the lemon juice. Add each artichoke to the lemon juice as soon as it is pared and sliced.

3. In a large skillet, heat olive oil. Drain and pat dry the artichoke pieces and add them to the skillet. Sauté until tender, about 15 minutes, stirring frequently. Add salami and garlic and sauté until the salami crisps.

4. Add cooked pasta, parsley, and the goat cheese. Toss well and top with Parmesan cheese.

CALIFORNIA ARTICHOKES

Almost all American artichokes come from the Monterey area in California, the setting of many John Steinbeck novels. Before selecting an artichoke, look closely at the leaves. Lightly browned edges indicate that the artichoke was exposed to frost and will therefore be of poor quality. Choose pure green ones. Artichokes, trimmed and cooked plain, have about fifty calories each and are rich in minerals and vitamins.

Each serving		% of calories from fat 27	
Calories	462	Total Fat	14 g
Protein	20 g	Saturated Fat	4.6 g
Carbohydrates	68 g	Cholesterol	14 mg
Dietary Fiber	15 g	Sodium	436 mg

ARUGULA WITH BACON AND THIN SPAGHETTI

MAKES 4 SERVINGS

Arugula is also known as rocket or roquette. It used to be sold only in Italian markets, but it is now widely available. It is rich in beta-carotene and very high in vitamin C. Arugula has a peppery taste, and its flavor becomes stronger as it matures.

1 tablespoon extra-virgin olive oil
2 thin slices bacon, finely chopped
2 large cloves garlic, minced
1/2 teaspoon red pepper flakes
1 1/2 cups low-sodium, defatted chicken broth
1/2 pound thin spaghetti
2 cups finely chopped arugula (1 bunch)
4 tablespoons freshly grated Parmesan cheese

❶ Heat oil in a large skillet and sauté bacon until it is almost crisp. Add garlic and red pepper flakes, and cook 1 minute longer.

❷ Add the broth, bring to a boil, and reduce by one third, about 5 minutes.

❸ Cook the pasta according to package directions. Drain and add it to the skillet. Toss well over medium heat.

❹ Add the chopped arugula and toss well. Transfer the pasta to a bowl or a platter, add the cheese, and serve right away.

Each serving (incl. pasta)		% of calories from fat 25	
Calories	321	Total Fat	9 g
Protein	13 g	Saturated Fat	3 g
Carbohydrates	46 g	Cholesterol	14 mg
Dietary Fiber	5 g	Sodium	290 mg

FARFALLE WITH ROASTED GARLIC AND BROCCOLI PUREE

MAKES 4 TO 6 SERVINGS

Broccoli, garlic, and pasta team up here to make a special dish. Don't overprocess the broccoli. The sauce should have a lot of texture.

- 1 head garlic
- 1 bunch fresh broccoli or 2 packages (10 ounces each) frozen, thawed
- 2 cups cooking liquid from the broccoli
- 1 generous tablespoon extra-virgin olive oil
- juice of 1 lemon, about 3 tablespoons
- 1/4 cup finely chopped chives
- 3/4 pound farfalle
- 1/4 teaspoon salt
- freshly ground black pepper
- grated Parmesan cheese

❶ Cut off about 1/2 inch of the top of the garlic head. Spoon several drops of olive oil over the cut edge. Wrap in foil and bake 30 minutes or longer in a preheated 425°F oven until the cloves are tender. Cool. When cool enough to handle, squeeze the pulp from the cloves and put the pulp into the bowl of a processor.

❷ Cook broccoli until tender and drain, reserving 2 cups of liquid. Add broccoli, reserved liquid, 1 tablespoon oil, and lemon juice to the processor. Puree with several pulses.

❸ Cook the farfalle according to package directions. Drain the pasta and put it in a bowl. Add the puree, chives, salt, and a liberal amount of pepper and toss well. Serve with Parmesan cheese if you wish.

CHIVES

Related to onions, chives are thinner than scallions and look more like grass, but with hollow shoots. This verdant herb forms no bulbs, so only the shoots are used. Grow chives in a pot or in your garden and pick them fresh when you want to use them. Using scissors, snip them into your sauces and salsas or use them whole, as a garnish. They will add a lively touch of flavor and color to any savory dish. A perennial herb, when planted in the ground, chives will return the following spring.

Each serving		% of calories from fat 10	
Calories	281	Total Fat	3.4 g
Protein	11 g	Saturated Fat	0.4 g
Carbohydrates	52 g	Cholesterol	0 mg
Dietary Fiber	5 g	Sodium	22 mg

CAVATELLI WITH GARBANZOS IN A TOMATO SAUCE

MAKES 4 SERVINGS

This healthy and substantial dish is easy to prepare and is good reheated. You'll make this recipe often. Serve with a fresh green salad.

- 1 tablespoon extra-virgin olive oil
- 1 medium onion, diced
- 3 large cloves garlic, minced
- 1 tablespoon finely chopped rosemary or 1 teaspoon dried
- 1 can (28 ounces) plum tomatoes with juices, put through a food mill
- 3/4 cup canned garbanzos, rinsed several times
- 1/2 pound cavatelli
- 4 tablespoons freshly grated Pecorino cheese

❶ Heat oil in a large, nonstick skillet and sauté onions 3 minutes to soften. Stir in garlic and rosemary and cook 2 minutes, stirring all the time.

❷ Add tomatoes and cook uncovered 5 minutes. Add garbanzos and cook 5 minutes more.

❸ Meanwhile, cook cavatelli according to package directions. Drain and add to the skillet. Toss well 1 to 2 minutes over medium-high heat. Serve in a bowl or on individual plates. Top with Pecorino cheese.

HAIL ROSEMARY

Rosemary has many uses in cooking, especially with meats and pasta sauces. It is a unique flavoring agent. Use this herb sparingly because it has a strong flavor and may overtake other flavors. If you use it dried, be sure to crush the leaves to help release the flavor, but remember that a little goes a long way.

A lovely story about this herb says that the Virgin Mary spread her linen cloak over a white flowered rosemary bush, and thereafter, the flowers were as blue as her cloak. The herb is best fresh, and it is abundant in Virginia, North Carolina, and California.

Each serving		% of calories from fat 16	
Calories	454	Total Fat	8.5 g
Protein	18 g	Saturated Fat	1.9 g
Carbohydrates	74 g	Cholesterol	7 mg
Dietary Fiber	11 g	Sodium	448 mg

FEDELINI WITH GARLIC, LEMON, AND RADICCHIO

MAKES 4 SERVINGS

This dish is beautiful to look at and very elegant to serve as a main lunch dish or as a first course for eight.

1 tablespoon extra-virgin olive oil
2 large cloves garlic, minced
1/2 cup dry white wine
finely chopped zest of 1 lemon
juice of 1 lemon, about 3 tablespoons
1 cup finely diced radicchio
1/2 pound fedelini pasta (very thin spaghetti)
1/2 cup finely diced green pepper
4 teaspoons freshly grated Parmesan cheese
freshly ground black pepper

❶ Heat oil in a large, nonstick skillet and sauté garlic 1 minute. Carefully add wine and cook 2 minutes to reduce it by about half. Stir in zest, lemon juice, and radicchio. Remove from the heat and set aside.

❷ Cook the fedelini according to package directions. Drain, reserving a cup of the cooking liquid, and put the pasta in the skillet. Add uncooked green pepper and several tablespoons of the cooking liquid and toss well. Heat for 2 minutes. If the pasta seems too dry, add more cooking liquid and toss.

❸ To serve, transfer the pasta to a warmed large platter or individual plates. Add the Parmesan cheese and a liberal amount of black pepper. Serve right away.

Each serving		% of calories from fat 15	
Calories	300	Total Fat	5 g
Protein	9 g	Saturated Fat	1 g
Carbohydrates	49 g	Cholesterol	2 mg
Dietary Fiber	5 g	Sodium	45 mg

FEDELINI WITH GRILLED PEPPERS AND ZUCCHINI

MAKES 8 SERVINGS

Fedelini is a string pasta that is dried. It is narrower than spaghetti yet thicker than angel hair. It is one of my favorite string pastas.

- 4 tablespoons extra-virgin olive oil
- 3 tablespoons seasoned rice vinegar
- freshly ground black pepper
- 4 small zucchini, rinsed, ends removed, and sliced once lengthwise
- 1 large red onion, cut into 1/2-inch slices
- 2 large garlic cloves, minced
- freshly ground black pepper
- 2 large red, yellow, or orange bell peppers, grilled, peeled, seeded, and cut into 3/4-inch cubes, or jar of roasted peppers, drained
- 1 cup finely chopped fresh or canned tomatoes
- 1 1/2 cups low-sodium vegetable or defatted chicken broth
- 1 pound fedelini or other thin string pasta such as spaghettini
- 1/4 cup each finely chopped fresh basil and flat leaf parsley
- 8 slivers of curled, sliced Parmesan cheese, or 1/2 cup freshly grated

❶ Combine oil, vinegar, and pepper in a large, shallow bowl. Marinate the zucchini, onions, garlic, and pepper 30 to 40 minutes. Drain the vegetables, reserving the marinade.

❷ When the fire is ready, spray oil on the grill, add the zucchini and onions and grill them about 5 minutes per side. When done, remove vegetables from the grill, cool, and cut zucchini and onion into 3/4-inch pieces.

Continued on next page

❸ Put reserved marinade in a large saucepan. Add cubed zucchini and onion, peppers, tomatoes, and broth, and bring just to the boil. Turn off heat.

❹ Cook the pasta according to package directions. Drain well and add it to the vegetables and sauce. Toss well with the basil and parsley, and heat 2 to 3 minutes.

❺ To serve, spoon onto individual plates and add a curl of Parmesan cheese on the top or let people add their own grated cheese.

Each serving		**% of calories from fat 26**	
Calories	346	Total Fat	10 g
Protein	12 g	Saturated Fat	2 g
Carbohydrates	52 g	Cholesterol	5 mg
Dietary Fiber	6 g	Sodium	213 mg

FETTUCCINE AL FRESCO

MAKES 6 SERVINGS

The only cooked ingredient here is the pasta. Be sure to use really ripe tomatoes and to make the bread crumbs fresh. This is a summer dish when the tomatoes and herbs come from the garden. But if you can get juicy ripe tomatoes at your market at other times, be sure to try this dish all year long.

- 2 pounds ripe tomatoes, peeled (page 76), seeded, and cut in 1/2-inch pieces
- 1 cup thinly sliced celery hearts
- 1 cup finely chopped onion
- 3/4 cup finely chopped fresh basil
- 1/2 cup finely chopped flat parsley
- 2 tablespoons extra-virgin olive oil
- 2 tablespoons balsamic vinegar
- 3/4 pound fettuccine, cooked and drained
- 1/2 cup freshly grated Parmesan or Pecorino cheese
- freshly ground black pepper
- 1/4 cup freshly made bread crumbs, toasted
- 2 teaspoons minced or finely grated orange or lemon zest
- 1 teaspoon dried oregano

❶ Place tomatoes, celery, onion, basil, parsley, olive oil, and vinegar in a large bowl. Toss and leave at room temperature for 30 to 60 minutes.

❷ Cook fettuccine according to package directions. Drain and transfer it to the tomato mixture.

❸ Add cheese and a liberal amount of ground black pepper and toss well. Combine the toasted bread crumbs with the zest and oregano, tossing lightly to mix. Distribute the pasta to individual plates and sprinkle some bread/zest mixture over each portion.

Each serving		% of calories from fat 27	
Calories	374	Total Fat	9 g
Protein	14 g	Saturated Fat	2.6 g
Carbohydrates	60 g	Cholesterol	7 mg
Dietary Fiber	7 g	Sodium	232 mg

GRILLED PEPPERS AND EGGPLANT WITH FETTUCCINE

MAKES 4 SERVINGS

1 medium eggplant
salt
2 medium red bell peppers
4 Italian fryer peppers
2 large garlic cloves, minced
1/2 cup fresh basil leaves
freshly ground black pepper
2 tablespoons balsamic vinegar
1 pound cherry or Italian plum tomatoes, trimmed and cut in small pieces
2 tablespoons extra-virgin olive oil
8 ounces fettuccine
1/4 cup finely chopped fresh flat leaf parsley

❶ Peel the eggplant, slice it 1/2 inch thick, and cut the slices into 1/2-inch cubes. In a colander, salt eggplant lightly and let drain 30 minutes.

❷ Trim the peppers and cut them into 1/2-inch pieces.

❸ Cut off a large piece of foil and turn up the edges. To the packet, add the eggplant, peppers, garlic, basil, black pepper, vinegar, tomatoes, and 1 tablespoon oil. Toss the vegetables and leave the packet partially open.

❹ Carefully place the packet on a hot grill, close the grill cover, and cook 20 to 30 minutes or until the vegetables are tender. Test with a wooden skewer. Remove and let the packet rest.

❺ Cook the pasta according to package directions. Drain, add remaining oil, and toss. Add the cooked vegetables and the fresh parsley. Toss lightly but well. Serve hot or at room temperature.

Each serving		% of calories from fat 26	
Calories	392	Total Fat	9 g
Protein	11 g	Saturated Fat	1 g
Carbohydrates	70 g	Cholesterol	0 mg
Dietary Fiber	11 g	Sodium	25 mg

FRESH SPINACH PASTA (FETTUCCINE VERDI)

MAKES 8 SERVINGS WITH 1 1/2 POUNDS OF PASTA

Fettuccine is one of the most popular pasta shapes in all Italy. It is rolled out thinly and cut a little less than 1/2 inch wide. Spinach fettuccine is especially colorful. Moreover, fettuccine is healthy and low in fat. After boiling it, add it to 2 cups of low-sodium, defatted chicken or vegetable broth. Serve with a heaping tablespoon of freshly grated Parmesan cheese or top with thinly sliced fresh spinach. If you like, you can make this dish with egg whites. You will need six to seven egg whites depending on size.

- 1 bag fresh spinach (10 ounces), stemmed, rinsed and spun dry; save a few uncooked leaves for garnish
- 3 cups unbleached all-purpose flour
- 1/2 teaspoon ground white pepper
- 2 large eggs
- 1 large egg white

1. Prepare several uncooked spinach leaves for garnish and set aside.

2. Steam the remaining spinach for 3 or 4 minutes until still somewhat al dente. Remove spinach. When cool enough to handle, squeeze out as much liquid as possible. Transfer spinach to the bowl of a food processor.

3. Add flour and white pepper to the spinach and pulse until flour is sprinkled with green, 5 or 6 times.

4. Beat eggs and egg white in a separate bowl until frothy. While the processor is on, add beaten eggs. The mixture should take on a coarse texture, like cooked farina. If it is too moist, add a spoonful of flour; if too dry, add a spoonful of water. Transfer the pasta dough to a floured work surface and divide and form it into quarters. Cover with plastic wrap or a large bowl and let it rest for 30 minutes.

Continued on next page

❺ Roll the quarters into thin sheets in your pasta machine, flouring if needed, but using only a minimal amount. The pasta sheets should be cut into strips about 8 inches long, 1/8-inch thick, a little under 1/2-inch wide. Set the cut pasta on a pizza pan or cookie tray.

❻ Either cook pasta immediately or freeze it on the tray. After it is frozen, transfer it to a plastic bag and place it in the freezer for 1 to 2 months. Frozen pasta will cook very quickly. As soon as the pasta rises to the surface of the lightly salted water, it will be done, but test a strand. Use as suggested earlier or in a variety of ways described in the many recipes in this book.

Each serving		**% of calories from fat 8**	
Calories	200	Total Fat	1.8 g
Protein	8 g	Saturated Fat	0.4 g
Carbohydrates	37 g	Cholesterol	53 mg
Dietary Fiber	2 g	Sodium	52 mg

LINGUINE AND ASPARAGUS WITH SPINACH PESTO

MAKES 6 SERVINGS

8 cups packaged fresh spinach (1 10-ounce package), rinsed, spun dry, and stemmed
1/2 cup coarsely chopped walnuts
6 tablespoons freshly grated Parmesan cheese
3 large cloves garlic, minced
1/4 cup low-sodium, defatted chicken broth
1/4 cup chopped fresh basil leaves
3 tablespoons fresh lemon juice
salt
freshly ground black pepper
1/2 pound linguine
2 cups red potatoes, diced
18 asparagus spears, trimmed, cut into 1-inch pieces (about 2 cups)
1 tablespoon extra-virgin olive oil
1/2 cup thinly sliced scallions

❶ To make the pesto, put half of the spinach, half of the walnuts, half of the cheese, garlic, and broth in the bowl of a food processor. Pulse 5 or 6 times. Transfer to a large bowl. Process the remaining spinach and add it to the bowl. Fold in the remaining cheese, basil, lemon juice, salt, and pepper.

❷ To prepare the pasta and vegetables, cook the linguine and the potatoes in lightly salted boiling water 8 minutes. Add the asparagus and continue cooking until the pasta is al dente, 10 to 12 minutes total cooking time. Drain well. Add olive oil and toss lightly.

❸ Add pasta and vegetables to the bowl of pesto, along with the remaining walnuts. Toss well. Sprinkle with scallions and serve.

Each serving	% of calories from fat 29
Calories 353	Total Fat 11.5 g
Protein 16 g	Saturated Fat 2 g
Carbohydrates 50 g	Cholesterol 5 mg
Dietary Fiber 10 g	Sodium 158 mg

ASPARAGUS

Buy asparagus with firm, closed tips; their stalks should be straight and green for most of their length. To store before cooking, wrap the stalk bottoms in a damp cloth or paper towel and keep in the refrigerator crisper or put the wrapped asparagus stalks in a plastic bag and store them in the coldest part of the refrigerator. To prepare them for cooking, rinse them in cool running water to rid them of any sand. Cut or break off the tough or white ends of the stalks. For thicker asparagus, peel the lower third of the stalks with a vegetable parer.

GARLICKY, ONIONY PASTA WITH MUSHROOMS AND PISTACHIOS

MUSHROOMS

The popular varieties include:

- White and off-white buttons.
- Brown buttons are the same as the white buttons but have a brown cap.
- Cepes are also known as bolete and porcini.
- Chanterelles are shaped like trumpets and range in color from yellow to orange.
- Enoki are native to Japan. Their small caps, less than 1/2 inch, are perched on long, thin stems.
- Morels have a strong flavor.
- Portobellos have large, flat tops and long, thick stems.
- Shiitakes have large, umbrella-shaped caps and are brown-black in color.

MAKES 4 SERVINGS

The pistachios add crunch and unusual flavor to this excellent pasta dish.

1 tablespoon extra-virgin olive oil
1/2 cup thinly sliced scallions
4 medium cloves garlic, minced
1 cup thinly sliced mushrooms
2 tomatoes, peeled, seeded, and chopped 1/2 inch
1/4 cup pistachios
1/4 cup finely chopped flat parsley
1/2 teaspoon each, dried thyme and oregano
1/4 teaspoon salt
freshly ground black pepper
1/2 pound fettuccine

❶ Heat oil in a large skillet and sauté the scallions until tender, about 5 minutes. Add garlic and sauté 1 minute longer.

❷ Stir in mushrooms, tomatoes, pistachios, parsley, thyme, oregano, salt, and pepper. Sauté only long enough to heat the vegetables thoroughly.

❸ Cook the pasta according to package directions. Drain and add it to the skillet. Toss well over medium heat for 1 to 2 minutes. Serve right away.

Each serving		% of calories from fat 23	
Calories	326	Total Fat	8.6 g
Protein	11 g	Saturated Fat	1 g
Carbohydrates	52 g	Cholesterol	0 mg
Dietary Fiber	7 g	Sodium	158 mg

GRILLED EGGPLANT WITH FETTUCCINE AND FRESH ARUGULA

MAKES 4 SERVINGS

Grilled eggplant is delicious with cooked pasta, and the peppery, chopped, fresh arugula makes this a wonderful dish any time of the year.

- 1 eggplant, about 1 pound, trimmed and sliced 1/4 inch thick
- spray oil
- 2 tablespoons extra-virgin olive oil
- 2 tablespoons white wine vinegar
- 1/4 cup finely chopped fresh basil leaves
- 2 large cloves garlic, minced
- 4 anchovies, rinsed well and dried
- 1 bunch fresh arugula, stems trimmed, rinsed and dried
- 1/2 pound fettuccine, cooked and drained
- 1/4 cup toasted pine nuts

❶ Ready a grill or broiler. Spray oil on the eggplant slices and cook 3 to 4 minutes per side until browned and tender.

❷ In the small bowl of a food processor, combine oil, vinegar, basil, garlic, and anchovies. Pulse until anchovies are combined into a sauce.

❸ Put the cooked pasta in a bowl or on a platter. Coarsely chop the eggplant and add it to the pasta along with the sauce.

❹ Chop the arugula into 1/2-inch pieces and add it to the pasta. Toss well. Garnish with toasted pine nuts. (To toast the pine nuts, put them in a small skillet over medium heat and sauté them until they begin to turn brown.)

Each serving		% of calories from fat 30	
Calories	375	Total Fat	12.7 g
Protein	12 g	Saturated Fat	1.9 g
Carbohydrates	54 g	Cholesterol	3 mg
Dietary Fiber	8 g	Sodium	154 mg

EGGPLANT

Eggplants available in the United States come in two basic shapes and colors: oblong and elongated, purple and white. The elongated variety sometimes is called Japanese eggplant. The smaller, deep-purple elongated ones are called Italian eggplant. White eggplants are readily available at vegetable stands and supermarkets. They seem to have firmer and moister flesh than the purple ones, but all egg-plant varieties are good for combining with pasta.

Buy eggplants that are firm and have bright green stems. To test for freshness, gently press your thumb into the eggplant; if the indentation refills quickly, the eggplant is fresh.

PENNE PASTA WITH GRILLED CORN AND LEEK SAUCE

MAKES 4 SERVINGS

spray oil
2 leeks, about 1 inch thick, thoroughly rinsed, thinly sliced crosswise using white and light green parts only
2 cups chopped tomatoes
2 large garlic cloves, minced
1/4 cup finely chopped fresh basil or 2 teaspoons dried
1 teaspoon sugar
1/2 teaspoon dried fennel seed
freshly ground black pepper
2 ears fresh corn, in husks
1/2 pound penne pasta, cooked
1/4 cup freshly grated Pecorino cheese

1. Cut two large sheets of foil, 18″ x 18″, put one on top of the other, and lightly spray oil on the top side.

2. Put leeks, tomatoes, garlic, basil, sugar, fennel seed, and pepper into the foil after cupping its four corners. Bring up the corners and fold them over.

3. Remove the silk from the corn without removing the husk. Rewrap and immerse in water for 10 minutes.

4. Prepare the grill. Lightly spray with oil. When the fire is ready, put the foil packet and the corn on it. Grill both about 20 minutes, turning the corn every 5 minutes or so.

5. Transfer contents of the foil packet to a bowl large enough to hold the pasta. Cut the kernels off the cobs and add them. Add the cooked pasta and toss well.

Each serving		% of calories from fat 10	
Calories	312	Total Fat	3.6 g
Protein	12 g	Saturated Fat	1.3 g
Carbohydrates	60 g	Cholesterol	7 mg
Dietary Fiber	5 g	Sodium	101 mg

THE PEPPER MILL AND OTHER SPICES

Just about everyone knows the difference between the flavorful, spicy bite of freshly ground black peppercorns and the weak-flavored, already-ground supermarket variety. Almost every recipe in this book calls for freshly ground black pepper, and it is especially important to use your pepper mill to get the full flavor of this spice on your food.

The difference in taste and aroma also is true of other freshly ground spices. When I visited Tortola, in the British Virgin Islands, I learned to appreciate the difference between freshly ground nutmeg and the store-bought ground variety.

PASTA WITH SPINACH, GARLIC AND LEMON

MAKES 4 TO 6 SERVINGS

I enjoy making this simple, elegant dish with very thin spaghetti, but you can use the recipe with other pastas such as linguine or fettuccine.

- 2 tablespoons extra-virgin olive oil
- 4 medium cloves garlic, minced
- 1 package (10 ounces) frozen or 1 pound fresh spinach, stemmed, rinsed, and coarsely chopped
- 1/2 pound thin spaghetti or other pasta
- juice of 1 lemon, about 3 tablespoons
- salt
- freshly ground black pepper

❶ Heat oil in a large skillet and sauté garlic 1 minute, stirring all the time.

❷ Add spinach by the handsful (it will overwhelm the skillet but it will fit with patience), toss carefully, and cook 2 or 3 minutes. Do not overcook. Remove from heat.

❸ Cook the spaghetti according to package directions. Drain well, reserving 1 cup of the cooking liquid, and add the spaghetti to the skillet. Over medium heat, toss spaghetti and spinach, adding the lemon juice, salt, and a liberal amount of pepper. If you wish, thin the sauce by adding some of the cooking liquid, a table-spoon at a time. Serve immediately on four warm plates.

Each serving		% of calories from fat 23	
Calories	212	Total Fat	5.6 g
Protein	7 g	Saturated Fat	0.8 g
Carbohydrates	34 g	Cholesterol	0 mg
Dietary Fiber	5 g	Sodium	61 mg

PENNE RIGATI WITH GRILLED VEGETABLES

MAKES 4 SERVINGS

You can be adventuresome and substitute zucchini for the eggplant. If you can't find Vidalia onions, use a large red onion. This pasta has a lot of flavor.

- 2 bell peppers of different colors
- spray oil
- 1 eggplant, about 1 pound, cut into 1/2-inch slices
- 8 ripe plum tomatoes, sliced in half lengthwise
- 1 medium Vidalia onion, peeled and sliced into 1/4-inch rings
- 2 anchovies, rinsed and dried
- 2 large cloves garlic, coarsely chopped
- 2 tablespoons chopped basil leaves
- 1/2 teaspoon freshly grated black pepper
- 2 tablespoons extra-virgin olive oil
- 1/2 pound penne rigati, cooked and drained

1. Heat a grill and blacken the peppers on all sides until the skin blisters. Put them in a paper sack and let stand 10 minutes. Meanwhile, spray oil on the eggplant and grill it for 4 minutes on each side until the slices are tender. Spray oil on the tomatoes and onion slices and grill them also. Put the tomatoes on the grill skin side down but do not turn them as you do the onion slices.

2. Peel the peppers and remove the stems, seeds, and ribs. Slice peppers 1/4-inch thick and put them in a large bowl. Cut the other grilled vegetables into small pieces and add them to the bowl also, but set aside half of the tomatoes.

3. In a small bowl of a food processor, add the reserved tomatoes, anchovies, garlic, basil, and black pepper. Pulse several times and add the oil. Pulse 3 or 4 more times. Transfer mixture to the vegetable bowl.

4. Add the cooked pasta to the bowl, toss well, and serve warm.

Each serving		% of calories from fat 22	
Calories	344	Total Fat	8.6
Protein	11 g	Saturated Fat	1.2 g
Carbohydrates	59 g	Cholesterol	2 mg
Dietary Fiber	8 g	Sodium	92 mg

VEGETABLE AND TOMATO SAUCE WITH THIN SPAGHETTI

MAKES 6 SERVINGS

This may be low in fat but it is a rich-tasting pasta. You'll cook this more than once.

1 tablespoon extra-virgin olive oil
1 small onion, peeled and finely diced
1/2 green bell pepper, seeded and finely diced
1 large clove garlic, minced
1/2 teaspoon red pepper flakes
2 small zucchini, trimmed, rinsed, and grated in largest holes of grater
1/4 pound mushrooms, thinly sliced
2 teaspoons each of dried basil and oregano
1/2 teaspoon salt
1 can (28 ounces) tomato puree
1/3 cup dry red wine
3/4 pound thin spaghetti
6 tablespoons freshly grated Parmesan cheese

❶ Heat oil in a large, nonstick skillet and sauté onion, pepper, garlic, and red pepper flakes 5 minutes until onion becomes limp.

❷ Add the zucchini, mushrooms, basil, oregano, and salt. Cook, uncovered, 5 minutes to allow the mushrooms to render some of their juices.

❸ Add tomato puree and the wine, bring to a boil, lower the heat, and simmer, uncovered, 20 minutes. Stir frequently.

❹ Meanwhile, cook the spaghetti according to package directions. Drain the pasta and place it in a bowl. Add half of the cooked sauce and toss. Divide among six plates. Add the remaining sauce and pass the Parmesan cheese. Serve right away.

Each serving		% of calories from fat 14	
Calories	348	Total Fat	5.6 g
Protein	13 g	Saturated Fat	1.7 g
Carbohydrates	61 g	Cholesterol	5 mg
Dietary Fiber	8 g	Sodium	842 mg

RADICCHIO AND RIGATONI

RADICCHIO

There are three varieties:

- The radicchio with variegated leaves from Castelfranco (in the Veneto region) grows in small, round sizes like a head of cabbage. It is called a rosette because its yellow-green leaves are flecked with red.
- The radicchio from Treviso, a chic city north of Venice, is long and feathery. Its color runs pink to ox-blood with white ribs.
- The baby radicchio, called radicchietto, has tiny, tear-shaped green leaves that are especially good in salads.

MAKES 4 SERVINGS

Radicchio is one of Italy's favorite vegetables; it is a crisp salad green belonging to the chicory family. It is also popular here and can be found in almost every greengrocery and in the fresh produce sections of supermarkets. See the accompanying sidebar for different kinds of radicchio.

2 tablespoons extra-virgin olive oil
4 cups finely chopped radicchio leaves
1/2 cup finely chopped onion
1/2 cup dry red wine
1/2 pound rigatoni
1 cup balsamella sauce (page 26), heated
4 tablespoons freshly grated Pecorino cheese

❶ Heat oil in a large skillet and sauté onion and 3 cups of chopped radicchio until onion seems done, 6 to 8 minutes.

❷ Add wine and let half of it cook off, about 5 minutes.

❸ Meanwhile, cook pasta according to package directions. Drain well and add pasta and balsamella to the skillet. Also add remaining uncooked, chopped radicchio. Toss and heat thoroughly.

Each serving		% of calories from fat 28	
Calories	405	Total Fat	13 g
Protein	13 g	Saturated Fat	3 g
Carbohydrates	54 g	Cholesterol	9 mg
Dietary Fiber	2 g	Sodium	160 mg

SPICY GRILLED TOMATO AND LEEK SAUCE OVER RIGATONI

MAKES 6 SERVINGS

The delicious grilled flavor is doubled here when two very tasty ingredients, tomatoes and leeks, are combined. Together, they make a robust sauce for rigatoni.

6 large ripe globe tomatoes, trimmed, cut in halves
1/4 cup finely chopped fresh oregano or 1 tablespoon dried
spray oil
2 large leeks, trimmed, rinsed carefully, and sliced lengthwise
2 large cloves garlic, minced
4 tablespoons extra-virgin olive oil
1/3 teaspoon red pepper flakes
1 teaspoon sugar
3/4 pound rigatoni, cooked and drained
2 tablespoons Pecorino cheese
3 tablespoons finely chopped flat parsley

❶ Prepare the grill. Squeeze the seeds out of the tomatoes, discard the seeds, and season tomatoes with oregano. Spray oil on tomatoes. When the fire is ready, grill the tomatoes with the cover down 5 minutes per side. Spray oil on leeks and grill them at the same time; the leeks may take a little longer to grill, depending on their size.

❷ Transfer the grilled tomatoes and leeks to the bowl of a processor. Add garlic, oil, pepper flakes, and sugar, and pulse to make a chunky sauce.

❸ Put cooked pasta on a large bowl or platter, add all the sauce, toss, and serve. Top with cheese and parsley.

Each serving		% of calories from fat 28	
Calories	349	Total Fat	11 g
Protein	10 g	Saturated Fat	1.7 g
Carbohydrates	54 g	Cholesterol	2 mg
Dietary Fiber	3 g	Sodium	47 mg

SPICY, LEMONY PASTA WITH ARTICHOKES AND OLIVES

THE MAGICAL LEMON

The juice of a fresh lemon (or lime) will add zest to any food, and you should have both in your refrigerator. They are available year round and, unlike other citrus fruit, lemons do ripen off the tree. Lemons and limes are excellent sources of vitamin C. One lemon will juice to about three tablespoons and yield one tablespoon of grated zest. Limes will juice to about two tablespoons and yield about one-and-a-half teaspoons of grated zest.

MAKES 4 SERVINGS

Here is another easy-to-make pasta dish with a tasty combination of flavors. Be sure to use fresh lemon juice.

- 1 can (1 pound) artichoke hearts
- 1/3 cup sliced, pitted cured black olives
- juice of 1 lemon, about 3 tablespoons
- 3 tablespoons extra-virgin olive oil
- 2 cloves garlic, minced
- 1/4 cup finely chopped flat parsley
- 1/4 cup thinly sliced scallions
- 1/4 teaspoon red pepper flakes
- 1/2 pound gemelli pasta, cooked and drained

1. Drain and rinse artichokes; dry them well. Slice artichokes lengthwise into thin strips, about 1/4 inch wide.
2. In a bowl, combine the remaining ingredients, except the pasta. Add artichokes, stir well, and leave at room temperature 1 hour.
3. Add the cooked pasta, toss well, and serve.

Each serving		% of calories from fat 30	
Calories	359	Total Fat	12.4 g
Protein	10 g	Saturated Fat	1.7 g
Carbohydrates	53 g	Cholesterol	0 mg
Dietary Fiber	7 g	Sodium	308 mg

TOMATO SAUCE WITH SAUTÉED VEGETABLES

MAKES 4 SERVINGS WITH 1/2 POUND OF ANY THIN PASTA

This recipe is one of the easiest ways to cook pasta. The vegetables add flavor. A more complex vegetable/tomato sauce follows. It is also delicious and very low in fat.

- 2 pounds ripe plum tomatoes, skinned, seeded, and coarsely chopped or 2 cups canned Italian plum tomatoes put through a food mill
- 1 tablespoon extra-virgin olive oil
- 1/2 cup finely chopped onion
- 1/3 cup finely chopped celery, including the pale green leaves
- 1/3 cup finely chopped carrot
- 1/3 cup low-sodium, defatted chicken broth
- 1 teaspoon sugar
- salt
- freshly ground black pepper
- 1/2 pound thin pasta such as spaghettini, cooked and drained

1. Prepare tomatoes and set them aside.

2. Heat oil in a large skillet and sauté onion, celery, and carrot for 10 minutes until the vegetables become somewhat tender. If the skillet dries, add 1 or 2 tablespoons of broth as the vegetables cook.

3. Add tomatoes, sugar, the remaining broth, salt (if you wish), and pepper. Cook, uncovered, at a bare simmer for 20 minutes, stirring frequently. Serve over freshly cooked pasta.

Each serving (incl. pasta)		% of calories from fat 15	
Calories	320	Total Fat	5.4 g
Protein	10 g	Saturated Fat	0.8 g
Carbohydrates	59 g	Cholesterol	0 mg
Dietary Fiber	8 g	Sodium	44 mg

ZUCCHINI AND SUN-DRIED TOMATOES WITH ROASTED PEPPER PASTA

MAKES 6 SERVINGS

3 small zucchini, ends removed, cut lengthwise in four and sliced 1/4 inch
2 medium red bell peppers, diced 1/2 inch
6 scallions, thinly sliced, including tender green part
4 large sun-dried tomatoes, softened in red wine or warm water, finely diced
2 large cloves garlic, minced
2 tablespoons finely chopped fresh oregano or 1 teaspoon dried
1 tablespoon finely chopped fresh thyme or 1/2 teaspoon dried
salt
freshly ground black pepper
1/2 cup vegetable or low-sodium chicken broth
3/4 pound roasted pepper pasta

❶ Prepare the vegetables and herbs and set them aside.

❷ Heat a large skillet, add the broth, and all the ingredients except the pasta and cheese. Bring to a boil, cover, lower the heat, and simmer 15 minutes or until the vegetables are tender.

❸ While the vegetables are cooking, cook the pasta according to package directions. Drain and add pasta to the skillet. Toss over low heat and serve.

Each serving		% of calories from fat 10	
Calories	313	Total Fat	3.7 g
Protein	14 g	Saturated Fat	1.5 g
Carbohydrates	58 g	Cholesterol	5 mg
Dietary Fiber	7 g	Sodium	507 mg

THE SAVORY SCALLION

Scallions are in the market year-round and play an important role in cooking. They look like skinny leeks, but they are really young onions; they are picked before a full bulb is developed. Green onions are more mature scallions; they are picked later and have bulbs. Many recipes in this book call for scallions.

What is so special about scallions, besides their savory flavor, is that the green tops have about five times more vitamin C than full-grown onions. Scallions generally are sold in small bunches of six to ten. Purchase ones with crisp, green tops and clean, white bottoms.

CHAPTER 7
GLORIOUS PASTA WITH SEAFOOD

INTRODUCTION

Seafood is one of the great culinary delights. Unlike a thick beefsteak, the creatures of the ocean and sea deliver high-quality protein that is often low in cholesterol and fat. It is true that cold water fish such as anchovies, herring, mackerel, and salmon are higher in fat than others; however, they are packed with omega-3 fatty acids that do not harden when cooled as saturated fat does. These fish oils are less likely to stick to artery walls.

Research has shown that fish oils seem to hinder the formation of blood clots that can cause heart attacks and strokes and that they reduce high blood triglyceride levels, a risk factor for coronary disease. And there is some evidence that fish oils help prevent heart rhythm abnormalities.

The variety of combinations of fish with pasta offers nutritional choice. For example, a leaner fish such as cod may be eaten one day, and a fattier fish such as mackerel can be eaten another. Keep in mind that clams, oysters, mussels, and scallops are very low in fat and dietary cholesterol. The crustaceans, such as lobster, shrimp, and crab, contain more cholesterol because they are meat eaters.

Fish could keep calories under control. A four-ounce serving of fish provides 140 calories, most of it coming from its high-protein content. This four-ounce portion also gives the body about half its protein needs for the day.

The demand for fish has ignited a cross-country increase in the number of supermarket seafood sections and fish specialty stores. Improved air and other forms of transportation have made fish from Australia almost as common as that from Atlantic cities in the United States, but there has also been a tremendous growth in the number of farm fisheries. One fishmonger recently remarked that most of the fish he sells comes from Chile. There is no question that more and more people are cooking fish whether farm-raised or wild.

BUCATINI WITH SARDINES AND FRESH FENNEL

MAKES 6 SERVINGS

I don't know the origin of this dish, but I first had a similar dish a long time ago at the home of Sicilian friends in New York. It is reasonably low in fat and has a lot of flavor.

- 1 fresh fennel bulb, trimmed and chopped into 1/2-inch pieces
- 2 sun-dried tomatoes, finely chopped
- 2 tablespoons currants
- pinch of saffron threads
- 2 tablespoons extra-virgin olive oil
- 1 medium onion, finely chopped
- 6 anchovy fillets, drained and rinsed 2 or 3 times
- 1/4 cup pine nuts
- 2 cans (4 ounces each) boneless sardines
- freshly ground black pepper
- salt
- 1/2 pound bucatini pasta

❶ Bring 4 to 5 quarts of lightly salted water to a boil in a large pot and cook the fennel pieces about 10 minutes, or until al dente. Drain the fennel and reserve the liquid for cooking the pasta.

❷ Combine tomatoes, currants, saffron threads, and 1/2 cup of cooking liquid in a bowl and let stand 15 minutes.

❸ Heat olive oil in a large skillet and sauté onion until it is transparent, about 3 minutes. Add anchovies, breaking them up with a wooden spoon. Add tomato mixture, cooked fennel, pine nuts, and sardines. Bring to a boil. If the sauce is too dry, add more cooking liquid by spoonfuls. Liberally add black pepper and some salt, if needed. Transfer half of the sauce to a bowl.

❹ Cook pasta in the reserved cooking liquid, drain, and add it to the skillet. Toss well. Transfer to a baking dish, top with remaining sauce, cover, and bake 5 minutes in a preheated oven at 375°F.

Each serving		% of calories from fat 35	
Calories	333	Total Fat	13 g
Protein	18 g	Saturated Fat	2.3 g
Carbohydrates	36	Cholesterol	34 mg
Dietary Fiber	3 g	Sodium	520 mg

CREAMY WHITE CLAM SAUCE

MAKES 4 SERVINGS WITH 1/2 POUND OF PASTA

There is neither butter nor heavy cream in this sauce; instead, buttermilk and a little cornstarch are used to thicken it. It is tasty, easy to prepare, and healthful.

spray oil
1/2 teaspoon dried fennel seeds
3 large cloves garlic, minced
1/2 large onion, finely diced
1/2 cup dry white wine
1/2 cup bottled clam juice
1 cup buttermilk
1 teaspoon cornstarch dissolved in 2 teaspoons water
1 tablespoon freshly grated Parmesan cheese
1 can (6 1/2 ounces) minced clams and their juices
Tabasco sauce to taste
1/3 cup finely chopped chives
1/2 pound pasta, cooked and drained

❶ Spray oil on a large, nonstick skillet and put it over medium high heat. Add fennel seeds and toast them 1 minute, stirring all the time.

❷ Add garlic and onion and sauté 2 minutes. Add wine and clam juice and cook until the liquid is reduced by about half, 3 to 5 minutes. Lower the heat.

❸ Stir in the buttermilk and cornstarch mixture and cook to thicken, about 2 minutes. Stir in the cheese, minced clams, and their juices. Add Tabasco to taste.

❹ When the sauce is thoroughly heated, add cooked pasta to the skillet and toss well over medium heat for 1 to 2 minutes. Serve in a bowl or on individual plates, garnishing with chives.

Each serving		% of calories from fat 5	
Calories	324	Total Fat	2 g
Protein	14 g	Saturated Fat	0.8 g
Carbohydrates	56 g	Cholesterol	11 mg
Dietary Fiber	5 g	Sodium	410 mg

THE LEAN FISH IN THE SEA

These saltwater fish have a fat content between 1 and 5 percent. Most have mild flavored, firm, white flesh.

- COD is the key fish in New England and the Atlantic cod is king of the catch.
- FLATFISH are found on both coasts. On the West Coast there are the petrale, Pacific halibut, and Dover sole. On the East Coast, there is the flounder family including lemon sole or fluke.
- SNAPPER is one of the best-tasting fish, coming from the warmer Atlantic waters extending from North Carolina to Florida as well as in the Gulf of Mexico.
- PORGY are sweet, but a bit textured.
- SKATE and RAY used to be thrown away because most of the fish is inedible, but the wings are sweet and taste like scallops.
- DRUM are found in the East, the South, and the West and include the white sea bass.

CAPELLINI WITH LEMONY BAY SCALLOPS

MORE LEAN FISH

- SEA BASS is quite common. The striped bass is sometimes called the rockfish and can be found on both coasts. Black sea bass, grouper, and white perch are Atlantic fish, although grouper is also subtropic. The giant sea bass is found on the West Coast.
- ROCKFISH include fish that are white to pink in color such as the highly marketed ocean perch (called redfish) and the vermilion rockfish from the West Coast.
- WOLF FISH is probably the least known, but when it is in the markets, it is sold as ocean catfish.

MAKES 6 SERVINGS

Lemon is the spark here. Always use fresh lemon juice; never make the mistake of using bottled juice because it is just not the same.

1 pound fresh bay scallops
juice of 1 lemon, about 3 tablespoons
2 tablespoons extra-virgin olive oil
8 shallots, peeled and thinly sliced
1/2 cup dry white wine
2 cups canned Italian plum tomatoes, put through a food mill
12 ounces clam juice
1/2 teaspoon dried fennel seed
freshly ground black pepper
1 tablespoon butter
1 pound capellini (very thin pasta)
1/2 cup finely chopped flat parsley
1 tablespoon finely chopped lemon zest

1. Marinate scallops in lemon juice 30 minutes.

2. Meanwhile, prepare sauce. In a skillet, heat oil and sauté shallots until they begin to turn color, 3 to 5 minutes. Add wine, tomatoes, clam juice, fennel seed, and a liberal amount of pepper. Simmer 10 minutes.

3. Drain and sauté scallops in butter over high heat for 3 minutes. Add to the sauce for the last minute of cooking.

4. Cook the pasta according to package directions. Drain and return it to the pot in which it was cooked. Add the sauce with the scallops, parsley, and lemon zest. Toss well and serve immediately.

Each serving		% of calories from fat 15	
Calories	492	Total Fat	8.5 g
Protein	24 g	Saturated Fat	2.3 g
Carbohydrates	74 g	Cholesterol	30 mg
Dietary Fiber	7 g	Sodium	536 mg

CONCHIGLIE WITH CLAMS AND SQUID

MAKES 6 SERVINGS

Conchiglie are large pasta shells that can be found boxed in most supermarkets, although they may be there with a different name. While these are large shells, they are not the largest, which are usually used for stuffing.

1/4 cup extra-virgin olive oil
4 large cloves garlic, minced
1/2 teaspoon dried fennel seed
2 cans (6 1/2 ounces each) minced clams
1/2 pound thinly sliced cleaned squid
1/2 cup dry white wine
3/4 pound conchiglie, cooked and drained well
1/2 cup thinly sliced scallions including tender green parts
freshly ground black pepper

1. In a large skillet, heat the oil and sauté garlic and fennel seeds 1 to 2 minutes until the garlic is lightly browned. Add the clams and their liquid, the squid, and the wine and cook 5 to 7 minutes until the squid is tender.
2. Add the cooked pasta to the skillet. Over medium heat, toss the pasta and the fish sauce for 2 to 3 minutes.
3. Serve on individual plates, topped with the sliced scallions and freshly ground pepper.

FRESH FISH

Fish and shellfish are best when fresh. Look your fish in the eye—bright, clear eyes are the surest signs of freshness. Freshness also means that whole fish, fillets, and steaks should have moist, lustrous flesh and shouldn't give off a "fishy" odor.

Take fish home immediately after buying it and put it in the coldest part of the refrigerator until ready to use, preferably in one day. To preserve nutrients, rinse (a very common recipe term) fish in a bowl of cold water by dipping rather than rinsing under cold running water.

Each serving		**% of calories from fat 24**	
Calories	411	Total Fat	11 g
Protein	22 g	Saturated Fat	1.6 g
Carbohydrates	50 g	Cholesterol	110 mg
Dietary Fiber	2 g	Sodium	119 mg

CRESPELLE WITH PARSLEY PESTO AND SPICY SHRIMP

MAKES 4 SERVINGS

For the pesto:

3 large cloves garlic, coarsely chopped
2 tablespoons walnut pieces
1 1/2 cups loosely packed flat parsley leaves
1/4 cup bottled clam juice
juice of 1 lemon, about 3 tablespoons

For the pasta:

8 crespelle (page 13)
spray oil
roasted tomato and onion sauce (page 82)

For the shrimp:

16 large shrimp, about 1 pound, peeled, deveined, rinsed, and dried
1 tablespoon blackening or Cajun seasoning
1/2 teaspoon fennel seed
juice of 1 lemon, about 3 tablespoons

❶ To make the pesto, put all the ingredients in the bowl of a processor and pulse to make a paste.

❷ Lay the crespelle on a flat work surface and divide the pesto among them, spreading the pesto over the crespelle with the back of a spoon. Roll up each crespelle and arrange them side by side, seam side down, in an oiled 8 x 8-inch baking dish. Spoon some roasted tomato and onion sauce over each crespelle and heat the dish in a preheated 350°F oven 20 minutes.

❸ While the crespelle are heating, spray oil on a large, nonstick skillet and put it over high heat. Dust the shrimp with the blackening or Cajun seasoning and sauté them 2 minutes per side or until crisp tender. Add fennel seeds to the skillet as the shrimp are sautéeing. Sprinkle the lemon juice over all and remove from the heat. To serve, put two crespelle with the sauce on each of four plates and add four shrimp to each.

Each serving		% of calories from fat 23	
Calories	217	Total Fat	5.6 g
Protein	13 g	Saturated Fat	1 g
Carbohydrates	30 g	Cholesterol	143 mg
Dietary Fiber	3 g	Sodium	567 mg

LASAGNA SQUARES WITH SNAPPER, MINT, AND WINE

FISH FILLETS

A fillet is the boneless strip of flesh that results when the fish is cut, lengthwise, away from the rib bones. Fillets can be cooked with or without the skin. I usually remove the skin, unless the fillet is very small and tender. In that case, I remove it after the fish has cooked.

If your fishmonger won't skin the fillet, you can do it at home. Using a sharp knife, move the blade just under the skin while pulling the skin away from the flesh with your free hand. Because the skin is oily, and therefore slippery, use a paper or kitchen towel to get a better grip.

MAKES 4 SERVINGS

Lasagna squares do not always need to have fillings between layers. Here is a different way to present lasagna that is tasty and imaginative. I use snapper because it is always fresh and available where I live, but grouper, sea bass, or any other light white fish works well.

4 snapper fillets, about 1 pound
salt
freshly ground black pepper
1 cup canned Italian plum tomatoes, put through a food mill
1/2 cup dry white wine
1/2 cup fish broth or bottled clam juice
1/4 cup finely chopped fresh mint (reserve half for garnish)
1/4 cup finely chopped onions
12 lasagna squares, 4 x 4 inches, about 1/2 pound

1. Lightly salt and liberally pepper the snapper. Arrange fillets in one layer in a large skillet.

2. Combine tomatoes, wine, fish broth, half the mint, and onions. Pour over the fish fillets, bring to a boil, lower the heat, and simmer uncovered 5 minutes. Remove the fish to a plate. Cook the sauce another 5 minutes to reduce it by one third.

3. Cook the lasagna according to package directions. Drain, cut into squares, and arrange three squares in each of four large shallow bowls with rims. The squares should be reasonably flat but overlap.

4. Spoon the sauce over the squares. Add some fish and garnish with the remaining mint.

Each serving		% of calories from fat 7	
Calories	346	Total Fat	2.6 g
Protein	31 g	Saturated Fat	0.5 g
Carbohydrates	42 g	Cholesterol	42 mg
Dietary Fiber	3 g	Sodium	312 mg

PASTA, SICILIAN STYLE, WITH ANCHOVIES AND BREAD CRUMBS

MAKES 6 SERVINGS

This classic Sicilian dish has been modified to lower the fat. It is simple to prepare. The "toasted" bread crumbs add an interesting texture.

3 tablespoons extra-virgin olive oil
2 large cloves garlic, minced
big pinch red pepper flakes
1 can (4 ounces) of flat fillet anchovies
1/2 pound thin spaghetti
1/4 cup finely chopped flat parsley
1 cup fresh bread crumbs
freshly ground black pepper

1. Heat olive oil in a large skillet and sauté garlic until lightly browned, 1 to 2 minutes. Add pepper flakes and anchovies. Mash anchovies with the back of a wooden spoon. Remove from heat.

2. Cook pasta according to package directions. Drain, reserving about 1 cup of the cooking liquid.

3. Add 1/4 cup of the reserved water to the skillet to thin the sauce. Add the pasta and parsley and toss well. If more liquid is needed, add by tablespoons.

4. Put bread crumbs on a cookie sheet and broil until they begin to brown, 1 to 2 minutes. Do not scorch them.

5. Divide the pasta among six plates. Sprinkle some bread crumbs and a liberal amount of black pepper over each and serve.

EAT FISH FOR PROTEIN

The average person needs about 55 grams of protein a day. Most Americans consume more than that because they eat large quantities of red meat and poultry. Health experts advise that we cut down on red meat—eating it only two or three times a week—remove the skin from poultry, and eat more whole grains and legumes, which are low in fat. They also encourage us to eat more fish because it is low in calories, low in fat, and high in protein. Fish also has important omega-3 fatty acids, which, according to current literature, seem to help prevent heart disease.

Each serving		% of calories from fat 29	
Calories	321	Total Fat	10 g
Protein	15 g	Saturated Fat	1.8 g
Carbohydrates	43 g	Cholesterol	16 mg
Dietary Fiber	3 g	Sodium	851 mg

GEMELLI IN A SPICY SNAPPER FISH SAUCE

MAKES 6 SERVINGS

Any snapper fish fillet, including red snapper, can be the basis for this refreshing and tasty pasta sauce, which is spooned over gemelli. Gemelli looks like two small strands of pasta braided together.

3 tablespoons extra-virgin olive oil
1 large red bell pepper, cored, seeded, and diced 1/2 inch
1/2 cup diced fresh fennel or 1/2 teaspoon dried fennel seed
1 medium onion, diced 1/2 inch
1 large clove garlic, minced
6 anchovy fillets, rinsed and dried
3 cups canned Italian plum tomatoes, put through a food mill
1/2 teaspoon red pepper flakes
1 pound snapper fillets, rinsed, dried, and cut into 2-inch squares
1 tablespoon fresh lemon juice
1 pound gemelli
6 sprigs fresh flat parsley

❶ Heat oil in a heavy saucepan and add bell pepper, fennel, onion, garlic, and anchovies. Cook 5 minutes, stirring frequently. Break up the anchovies while stirring.

❷ Add tomatoes and red pepper flakes and bring to a boil. Lower the heat and simmer, uncovered, 10 minutes. Add the snapper and lemon juice and cook a few minutes until the fish turns white.

❸ Cook the gemelli according to package directions. Drain. Put the pasta in a large platter or bowl or divide it among six plates. Spoon the fish and the sauce over the pasta and top with a parsley sprig. Serve right away.

Each serving		% of calories from fat 17	
Calories	484	Total Fat	9.6 g
Protein	29 g	Saturated Fat	1.5 g
Carbohydrates	68 g	Cholesterol	31 mg
Dietary Fiber	8 g	Sodium	421 mg

PENNE RIGATI WITH WHITE CLAM SAUCE

SHELLFISH

When buying clams, oysters, and mussels, make sure that they are alive. The shells should be tightly closed or should close if you touch them. Steamer (soft-shell) clams are an exception. Their shells always gap somewhat, but, if they are alive, the neck will constrict when touched.

Crabs and lobsters should be alive and lively. If lobsters and king crabs have been frozen, they should not have any white freezer-burn spots. All shellfish should have a clean, fresh aroma. A faint iodine odor is caused by habitat and is not a sign of spoilage. A smell of ammonia, however, is a bad sign.

MAKES 8 SERVINGS

Cooking down the broth is important in this recipe because it intensifies the flavor. Making fish broth is really quite a simple task; you should try it.

2 tablespoons extra-virgin olive oil
3 large cloves garlic, minced
1 1/2 quarts fish broth or bottled clam juice
1 1/2 cups dry white wine
3 cans (6 1/2 ounces each) minced clams
1/2 teaspoon red pepper flakes
1 tablespoon vegetable oil spread
1 pound penne rigati pasta, cooked and drained
1/2 cup finely chopped scallions

1. In a large saucepan, heat oil, and sauté garlic 1 minute. Carefully add broth (so it won't sputter) and wine. Bring to a boil. Lower the heat to simmer.

2. Add clams and pepper flakes and simmer uncovered until the broth is reduced by almost half, 15 to 20 minutes.

3. While the broth is cooking, prepare pasta according to package directions. Drain and transfer it to a large bowl. Add the vegetable oil spread and toss well. Add half of the clam sauce.

4. Serve, topping with more sauce and the sliced scallions.

Each serving		% of calories from fat 17	
Calories	319	Total Fat	6 g
Protein	18 g	Saturated Fat	0.8 g
Carbohydrates	47 g	Cholesterol	24 mg
Dietary Fiber	2 g	Sodium	856 mg

SHRIMP, SQUID, AND SPAGHETTI

MAKES 6 SERVINGS

Squid has become quite popular in the United States and you can find it in the fish sections of most supermarkets. It also comes cleaned and frozen. It is very tasty when prepared with pasta.

- 12 fresh baby squid (calamari)
- 24 medium shrimp
- juice of 1 lemon, about 3 tablespoons
- 1 tablespoon unsalted butter
- 2 tablespoons extra-virgin olive oil
- 1/2 teaspoon red pepper flakes
- 1 pound thin spaghetti
- freshly ground black pepper
- 1 1/2 cups fish broth or bottled clam juice, heated
- 1/2 cup finely chopped flat parsley

1. Prepare the squid (see accompanying sidebar).
2. Peel, devein, and rinse the shrimp carefully. Pat dry and combine with the lemon juice. Set aside.
3. Heat butter and oil in a large skillet until the butter melts and the oil bubbles. Add squid pieces and sauté 15 minutes or until tender.
4. Five minutes before the squid are done, add the shrimp and sauté until they turn pink. Do not overcook the shrimp. Add the red pepper flakes.
5. Cook the pasta according to package directions. Drain and return it to the pot. Add ground pepper, fish broth or clam juice, half of the squid-shrimp mixture, and parsley. Toss well and transfer to a large platter. Add the remaining squid and shrimp and serve right away.

Each serving		% of calories from fat 19	
Calories	469	Total Fat	10 g
Protein	29 g	Saturated Fat	2.5 g
Carbohydrates	64 g	Cholesterol	246 mg
Dietary Fiber	3 g	Sodium	470 mg

CLEANING SQUID

Lay the squid on a flat surface and stretch it lengthwise. With a sharp knife, cut just below the eyes. There are ten tentacles, in the center of which is the mouth. Pull or cut it off and discard it.

Pull off whatever skin you can from the tentacles. The tentacles can be chopped and added to the sauce with the rest of the squid.

Squeeze the body and pull out the head. The viscera will slip out of the body easily. Discard all this. Now pull out the transparent center bone.

What remains of the squid is a sack. Rinse this well and peel off the outer skin.

Rinse again and slice it crosswise to make thin circles or cut it lengthwise. If the squid is to be stuffed, no slicing is needed.

HERBED TUNA AND PASTA WITH OLIVES

MAKES 4 SERVINGS

Fresh tuna is delicious cooked with pasta. Here's an easy dish combining both. Be sure to use cured olives.

- spray oil
- 1 pound fresh tuna steak, 3/4 inch thick, cut into 3/4-inch cubes
- 1 teaspoon dried fennel seeds
- 3 large cloves garlic, minced
- 1/4 cup each large, pitted cured green and black olives, chopped
- 1 teaspoon minced lemon zest
- juice of 1 lemon, about 3 tablespoons
- 1/2 teaspoon red pepper flakes
- 3/4 cup dry white wine
- 1/2 pound thin spaghetti, cooked and drained, reserving 1/2 cup of the cooking liquid

❶ Heat a large skillet, spray oil on it, and quickly sear the tuna, 1 to 2 minutes. Remove the tuna.

❷ Add fennel seed and garlic to the skillet and sauté 2 minutes, stirring constantly. Add olives, lemon zest and juice, red pepper flakes, and wine. Bring to a boil and cook about 3 minutes to reduce the sauce.

❸ Return tuna to the skillet and heat 1 minute, stirring all the time.

❹ Add the pasta and toss over medium heat until well combined. Add some pasta cooking liquid to get desired sauce consistency. Serve immediately.

Each serving		% of calories from fat 15	
Calories	434	Total Fat	7.6 g
Protein	34 g	Saturated Fat	1.7 g
Carbohydrates	48 g	Cholesterol	43 mg
Dietary Fiber	5 g	Sodium	122 mg

SPIRAL PASTA WITH MUSSELS AND GARLIC

CLEANING MUSSELS

Use a clam knife to scrape any barnacles from the shells; remove the beardlike strands simply by pulling them by hand. Put the mussels in a large bowl and completely cover them with water. Move the mussels around with your hand, lightly hitting them against each other. Drain and discard the water. Do this two more times, and the water will become clear. Use the mussels immediately or refrigerate until ready to use. There is no need to steep them in water for 4 or 5 hours to rid them of sand, as you might have read.

MAKES 4 SERVINGS

Mussels, garlic, and pasta are a naturally delicious combination of food, and they can be prepared in a variety of ways. Here, they are joined with tomatoes and parsley.

2 quarts mussels, rinsed and scrubbed clean
2 tablespoons extra-virgin olive oil
4 medium cloves garlic, minced
2 cups canned Italian plum tomatoes, put through a food mill
salt
freshly ground black pepper
1/2 pound spiral pasta, cooked and drained
1/4 cup finely chopped flat parsley

❶ Spread cleaned mussels in one layer in a large pan and bake in a preheated 325°F oven 4 to 5 minutes until the mussels open. Check frequently because it does not take long for mussels to open their shells. Remove mussels from the shells, discard the shells, and strain pan juices through two layers of cheesecloth.

❷ In a large skillet, heat oil and sauté garlic 1 minute. Add the tomatoes and the strained mussel liquid and simmer, uncovered, for 12 to 14 minutes. Add mussels and cook 3 or 4 minutes longer. Don't overcook or the mussels will toughen. Add a little salt and a liberal amount of pepper.

❸ Add cooked pasta to the skillet. Toss to coat it with the sauce. Serve in a platter or on individual plates after garnishing with chopped parsley.

Each serving		% of calories from fat 23	
Calories	544	Total Fat	14 g
Protein	44 g	Saturated Fat	2.8 g
Carbohydrates	55 g	Cholesterol	84 mg
Dietary Fiber	3 g	Sodium	1080 mg

THIN SPAGHETTI WITH CRABMEAT

MAKES 6 SERVINGS

Fresh crabmeat is expensive, but the cost per serving is reduced when you prepare this recipe as a main dish for six people. This would also be an excellent buffet item. I find good, fresh lump crabmeat in containers in the fish sections of most supermarkets.

- 3 tablespoons extra-virgin olive oil
- 3 small white onions, finely chopped
- 3 inner celery ribs, thinly sliced
- 2 large cloves garlic, minced
- 1/4 cup finely chopped flat parsley
- freshly ground black pepper
- 2 teaspoons paprika
- 1 to 1 1/2 cups fish broth or bottled clam juice
- 1 pound fresh or canned lump crabmeat, flaked
- 1 pound thin spaghetti

1. In a saucepan, heat the oil and sauté onions, celery, and garlic until the onions begin to turn color, about 3 to 5 minutes.

2. Add parsley, pepper, paprika, and 1 cup of fish broth and simmer 10 minutes. Stir in crabmeat and simmer 3 minutes. Adjust seasoning by adding more freshly ground pepper as necessary.

3. Cook the spaghetti according to package directions. Drain and toss with half the sauce. If the pasta seems dry, add the remaining fish broth. Spoon the remaining sauce on top. Serve at once.

CHOLESTEROL

Studies at the University of California at Berkeley have shown that the cholesterol content of most shellfish is only 50 to 70 milligrams per 3 1/2-ounce serving; this is less than that of cooked, skinless chicken or turkey breast. Even shellfish with the highest cholesterol levels are only slightly higher in cholesterol than lean beef, veal, or pork. The exceptions are shrimp and crayfish, which have nearly twice as much cholesterol as a same-size serving of lean beef. Shellfish are also low in total fat and saturated fat—factors that have a greater impact on blood cholesterol. Additionally, shellfish, like fish, contain omega-3 fatty acids that appear to offer protection against heart disease.

Each serving		% of calories from fat 19	
Calories	457	Total Fat	9.9 g
Protein	27 g	Saturated Fat	1.3 g
Carbohydrates	65 g	Cholesterol	76 mg
Dietary Fiber	7 g	Sodium	400 mg

SAUTÉED SCALLOPS ON LASAGNA SQUARES WITH CHILI CREAM SAUCE

MAKES 4 SERVINGS

I prepare this stylish dish for company. It looks so elegant and, of course, its taste is exquisite.

8 lasagna squares, each 4 x 4 inches
1 1/2 pounds fresh sea scallops, rinsed, drained, and dried
2 1/2 tablespoons all-purpose flour
2 teaspoons canola oil
1 teaspoon chili powder
1/2 teaspoon curry powder
3/4 cup low-fat milk (1%)
pinch of salt
1/4 cup finely sliced scallions including green part
dash of soy sauce

❶ If possible, use fresh lasagna squares cut to size. Cook until pasta rises to top in lightly salted boiling water, 2 or 3 minutes. Drain lasagna, transfer to a bowl, cover with plastic wrap, and keep warm.

❷ Combine the scallops with 2 tablespoons of flour (reserve the remaining half tablespoon for the sauce) and toss well to coat. Heat oil in a skillet and sauté the scallops until lightly browned, about 2 minutes per side. Remove the scallops and set aside.

❸ Add the remaining flour, chili powder, and curry powder to the skillet and stir with a wooden spoon for 1 minute. Add milk slowly, stirring continuously, and cook until the sauce thickens enough to coat the spoon, about 3 minutes. Add salt. Return scallops to skillet, toss, and reheat 1 minute.

❹ Arrange two lasagna pieces on each of four plates. Distribute the scallops and the sauce over the lasagna. Dot with scallion slices and add 1 or 2 drops of soy sauce to the top of each serving.

Each serving		% of calories from fat 12	
Calories	367	Total Fat	5 g
Protein	36 g	Saturated Fat	1.2 g
Carbohydrates	42 g	Cholesterol	58 mg
Dietary Fiber	2 g	Sodium	306 mg

THIN SPAGHETTI WITH ITALIAN TUNA AND TOMATOES

MAKES 6 SERVINGS

The combination of tuna, pasta, and parsley is traditional in Italy. It is not as popular in this country because it is not as well known as other pasta dishes. This dish is quite tasty and low in fat.

1 can (6 1/2 ounces) tuna packed in oil
1 medium onion, peeled and diced
3 medium cloves garlic, minced
1 can (28 ounces) Italian-style plum tomatoes, put through a food mill
3/4 pound thin spaghetti
1/4 cup finely chopped flat parsley
1/2 teaspoon red pepper flakes

❶ Drain the tuna, reserving the oil.

❷ In a large, nonstick skillet, heat the tuna oil (1 to 2 tablespoons) and sauté onions until translucent, 4 minutes. Stir in garlic and cook 1 minute longer.

❸ Add tomatoes, bring to a boil, lower the heat, and simmer until the sauce thickens, 15 to 20 minutes. Break up the tuna into flakes and add it to the tomato sauce. Simmer 5 minutes.

❹ While the tomatoes are cooking, prepare the thin spaghetti according to package directions. Drain and add it to the skillet with the red pepper flakes and half of the parsley. Toss well over medium heat, 1 to 2 minutes. Serve on a platter or on individual plates topped with a sprinkle of parsley.

Each serving		% of calories from fat 10	
Calories	321	Total Fat	3.6 g
Protein	18 g	Saturated Fat	0.6 g
Carbohydrates	51 g	Cholesterol	6 mg
Dietary Fiber	6 g	Sodium	353 mg

THIN SPAGHETTI WITH SHRIMP AND BASIL SAUCE

MAKES 6 TO 8 SERVINGS

Basil, parsley, and red pepper flakes accent this simple, tasty pasta dish. Don't overcook the shrimp or they will toughen.

1 pound thin spaghetti
4 tablespoons extra-virgin olive oil
1/2 medium onion, finely chopped
4 medium cloves garlic, minced
pinch red pepper flakes
salt
freshly ground black pepper
3/4 pound medium shrimp, peeled, deveined, sliced lengthwise in half
1 cup white wine
1/2 cup loosely packed chopped fresh basil
1/4 cup loosely packed chopped flat parsley
2/3 cup reserved water from the pasta pot

❶ Cook the spaghetti according to package directions. Meanwhile, make the sauce.

❷ In a large skillet, heat oil and sauté onion until it is translucent, about 3 minutes. Add garlic and cook 1 minute longer. Add red pepper flakes, salt, pepper, and shrimp and cook 3 minutes. Add wine, bring to a boil, and remove the shrimp with a slotted spoon. Add basil, parsley, and water from the pasta pot. Bring to another boil over high heat.

❸ Add the shrimp and the drained pasta to the sauce. Toss well over the heat. Distribute pasta and sauce to six or eight plates or serve all the pasta in a warm bowl.

Each serving		% of calories from fat 22	
Calories	353	Total Fat	8.6 g
Protein	17 g	Saturated Fat	1.2 g
Carbohydrates	47 g	Cholesterol	65 mg
Dietary Fiber	5 g	Sodium	68 mg

HOW TO CLEAN SHRIMP

It is best to clean shrimp near a sink with water running. Use the tips of your fingers to peel off the shell carefully so the shrimp is not torn or broken, especially at the tail end. With a small, sharp paring knife, make a shallow cut along the back (the curved edge) of the shrimp. Carefully pull out and discard the dark intestinal vein, which also can be grayish. Rinse your hands and the shrimp under the running water. Dry the shrimp before adding to a recipe. Discard the shells or use them with other seafood to make fish broth.

SPICY CURRIED SHRIMP WITH THIN SPAGHETTI

MAKES 4 SERVINGS

Oriental flavors predominate in this recipe, which makes an excellent buffet dish.

1 teaspoon grated lemon zest
juice of 1 lemon, about 3 tablespoons
3 tablespoons low-sodium tamari sauce
3 tablespoons red curry paste
2 tablespoons sugar
1 tablespoon chili or canola oil
1 pound medium shrimp, peeled and deveined, cut in halves lengthwise
1 cup yellow, orange, or red bell pepper, diced
1/3 cup thinly sliced scallions
2 tablespoons finely chopped cilantro
1/2 pound thin spaghetti, cooked and drained, reserving 1/2 cup of the cooking liquid
spray oil
4 teaspoons chopped cashew nuts

1. Combine lemon zest, lemon juice, tamari sauce, curry paste, sugar, and oil in a small bowl. Mix well.

2. Put the shrimp in a bowl and add half of the marinade made in Step 1. Cover the bowl and marinate 40 minutes (30 minutes in the refrigerator, 10 at room temperature).

3. Add the remaining marinade to the peppers, scallions, cilantro and the spaghetti. Set aside.

4. Spray oil on a large skillet and sauté the shrimp until tender, 4 to 5 minutes. Add any leftover marinade during the last minute of cooking. Add the shrimp to the pasta mixture, toss well, and add some cooking liquid if you want a moister dish. Serve with a garnish of chopped cashews.

Each serving		% of calories from fat 17	
Calories	439	Total Fat	8 g
Protein	32 g	Saturated Fat	1 g
Carbohydrates	57 g	Cholesterol	172 mg
Dietary Fiber	5 g	Sodium	677 mg

CILANTRO AND CORIANDER

Cilantro grows everywhere in India and it is used in cooking much as we use parsley. Cilantro and its seeds, coriander, have been popular in Asian and Mediterranean cooking for centuries. This herb also grows wild in northern Africa. Its leaves, also called Chinese parsley, are dark green, flat, and round with jagged edges; they have a pungent, refreshing taste that gives many salsas their unique flavor. Its seeds are small, round, and yellowish, with a strong perfume. Coriander seeds should be heated in a lightly oiled skillet to release their flavor, before being used in a recipe. You can buy the seeds whole or ground.

VERMICELLI WITH SEAFOOD (LOBSTER CLAWS, CLAMS, SQUID, AND SOLE)

MAKES 6 SERVINGS

This is similar to a good fish soup poured over pasta. Fish sauces over pasta are not appreciated in the United States as much as they are elsewhere. Try this; you'll really enjoy it.

4 cups fish broth or clam juice
1/2 cup dry vermouth
1/4 pound squid pieces
1 pound lobster claws, chopped
1/2 pound finely chopped clams, fresh or canned
1 pound fillet of sole or other white fish, cut into large chunks
freshly ground black pepper
1 pound vermicelli
1 tablespoon finely chopped flat parsley
2 tablespoons thinly chopped scallions

❶ Bring broth and vermouth to a boil in a medium saucepan. Add the squid, lower heat, and simmer 25 minutes.

❷ Add lobster and clams and cook 2 minutes longer. Add the fish and cook 2 additional minutes. Sprinkle with a liberal amount of freshly grated black pepper. The fish will cook very quickly-it will turn white. Do not overcook it. Try not to break the fillet pieces, although they will invariably flake apart a little. The point is not to end up with fish looking like mashed potatoes. Remove saucepan from the heat and set aside.

❸ Cook the vermicelli according to package directions. Drain and transfer it to a large, deep platter or bowl. Pour the fish and sauce over the vermicelli. Garnish with parsley and scallions and serve immediately.

Each serving		% of calories from fat 6	
Calories	537	Total Fat	4 g
Protein	52 g	Saturated Fat	0.7 g
Carbohydrates	64 g	Cholesterol	189 mg
Dietary Fiber	3 g	Sodium	737 mg

CHAPTER 8
PASTA AND POULTRY: THE PERFECT PAIR

INTRODUCTION

Chicken, turkey, and other poultry make excellent partners with pasta and can be prepared in a variety of ways to make tasty, low-fat dishes. As in other chapters, the techniques and procedures in the recipes are easy and include sautéing with nonstick pans, using vegetable spray oils, eliminating fat by removing poultry skin and all other animal fat, and increasing the use of herbs and spices. Although fat is kept to a minimum, the recipes do not sacrifice taste and flavor despite the absence of butter and cream. Also the use of non- and low-fat yogurt, sour cream, and cream cheese, as well as other low-fat cheese, adds flavor without extra calories.

I have concentrated on chicken breasts because of their distinct advantages over other cuts of poultry. A breast is usually divided into two halves and, in most cases, half a breast is more than adequate as a serving. Although the average half-breast size is about six ounces, you can either ask for smaller breasts or consider using chicken breast "fillets" or "tenders" (these are packed separately and can be found in most supermarket meat and poultry sections). Frozen breasts are probably the least expensive; these should be thawed in the refrigerator and not at room temperature. So, if you use frozen chicken breasts, allow enough time for defrosting in the refrigerator before proceeding with a recipe. Boned and skinned breasts are more expensive but remember that they have almost no waste. Free-range chicken breasts are the most costly, but you may find that they are worth the extra money. A six-ounce chicken breast half has about 170 calories and 5 grams of fat—excellent reasons to choose boned, skinned chicken breasts for low-fat pasta meals. Besides, they're the best sources of low-fat protein available.

If possible, buy your poultry at counters where a butcher is on duty rather than opting for the shrink-wrapped packets. You will get fresher, better cuts of poultry. If you must buy packaged goods, be sure to check the sell-by dates for freshness. More and more supermarkets are offering better grade chickens, such as free-range, that you might want to consider.

Here are various ways to incorporate this low-fat product into tasty pasta preparations.

GEMELLI WITH WALNUTS, TURKEY BACON, AND PEPPERS

MAKES 4 SERVINGS

The flavor of walnuts is enhanced when they are toasted, which is very easy to do. The dish contains little meat, but the bacon flavor is evident. This recipe is somewhat high in total fat, but very low in saturated fat.

3/4 cup walnut halves
2 tablespoons extra-virgin olive oil
1 large red bell pepper, cored, seeded, ribs removed, thinly sliced
3 large cloves garlic, minced
4 slices turkey bacon, crisped and crumbled
1/2 pound gemelli pasta
1/4 teaspoon salt
freshly ground black pepper
1/4 cup finely chopped chives

❶ Toast the walnuts on a cookie sheet in a preheated 350°F oven for 6 minutes. Stir walnuts once during baking. Remove from oven and set aside.

❷ Heat oil in a large, nonstick skillet and sauté the pepper pieces until they are tender, about 5 minutes. Stir in the garlic and sauté 1 minute longer. Add the crisped and crumbled bacon.

❸ Cook the pasta according to package directions. Drain, reserving a cup of the cooking liquid.

❹ Add pasta, walnuts, salt, and a liberal amount of pepper to the skillet. Toss well over medium heat 2 minutes. Add some cooking liquid by tablespoons if the pasta seems too dry. Serve on a platter and sprinkle with the chives.

Each serving		% of calories from fat 34	
Calories	367	Total Fat	14 g
Protein	12 g	Saturated Fat	2 g
Carbohydrates	47 g	Cholesterol	12 mg
Dietary Fiber	3 g	Sodium	335 mg

WHERE DO CALORIES COME FROM?

Proteins, carbohydrates, and fats are the three food elements that produce calories. Fat produces more than twice as many calories as equal amounts of carbohydrates or proteins. It is easy to understand, therefore, that the reduction of fat is the most efficient way to reduce calories. In equal-size servings of food, the portion containing less fat will have fewer calories.

CHICKEN AND GREEN PEPPER TOMATO SAUCE

ONIONS

An average-size onion has about sixty calories and provides B vitamins, vitamin C, and fiber. When buying onions, select those that are heavy for their size, and have dry skins with no bruises. Don't choose onions that are moldy or have visible sprouts.

Onions should be stored in the warmest part of the refrigerator.

MAKES 4 SERVINGS

Green peppers and onions offer a lot of flavor to this simple sauce made with store-bought fat-free spaghetti sauce.

1 tablespoon extra-virgin olive oil
1 1/2 cups finely chopped onion
1 1/2 cups finely chopped green pepper
1 1/2 cups diced cooked chicken or 1 can (12.5 ounces) chicken, drained
2 cups fat-free spaghetti sauce
1/2 pound thin spaghetti, cooked and drained
1/4 cup finely chopped flat parsley

1. Heat olive oil in a large skillet and sauté the onions and peppers until lightly browned, about 10 minutes.

2. Add chicken and tomato sauce, lower heat, cover, and simmer 5 minutes.

3. Combine with cooked pasta, top with parsley, and serve right away.

Each serving (incl. pasta)		% of calories from fat 19	
Calories	449	Total Fat	9.6 g
Protein	29 g	Saturated Fat	2 g
Carbohydrates	62 g	Cholesterol	56 mg
Dietary Fiber	8 g	Sodium	89 mg

GARLICKY FUSILLI WITH PEAS AND CHICKEN

MAKES 6 SERVINGS

2 cups frozen peas, thawed
1 cup low-sodium, defatted chicken broth
1 tablespoon extra-virgin olive oil
1/4 cup finely chopped minced onion
3 large cloves garlic, minced
1 pound skinned, boned, chicken breasts, cut into 1/4-inch strips
freshly ground black pepper
1/4 teaspoon freshly grated nutmeg
3 cups fusilli, cooked and drained
6 tablespoons freshly grated pecorino cheese
3 teaspoons toasted pine nuts

❶ Combine 1 cup peas and the chicken broth in the bowl of a processor and pulse until a smooth sauce is produced. Pour mixture through a strainer and set it aside. Discard whatever is left in the strainer.

❷ Bring water to a boil in a small saucepan. Add the peas and cook for 1 minute. Drain immediately. Set the peas aside.

❸ Heat the oil in a large, nonstick skillet. Add onion and sauté 3 or 4 minutes until it begins to turn color. Add the garlic and sauté 1 minute, stirring all the time. Add the chicken strips and sauté 3 to 5 minutes, until thoroughly cooked. Add a liberal amount of pepper and the nutmeg.

❹ Add the strained pea sauce to the skillet and reheat. Add pasta and reserved boiled peas and cook over medium heat to bring the various flavors together. Just before serving, stir in cheese. Garnish with pine nuts and serve warm.

CHICKEN SAFETY

Always take care when storing, thawing, and cooking chicken to avoid bacterial contamination. Put the chicken or turkey in the refrigerator as soon as possible after purchase. Wrap the giblets and the bird separately when freezing. Do not thaw at room temperature. Instead, defrost the meat in the refrigerator or in a microwave, according to manufacturer's directions. The current recommendation from the U.S. Department of Agriculture is not to wash poultry as it may spread bacteria around the sink and surrounding area. Always clean the area where you have prepared the poultry. It is best to cook chicken well done; the meat should no longer be pink and the juices should be clear.

Each serving		% of calories from fat 19	
Calories	455	Total Fat	9.7 g
Protein	35 g	Saturated Fat	2.9 g
Carbohydrates	55 g	Cholesterol	53 mg
Dietary Fiber	5 g	Sodium	142 mg

SMOKED CHICKEN AND WATERCRESS SAUCE

MAKES 4 TO 6 SERVINGS WITH 3/4 POUND OF GNOCCHI

1 medium onion, peeled and coarsely chopped
3 large cloves garlic, peeled and coarsely chopped
4 cups watercress, stems trimmed, rinsed, and spun dry
1 cup nonfat sour cream
2 teaspoons mustard, preferably Dijon
juice of 1 lemon, about 3 tablespoons
freshly ground black pepper
1 tablespoon finely chopped fresh tarragon or 1 teaspoon dried
1 tablespoon butter, divided in half
2 cups diced smoked, boned, skinned chicken breasts (about two breast halves)
3/4 pound potato gnocchi
3 tablespoons finely chopped scallions
grated Parmesan cheese

❶ Mince the onion and garlic in a processor.

❷ Add watercress and mince. Add sour cream and mustard and process to make a thick sauce. Add the lemon juice, a liberal amount of pepper, and tarragon. Pulse and transfer the mixture to a large, nonstick skillet.

❸ Heat half of the butter in a small saucepan or skillet and sauté the chicken 2 minutes, tossing and stirring all the time. Add this to the sauce in the skillet.

❹ Cook the gnocchi according to package directions, drain well, and add the remaining butter. Stir and add to the skillet with the chicken and sauce. Heat thoroughly.

❺ Spoon onto four individual plates and sprinkle sliced scallions over the tops. If you wish, you can pass a small bowl of grated Parmesan cheese.

Each serving (incl. pasta)		% of calories from fat 33	
Calories	181	Total Fat	6.7 g
Protein	9 g	Saturated Fat	3.8 g
Carbohydrates	21 g	Cholesterol	28 mg
Dietary Fiber	1 g	Sodium	155 mg

POULTRY SKIN

A 3 1/2-ounce portion of cooked chicken breast with skin has 8 grams of fat; without skin, it has 4 grams of fat. A chicken leg with skin has 13 grams of fat; without skin, 8 grams. For the same amount of turkey, the breast with skin has 3 grams of fat; without skin, 1 gram of fat. A turkey leg with skin has 10 grams of fat; without skin, 4 grams of fat.

A 3 1/2-ounce portion of duck with skin has 28 grams of fat; without skin, it has 11 grams of fat.

To remove the skin from poultry, use a paper towel to pull it away from the meat.

LASAGNA SQUARES AND CHICKEN IN WHITE SAUCE WITH SUN-DRIED TOMATOES AND ASPARAGUS

MAKES 4 SERVINGS

In spite of some extra ingredients, this is quite an easy dish to prepare and a delightful and tasty one, too. Use dried or fresh lasagna sheets but remember that fresh pasta cooks in several minutes. To save on calories, use sun-dried tomatoes packed in plastic bags instead of in oil.

1/2 pound boned, skinned chicken breasts
1 1/2 cups dry white wine
1 tablespoon finely chopped fresh tarragon or 1 teaspoon dried
1/4 cup finely diced sun-dried tomatoes
1/2 cup boiling water
4 medium scallions, thinly sliced
1 cup thinly sliced cremini mushrooms
8 asparagus spears, trimmed, rinsed, and cut in 1-inch lengths
4 lasagna strips
1/4 cup low-sodium, defatted chicken broth
spray oil
4 cloves garlic, minced
1 tablespoon all-purpose flour
12 ounces evaporated skim milk
1/4 teaspoon red pepper flakes
1/3 cup finely chopped flat parsley

❶ Place chicken in a baking dish with the wine. Sprinkle chicken with tarragon and bake in a preheated 350°F oven 15 minutes or until the juices run clear. Slice the chicken into thin strips. Reserve the pan juices.

❷ As soon as the chicken goes into the oven, combine tomatoes and boiling water and let stand 15 minutes.

Continued on next page

❸ Heat a large, nonstick skillet and add the reserved pan juices. Add the scallions, mushrooms, asparagus, and drained tomatoes. Sauté about 5 minutes until the vegetables are tender. Set aside.

❹ Cook the lasagna strips according to package directions. Drain and cut each strip into four pieces. Put all the pasta squares into a bowl and add the chicken broth. Stir gently to coat well.

❺ Spray oil in a small saucepan and heat over medium heat. Add the garlic and sauté 1 minute. Add flour, milk, and pepper flakes and whisk until the mixture thickens, 3 to 5 minutes. With a rubber spatula, transfer the sauce to the vegetables in the skillet. Stir in the chicken and reheat.

❻ To assemble, layer four pieces of pasta in each dish spooning some of the sauce, chicken, and vegetables between the layers. End with some sauce, chicken, and vegetables on top. The pasta need not stack uniformly, but it should appear like a stack of pancakes. Sprinkle parsley over each dish and serve right away.

Each serving		**% of calories from fat**	**6**
Calories	313	Total Fat	2.3 g
Protein	24 g	Saturated Fat	0.6 g
Carbohydrates	35 g	Cholesterol	35 mg
Dietary Fiber	3 g	Sodium	226 mg

LEMON "CREAM" SAUCE WITH CHICKEN AND PASTA

HORMONES
Reports continue to surface concerning additives that are fed to chickens to make them grow faster and plumper. Most of the concern centers on hormone injections and the use of antibiotics in the poultry-farming industry. The Food and Drug Administration says there is nothing to worry about because any residual additives are few and harmless.

MAKES 4 SERVINGS

This is an easy-to-prepare dish with considerable taste—lemony and creamy.

- zest from 2 lemons
- juice from 2 lemons, about 6 tablespoons
- 1 cup balsamella sauce (page 26)
- 1/4 cup white wine
- 1 1/2 cups cooked cubed chicken without skin
- 1/2 pound thin spaghetti
- 2/3 cup freshly grated Parmesan cheese

1. Combine half the zest, all the lemon juice, and the balsamella sauce in a small saucepan, and bring it to a boil. Lower the heat and simmer for 3 minutes. Add wine and chicken, and cook 3 minutes longer. Set aside but keep warm.

2. Cook the pasta according to package directions. Drain and put it in a bowl. Add sauce and toss well. Add cheese and toss again. Serve right away.

Each serving		% of calories from fat 24	
Calories	487	Total Fat	13 g
Protein	33 g	Saturated Fat	5 g
Carbohydrates	55 g	Cholesterol	63 mg
Dietary Fiber	5 g	Sodium	425 mg

PAPPARDELLE AND TURKEY WITH HOT AND SWEET PAPRIKAS

MAKES 6 SERVINGS

If you can't find pappardelle pasta, use fettuccine. The paprikas add a spicy touch to this easy-to-make dish.

1 1/2 pounds turkey breast cutlets
2 tablespoons all-purpose flour
freshly ground black pepper
spray oil
1 large onion, finely chopped
3 large cloves garlic, minced
1 tablespoon sweet Hungarian paprika
1 teaspoon hot Hungarian paprika
2 cups low-sodium, defatted chicken broth
2 cups chopped, peeled, seeded tomatoes (4 small to medium tomatoes or use canned)
2 tablespoons tomato paste
3/4 pound pappardelle
1 tablespoon extra-virgin olive oil
1/4 cup finely chopped flat parsley

❶ Pat dry the turkey cutlets and flour and pepper both sides of each cutlet. Spray oil on a large, nonstick skillet and sauté the cutlets 2 to 3 minutes per side, or until lightly browned. Remove from the skillet, slice into 1/2-inch-thick strips, and set aside.

Continued on next page

❷ Add onion to the skillet and sauté until translucent, about 4 minutes. Add garlic and cook 1 minute longer. Add both paprikas and, stirring continuously, cook 2 minutes longer. Add chicken broth and tomatoes. Stir in tomato paste. Bring to a boil, lower the heat, and simmer, uncovered, 5 minutes to reduce the sauce a little. Add turkey slices and cook until the turkey is tender and cooked through, 3 minutes or so. Set aside.

❸ Cook the pasta according to package directions, drain well, add oil, and toss. Divide among six plates and spoon the turkey strips and sauce over the pasta. Garnish with the parsley and serve right away.

Each serving		**% of calories from fat**	**6**
Calories	389	Total Fat	2.6 g
Protein	39 g	Saturated Fat	0.7 g
Carbohydrates	51 g	Cholesterol	84 mg
Dietary Fiber	3 g	Sodium	103 mg

RIGATONI AND CHICKEN IN A CABERNET SAUCE

MAKES 6 SERVINGS

A little wine goes a long way here. Wine is a great addition to pasta sauces. In most recipes, however, nearly all of the alcohol cooks off, so only the flavor remains.

2 tablespoons extra-virgin olive oil
1 1/2 pounds skinned, boned chicken breasts, cut into 1-inch cubes
freshly ground black pepper
1/4 cup finely chopped onions
2 tablespoons finely chopped carrots
2 tablespoons finely chopped celery
1/2 teaspoon finely chopped fresh rosemary, or a pinch dried
1/4 cup Cabernet Sauvignon wine or a comparable substitute
1/4 cup low-sodium, defatted chicken broth
2 medium tomatoes, peeled, seeded, and chopped
3/4 pound rigatoni
6 tablespoons finely grated pecorino cheese
1/4 cup finely chopped chives

1. Heat oil in a large, nonstick skillet and sauté chicken until it browns on all sides. Add pepper to taste. Spoon the chicken into a bowl and set aside.

2. Add onions, carrots, celery, and rosemary to the same skillet and cook for 2 or 3 minutes over moderate heat. Add wine, broth, and tomatoes. Bring to a boil, lower the heat, and simmer 6 to 8 minutes.

3. While the sauce is cooking, cook the rigatoni according to package directions, drain, and put on a platter.

4. Add the chicken pieces to the sauce and any liquid in the bowl. Heat over medium flame. Pour sauce over the pasta and toss well. Top with cheese and garnish with chives. Serve immediately.

Each serving		% of calories from fat 21	
Calories	418	Total Fat	10 g
Protein	33 g	Saturated Fat	2.6 g
Carbohydrates	46 g	Cholesterol	69 mg
Dietary Fiber	2 g	Sodium	146 mg

SPICY SOY CHICKEN WITH YELLOW AND GREEN TAGLIATELLE

MAKES 4 TO 6 SERVINGS

This recipe makes one of the most colorful pasta dishes in the book because of the two-colored pasta, the green zucchini, and the red bell pepper. This recipe idea came from the popular pasta in Italy called *paglia e fieno,* which means straw and hay.

For the chicken marinade:

- 1/4 cup dry white wine
- 2 scallions, thinly sliced
- 2 large cloves garlic, coarsely chopped
- 2 tablespoons low-sodium soy sauce
- 2 tablespoons seasoned rice vinegar
- 2 tablespoons grated fresh ginger
- 1 tablespoon Dijon mustard
- juice of 1/2 lemon
- 1 small jalapeño pepper, stemmed, seeded and ribs removed, coarsely chopped

For the pasta:

- 1/2 pound boned, skinned chicken breasts
- 2 small zucchini, 1 x 6 inches each, trimmed and cut into 1 1/2-inch matchsticks
- 1 small red bell pepper, stemmed, seeded and ribs removed, cut into 1 1/2-inch matchsticks
- 4 ounces yellow tagliatelle
- 4 ounces green tagliatelle
- 1/2 cup low-sodium, defatted chicken broth
- 4 scallions thinly sliced

Continued on next page

GLORIOUS GINGER

Ginger comes from the tuberlike root of a tropical plant. The root has a paper-thin, light-brown skin that can be removed easily with a vegetable peeler or a paring knife. Ginger freezes well. It is a popular ingredient not only in gingerbread and ginger cookies but also in pasta, especially in the south of Italy.

Ginger is deeply rooted in history and is used in the cuisines of most civilizations, including Arabic, Chinese, Greek, Indian, Roman, and Asian. It is indigenous to India, China, south Asia, and the West Indies.

❶ Put all the ingredients for the marinade in the bowl of a processor and pulse until well blended. Divide the marinade in half.

❷ Put half of the marinade and the chicken in a small baking dish and let stand 30 minutes. Then bake the chicken and its marinade in a preheated 350°F oven 15 minutes or until the juices run clear. Cut the chicken into 1 1/2-inch matchsticks and transfer the pan juices to a large, nonstick skillet.

❸ While the chicken is baking, bring a large pot of lightly salted water to boil and prepare the vegetables.

❹ Heat the pan juices in the skillet over medium-high heat and add the zucchini and red peppers. Sauté until they become tender, 4 to 5 minutes.

❺ Cook the pasta according to package directions. Drain the pasta and put it in a bowl. Add chicken broth and stir. Add chicken, vegetables, and reserved half of the marinade. Toss well. Garnish with scallions and serve right away.

Each serving		**% of calories from fat**	**8**
Calories	216	Total Fat	2 g
Protein	14 g	Saturated Fat	0.4 g
Carbohydrates	33 g	Cholesterol	21 mg
Dietary Fiber	4 g	Sodium	395 mg

ROTELLE AND PEPPERS WITH LEMON-SCENTED CHICKEN

MAKES 4 TO 6 SERVINGS

3 tablespoons low-sodium tamari sauce
juice of 2 lemons, about 6 tablespoons
1 pound boned, skinned chicken breasts, diced 1 inch
2 tablespoons grated lemon zest
2 tablespoons seasoned rice vinegar
1 tablespoon honey
2 teaspoons cornstarch, dissolved in 1 tablespoon water
freshly ground black pepper
1 teaspoon chili oil
2 large bell peppers, one red and one yellow, trimmed and cut into 1-inch squares
1/2 pound rotelle pasta
1/2 cup finely chopped chives

❶ Combine 2 tablespoons of tamari sauce with 2 tablespoons of lemon juice in a bowl and add the chicken. Toss and marinate for 15 minutes.

❷ In another bowl, add remaining tamari sauce, remaining lemon juice, zest, vinegar, honey, cornstarch mixture, and pepper. Stir well and set aside.

❸ Heat chili oil in a large, nonstick skillet and sauté the chicken over high heat, 3 minutes. Remove chicken with a slotted spoon and put into a dish. Add bell peppers and any leftover marinade from the chicken bowl and sauté until the edges of the peppers begin to brown, 4 or 5 minutes. Return chicken to the skillet with the reserved lemon juice mixture. Bring to a boil, lower the heat, and simmer 2 or 3 minutes. Set aside.

❹ Cook the rotelle according to package directions, drain well, and add to the skillet with the chicken and the sauce. Over high heat, toss the pasta and sauce until heated thoroughly. Spoon into individual dishes or serve in a large bowl or platter. Sprinkle chopped chives over all.

Each serving		% of calories from fat	18
Calories	273	Total Fat	5.5 g
Protein	21 g	Saturated Fat	1.3 g
Carbohydrates	35 g	Cholesterol	48 mg
Dietary Fiber	3 g	Sodium	499 mg

SPINACH AND CHICKEN RAGOUT OVER RIGATONI RIGATI

MAKES 4 SERVINGS

1 teaspoon extra-virgin olive oil
4 chicken legs, skin removed
4 chicken thighs, skin removed
1 large onion, thinly sliced
3 large cloves garlic, minced
1 package (10 ounces) spinach or 1 pound fresh spinach, stemmed and coarsely sliced
1 can (28 ounces) plum tomatoes including their juices, put through a food mill
2 medium red bell peppers, roasted, peeled, with stems, seeds, and ribs removed, and diced 1/2 inch (see page 254)
1/2 cup low-sodium, defatted chicken broth
1/2 pound rigatoni rigati
1 tablespoon balsamic vinegar
freshly ground black pepper

❶ Heat oil in a large, nonstick skillet and brown the chicken 5 minutes per side. Remove chicken and set aside.

❷ Add onion to the skillet and sauté until soft, 3 or 4 minutes. Add garlic and sauté 1 minute longer, stirring all the time. Add spinach by the handfuls and, as it softens, add more until all of it is in the skillet.

❸ Add chicken, tomatoes, roasted peppers, and broth. Bring to a boil, lower the heat, and simmer until the chicken is tender, about 40 minutes.

❹ While the chicken is simmering, cook the pasta according to package directions. Drain the pasta and divide it into four warm bowls.

❺ Add vinegar to the ragout, stir well, and spoon it over the pasta, giving each portion one leg and one thigh. Liberally add the black pepper to the top of each dish. Serve right away.

Each serving		% of calories from fat 19	
Calories	512	Total Fat	11 g
Protein	39 g	Saturated Fat	2.7 g
Carbohydrates	62 g	Cholesterol	91 mg
Dietary Fiber	8 g	Sodium	494 mg

SMALL ZITI WITH MASCARPONE AND SMOKED TURKEY

MAKES 4 SERVINGS

This is richer than most other pasta dishes in this book, and the mascarpone is responsible. It is so good that you'll want to make it often.

1/2 pound small ziti
4 ounces mascarpone cheese
2 tablespoons white wine vinegar
1 tablespoon extra-virgin olive oil
1/3 cup thinly sliced scallions
2 zucchini, trimmed and sliced into small matchsticks
1/2 pound boned pre-cooked smoked turkey, sliced into small matchsticks
1/2 teaspoon red pepper flakes, optional

❶ Cook the pasta according to package directions. Reserve 1 cup of the cooking liquid while draining.

❷ In a small saucepan, heat mascarpone and vinegar over low heat just to melt the cheese. Keep warm.

❸ Heat olive oil in a small skillet and sauté the scallions and zucchini until tender, about 5 minutes.

❹ In a large bowl, toss the pasta with the cheese sauce, scallions, zucchini, turkey, and optional pepper flakes. Add a tablespoon or more of the cooking liquid if the pasta seems too dry.

Each serving		% of calories from fat 33	
Calories	389	Total Fat	14.5 g
Protein	24 g	Saturated Fat	6.6 g
Carbohydrates	40 g	Cholesterol	49 mg
Dietary Fiber	2 g	Sodium	1035 mg

THIN SPAGHETTI WITH CHICKEN AND LENTILS

MAKES 6 SERVINGS

Pasta and lentils are an almost perfect combination. One of the more popular soups in Italy is made with this duo. In this recipe, chicken enhances the combination of pasta and lentils to make a unique dish and the touch of balsamic vinegar cuts the richness of both the pasta and the lentils.

3/4 cup dried lentils
1 1/2 cups water
1/4 teaspoon salt
1 tablespoon extra-virgin olive oil
1 pound skinned, boned chicken breasts, cut into very thin strips
1 cup low-sodium, defatted chicken broth
1/2 cup finely chopped scallions
4 medium cloves garlic, minced
freshly ground black pepper
3/4 pound thin spaghetti
1 tablespoon balsamic vinegar
1 tablespoon finely chopped fresh tarragon, or 1 teaspoon dried
1 1/2 cups thinly sliced fresh spinach leaves
1 large ripe tomato, peeled, seeded, and chopped
2 tablespoons freshly grated Parmesan cheese

1. Combine the lentils and the water in a saucepan, bring to a boil, lower the heat, and simmer until the lentils are tender, about 25 minutes. Salt, drain, and set aside.

2. Heat the oil in a large, nonstick skillet and sauté the chicken strips until done, about 4 minutes. If the pan becomes dry, add a tablespoon or two of the broth. Remove the chicken and set aside.

Continued on next page

3. In the same skillet, sauté the scallions for 3 or 4 minutes, or until they begin to brown. Add garlic and sauté 1 minute longer. If scallion and garlic stick to the pan, add more broth.

4. Add lentils and remaining chicken broth to the skillet. Add a liberal amount of pepper. Simmer for about 5 minutes. Then add chicken and reheat.

5. Cook the thin spaghetti according to package directions, drain, and add it to the skillet. Add tarragon and balsamic vinegar, and toss well. Add spinach and tomatoes and toss again for 1 or 2 minutes over medium heat.

6. Put on a platter or in individual dishes with a small topping of Parmesan cheese. Serve right away.

Each serving		**% of calories from fat 11**	
Calories	353	Total Fat	4.6 g
Protein	16 g	Saturated Fat	1.1 g
Carbohydrates	62 g	Cholesterol	2 mg
Dietary Fiber	12 g	Sodium	171 mg

THIN SPAGHETTI WITH GAME HEN AND PAPRIKA WALNUT SAUCE

MAKES 6 SERVINGS

This unusual dish comes from the very northern part of Italy.

1 quart chicken broth (page 59)
Three 1-pound Cornish game hens, or one 3-pound chicken
1 quart of water
4 slices white bread, crusts removed
1/2 cup walnut pieces
3 large cloves garlic, coarsely chopped
2 tablespoons extra-virgin olive oil
1 teaspoon paprika
pinch red pepper flakes
3/4 pound thin spaghetti, #9 or #10, cooked and drained

❶ Put chicken broth, hens or chicken, and 1 quart water in a large pot. Bring to a boil, lower the heat, and simmer, covered, for 1 hour and 15 minutes, or until the birds are tender. Remove the birds. When cool enough to handle, remove all skin, bones, and fat, and cut meat into 1 1/2-inch pieces.

❷ Strain and defat the broth.

❸ Soak bread in 1 cup of the defatted broth, squeeze the bread dry, and put it in the bowl of a food processor. Add the walnuts and garlic and pulse five or six times to make a textured paste. Add 1 1/2 cups more of the broth to thin the paste.

❹ In a small skillet, heat olive oil, paprika, and pepper flakes until oil turns red, 2 or 3 minutes. Remove the pan from the heat.

❺ Put the cooked pasta in a large bowl and add about one third of the walnut sauce. Toss well. Distribute the pasta to six individual plates, spooning more sauce over the top. Add about 1 teaspoon of red oil to each and serve.

Each serving		% of calories from fat 27	
Calories	515	Total Fat	16 g
Protein	36 g	Saturated Fat	3 g
Carbohydrates	57 g	Cholesterol	113 mg
Dietary Fiber	6 g	Sodium	253 mg

VERMICELLI AND CHICKEN WITH UNCOOKED BASIL AND TOMATO SAUCE

CHICKEN BUYING OPTIONS

Your first option is a pre-packaged chicken. These are processed according to regulations set by the U.S. Department of Agriculture. The second option is a natural chicken, which is fed a special diet but no antibiotic or growth hormones. The third option, free-range chickens, is probably the most natural. The chickens are allowed to move about freely and are fed grain and insects. They do not get antibiotics or hormones. Kosher chickens are another possibility.

MAKES 6 SERVINGS

For low-fat dining, there is nothing comparable to the uncooked sauces of basil and tomatoes. Here, the chicken adds protein and considerable taste but very little fat.

- 2 cups fresh chopped, peeled, seeded tomatoes
- 2 tablespoons extra-virgin olive oil
- 2 bacon slices, crisped and crumbled
- 1/4 cup finely chopped fresh basil leaves
- 1/4 cup finely chopped fresh flat parsley
- 1/4 cup finely minced shallots
- 1/4 teaspoon red pepper flakes
- 3/4 pound vermicelli
- spray oil
- 1 1/2 pounds skinned, boned chicken breasts, prepared as pounded cutlets
- 1/4 cup dry white wine
- 1 tablespoon capers, rinsed and dried
- 1/4 cup finely chopped scallions

1. Put tomatoes, oil, bacon, basil, parsley, shallots, and pepper flakes in a bowl. Toss well and marinate for 20 minutes or so.

2. Cook vermicelli according to package directions.

Continued on next page

❸ While the pasta is cooking, heat a large, nonstick skillet, spray with oil and sauté the chicken pieces until browned on both sides, about 3 minutes per side. Add wine and capers and cook 2 or 3 minutes longer. Remove chicken breasts and cut them into thin strips.

❹ Put the cooked and drained pasta on a large platter, add the juices from the chicken skillet and the tomato sauce and toss well. Add chicken strips on top of pasta and garnish with the sliced scallions. Serve hot.

Each serving		**% of calories from fat 23**	
Calories	445	Total Fat	11.6 g
Protein	33 g	Saturated Fat	3.3 g
Carbohydrates	49 g	Cholesterol	72 mg
Dietary Fiber	5 g	Sodium	203 mg

CHAPTER 9
SOME MEAT AND PASTA, LOW-FAT STYLE

INTRODUCTION

In considering low-fat foods with pasta, it is not necessary to eliminate beef, pork, veal, and lamb entirely. Instead, it is important to consider the amount served and the cut of the meat used in a low-fat pasta preparation.

Different cuts of meat have widely differing fat contents. Regular ground beef, f example, has five times the fat grams as top round. The leanest cuts come fro the tenderloin, sirloin, and round steak. This is true for beef as well as for lamb, pork, or veal. Try to buy meats that come from the loin or round and remove an visible fat. Pork tenderloins have about the same low-fat count as chicken breas but require some fine "fat tuning" because they have more fat on them than ne essary. Most importantly, portion size must be significantly reduced.

I think that it is next to impossible for some people to eat without meat. Howeve if meat is quantified and prepared properly, there is no reason to avoid it completely. I have included, therefore, some very tasty preparations, but remember that the portions are small. Don't be surprised that three ounces of cooked mea will register between five and ten grams of fat (look at the nutritional analysis on the bottom of each recipe). But if the rest of the meal is low in fat, you will get b For example, although the beef and pork meatballs have 38 percent fat calories, the total fat calories can be reduced significantly if the meatball is joined by low fat foods such as a low-fat pasta and tomato sauce and a green salad with a low or nonfat dressing.

BEEF AND PORK MEATBALLS WITH SPICY RED PEPPER

MAKES 24 MEATBALLS

I never thought that there could be a tasty low-saturated-fat meatball; well, here it is.

1 1/2 pounds ground lean beef and pork (3/4 pounds of each)
1 cup fresh bread crumbs
1/3 cup Pecorino cheese
1/2 cup tomato sauce
1/4 cup chopped flat parsley
3 large cloves garlic, minced
1 tablespoon Dijon-type mustard
1 teaspoon dried oregano
salt, optional
1/2 teaspoon red pepper flakes
spray oil

❶ Mix all ingredients in a large bowl with splayed fingers. Roll into 1 1/2- to 2-inch meatballs.

❷ Spray oil on a rimmed cookie sheet and place the meatballs on it. Bake in a 400°F preheated oven for 18 minutes.

Note: These meatballs can be reheated in the basic low-fat marinara sauce (page 30).

FAT! FAT! FAT!

A gram of fat has more than double the calories of carbohydrates or protein:

1 gram of fat = 9 calories

1 gram of carbohydrates or protein = 4 calories

Our bodies store fat in a concentrated form. Fat puts on weight, and stored fat undermines good health. This cookbook concentrates on low-fat foods for improved health. Animal fats, as we know, are the culprits where saturated fat is concerned.

Each meatball		% of calories from fat 38	
Calories	57	Total Fat	2.58 g
Protein	7 g	Saturated Fat	1.04 g
Carbohydrates	2 g	Cholesterol	16 mg
Dietary Fiber	1 g	Sodium	61 mg

CREAMY PERCIATELLI WITH ASPARAGUS AND GRILLED SAUSAGE

MAKES 6 TO 8 SERVINGS

This dish is tasty and pretty to look at. The bright orange carrots and the bright green asparagus stand out in the white sauce, which is accented by the grilled sausage.

2 cups perciatelli
2 cups sliced carrots
12 asparagus spears, about 1/2 pound, trimmed and sliced 1 inch thick
1 1/4 cups low-fat or skim milk
1 chicken bouillon cube
2 tablespoons flour
freshly ground black pepper
1/2 pound Italian sausage, grilled and sliced thinly
1/2 cup freshly grated Pecorino cheese

1. Cook together the carrots and the perciatelli according to package directions. After they have cooked 8 minutes, add asparagus pieces and continue cooking until the pasta is al dente. Drain well and reserve 1 cup of cooking liquid.

2. In a skillet, heat milk and bouillon cube until the cube dissolves. Sift the flour into the skillet and whisk constantly until well blended. Add the pepper and bring to a boil. Lower the heat and cook, whisking all the time, until the sauce is thick enough to lightly coat a spoon.

3. Add pasta, carrots, and asparagus to the skillet. Follow with sausage and cheese. Toss over high heat and serve. If the sauce is too thick, thin with some of the cooking liquid reserved from the pasta.

Each serving		% of calories from fat 26	
Calories	202	Total Fat	6 g
Protein	11 g	Saturated Fat	2.5 g
Carbohydrates	26 g	Cholesterol	19 mg
Dietary Fiber	2 g	Sodium	380 mg

GEMELLI WITH SHERRIED CHICKEN LIVERS AND MUSHROOMS

MAKES 6 TO 8 SERVINGS

A few chicken livers make this a tasty dish as do the mushrooms and the sherry. It is quite easy to prepare.

1 tablespoon extra-virgin olive oil
1/2 pound chicken livers, trimmed, rinsed, and dried
1/3 pound thinly sliced shiitake mushrooms
1/4 cup thinly sliced scallions
1/3 cup sliced black cured or Kalamata olives
freshly ground black pepper
1/2 cup dry sherry
1 pound gemelli pasta, cooked and drained
6 to 8 teaspoons freshly grated Parmesan cheese

❶ In a large skillet, heat oil and sauté livers 5 minutes until browned on the outside; they should be pink inside. Remove the livers and coarsely chop them.

❷ In the same skillet, add mushrooms and scallions and cook 5 minutes. Add the olives, pepper, and sherry and cook 5 minutes, deglazing the pan at the same time.

❸ Add cooked and drained pasta to the skillet, toss well, and serve on a large platter or on individual plates with cheese sprinkled on top.

Each serving		% of calories from fat 15	
Calories	291	Total Fat	5 g
Protein	12 g	Saturated Fat	1 g
Carbohydrates	46 g	Cholesterol	75 mg
Dietary Fiber	5 g	Sodium	106 mg

LEAN BEEF AND TOMATO SAUCE

MAKES 6 TO 8 SERVINGS WITH 1 POUND OF PASTA

This is a tasty pasta sauce made with beef. It is surprisingly low in fat but only if lean meat is used.

1 tablespoon extra-virgin olive oil
1 small carrot, finely chopped
1 small onion, finely chopped
1 large clove garlic, minced
1 pound very lean ground chuck
1/2 cup red wine
1 teaspoon sugar
6 cups ripe plum tomatoes, skinned, seeded, and coarsely chopped or canned plum tomatoes including pulp and liquid put through a food mill
1 tablespoon finely chopped fresh basil or 1/2 teaspoon dried
1 tablespoon tomato paste
salt
freshly ground black pepper

❶ In a heavy saucepan, heat oil and sauté carrot for 2 minutes. Add onion and garlic and cook over high heat for 3 minutes. Add meat and continue cooking about 5 minutes.

❷ Add the wine, sugar, pureed tomatoes, basil, tomato paste, and salt and pepper to taste. Bring to a boil, lower the heat, and simmer, half-covered, for 1 1/2-hours. Stir frequently, every 15 minutes or so, and serve over hot cooked pasta.

Each serving		% of calories from fat 18	
Calories	393	Total Fat	7.9 g
Protein	21 g	Saturated Fat	2.4 g
Carbohydrates	54 g	Cholesterol	21 mg
Dietary Fiber	6 g	Sodium	376 mg

LEAN LAMB MEATBALLS WITH MINT

MAKES 24 MEATBALLS

Most people don't consider lamb as a meat for meatballs, but they should. These are very tasty, low in saturated fat, and so easy to prepare.

1 1/2 pounds lean ground lamb
1 cup fresh bread crumbs
1/2 cup freshly grated Pecorino cheese
1/4 cup finely chopped fresh mint
4 medium cloves garlic, minced
2 small or 1 large egg white
salt
freshly ground black pepper
spray oil

❶ Use splayed fingers to mix all ingredients in a large bowl and form the meat mixture into 1 1/2- to 2-inch balls—making 24.

❷ Spray oil on a rimmed cookie sheet and place the meatballs on it. Bake in a preheated 400°F oven 18 to 20 minutes.

Note: These meatballs may be reheated in the basic low-fat marinara sauce (page 30).

INVISIBLE FAT

Butter, margarine, lard, vegetable shortening, vegetable oil, and salad dressings are obviously visible fats. Most cooks are well aware of their fat content and can easily and quickly cut back on the amount of these fats used in a recipe. But there are foods in which the fat is not so visible. Beware of the fat hidden in foods that most of us enjoy on a daily basis—these are the invisible fats.

Invisible fat can be found in egg yolks, cream, whole milk, chocolate, olives, nuts, coconuts, and cheese.

Each meatball		% of calories from fat 36	
Calories	60	Total Fat	2.5 g
Protein	7 g	Saturated Fat	1.2 g
Carbohydrates	1 g	Cholesterol	22 mg
Dietary Fiber	1 g	Sodium	44 mg

MARINARA SAUCE WITH SAUSAGE

MAKES 4 SERVINGS WITH 1/2 POUND OF PASTA

Boiling sausage first before adding it to sauce is certainly worth the time and effort. This step rids the sausage of a lot of fat but keeps its flavor.

1/2 pound Italian hot or sweet sausage (about 2 links)
2 cups basic low-fat marinara sauce (page 30)
1/2 pound of pasta
4 tablespoons freshly grated Pecorino cheese
1/4 cup finely chopped fresh parsley

1. Pierce sausages in several places with the point of a very sharp paring knife and add them to boiling water. Cook over moderate heat for 6 minutes. Remove and drain. When cool enough to handle, dry and slice them as thinly as you can.

2. Heat marinara sauce in a skillet or medium saucepan and add the sausage slices. Cook only until the sauce is heated through. Serve over hot pasta with a sprinkle of cheese and parsley.

Each serving (incl. pasta)		% of calories from fat 23	
Calories	378	Total Fat	10 g
Protein	17 g	Saturated Fat	3.9 g
Carbohydrates	54 g	Cholesterol	29 mg
Dietary Fiber	6 g	Sodium	374 mg

MEAT TORTELLINI IN A MUSHROOM AND MEAT SAUCE

MAKES 6 SERVINGS

I've used meat tortellini here, but you can use other varieties of stuffed pastas. This is richer in fat than other recipes so add a big green salad with a fat-free dressing to balance the meal.

spray oil
1/4 pound lean ground chuck
1 can (16 ounces) ready-to-use diced tomatoes and their juices
1/2 teaspoon hot pepper sauce
1/2 teaspoon Worcestershire sauce
2 ounces red wine
1 tablespoon extra-virgin olive oil
1/2 pound chicken livers, trimmed and diced
1/2 pound sliced mushrooms
3 large cloves garlic, minced
1 tablespoon finely chopped fresh oregano or 1 teaspoon dried
1 pound meat-filled tortellini
1/3 cup finely chopped flat parsley

1. Spray oil on a large, nonstick skillet and sauté the beef until it is no longer pink, 4 to 5 minutes, breaking it up with the back of a wooden spoon as it cooks.

2. Add tomatoes, hot pepper and Worcestershire sauces, and wine, and cook 10 to 15 minutes until the sauce thickens.

3. Heat olive oil in another skillet and sauté livers and mushrooms until the mushrooms begin to brown, about 10 minutes. Stir in garlic and oregano and cook 1 minute longer. Transfer the mushroom mixture to the other skillet. Keep warm.

4. Cook the tortellini according to package directions (fresh pasta should rise to the top in about 5 minutes). Drain tortellini and add them to the skillet. Toss 1 to 2 minutes over medium-high heat. Serve on a platter or individual plates and top with the parsley.

Each serving		% of calories from fat 39	
Calories	271	Total Fat	12 g
Protein	19 g	Saturated Fat	3.5 g
Carbohydrates	19 g	Cholesterol	199 mg
Dietary Fiber	2 g	Sodium	732 mg

SPAGHETTI WITH CHICKEN LIVERS, SAGE, AND MARSALA

MAKES 4 SERVINGS

This is a spicy southern Italian specialty from the Calabria region (the toe of the boot), and it is very low in fat. The sage and marsala wine add the flavor.

- 1/4 cup finely chopped pancetta or bacon
- 1/2 pound chicken livers, trimmed, rinsed and dried, cut in halves
- 3 medium cloves garlic, minced
- 1/2 teaspoon red pepper flakes
- 1 teaspoon dried crumbled sage
- 1/3 cup marsala wine
- 1/2 pound spaghetti, cooked and drained
- 1/4 cup low-sodium, defatted chicken broth
- 1/4 cup finely chopped flat parsley

❶ Heat a large skillet and sauté the pancetta or bacon until crisp. Add livers and cook 4 minutes until they are browned.

❷ Add garlic, red pepper flakes, and sage. Stir and cook 1 minute. Remove the livers and herbs from the pan with a slotted spoon.

❸ Add marsala and deglaze the pan. As the wine sauce thickens a little, add the cooked pasta and chicken liver mixture. Toss well in the pan over moderate heat. If the pasta seems too dry, add the chicken broth, a little at a time. Serve in four individual plates, and sprinkle some parsley over the tops of each.

Each serving		% of calories from fat 11	
Calories	321	Total Fat	4 g
Protein	16 g	Saturated Fat	1 g
Carbohydrates	48 g	Cholesterol	154 mg
Dietary Fiber	5 g	Sodium	153 mg

SPICY LIGHT AND DARK TURKEY MEATBALLS

MAKES 16 MEATBALLS

These meatballs are delicious, and you will want to use them in many ways (they can be added to most pasta preparations in this book). One secret is to add some dark meat to the light; a good mixture is three parts breast meat and one part dark meat. You can either ask your butcher to do this for you or bring home the chunk and chop the meat in your food processor. If you grind your own, use about ten pulses to get a properly ground mixture. Do not overwork the meat when forming the balls and do not add salt because the cheese gives a salty flavor. Add tomato sauce (page 76) to the meatballs, doubling both recipes if needed, and you will have an excellent buffet item.

1 1/2 pounds light and dark ground turkey
1 cup fresh bread crumbs
1/2 cup freshly grated Pecorino cheese
1/2 cup finely diced onions
1/4 cup finely chopped flat parsley
1/2 teaspoon red pepper flakes
3 medium cloves garlic, minced
2 small or 1 large egg white
spray oil

❶ With splayed fingers, mix all the ingredients in a large bowl. Using a 1/3-cup measure (loosely filled), form the meat mixture into 16 balls. Do not overwork the meat.

❷ Spray oil on a rimmed cookie sheet and place the meatballs on it. Bake in a 400°F preheated oven, 15 minutes or until cooked thoroughly. Place under the broiler for about 2 minutes to lightly brown the tops.

Each meatball		% of calories from fat 43	
Calories	83	Total Fat	4 g
Protein	9 g	Saturated Fat	1 g
Carbohydrates	2 g	Cholesterol	36 mg
Dietary Fiber	0.2 g	Sodium	83 mg

PORK MEATBALLS WITH MUSHROOMS AND ROSEMARY

MAKES 16 MEATBALLS

Low-fat pork makes an excellent meatball to be cooked in a tomato sauce or to be served as is with coleslaw, potato salad, or a crisp, green salad.

1 tablespoon extra-virgin olive oil
1 cup finely chopped onion
2 large cloves garlic, minced
1 pound ground lean pork
1/3 pound mushrooms, finely chopped, about 1 1/2 cups
1 teaspoon finely chopped rosemary
freshly ground black pepper
1 cup freshly made bread crumbs
2 egg whites, lightly beaten
1/2 teaspoon red pepper flakes, optional
spray oil

❶ Heat oil in a small skillet and sauté onion until tender, about 4 minutes. Add garlic and cook 1 minute longer.

❷ Put pork in a bowl and add onion and garlic. Also add the mushrooms, rosemary, pepper, bread crumbs, egg whites, and the optional red pepper flakes.

❸ With splayed fingers, toss the meat lightly to mix all the ingredients. Do not overhandle. Divide the meat mixture into 16 portions and lightly form meatballs with the palms of your hands. Do not overwork the meat.

❹ Spray oil on a baking sheet. Arrange the meatballs on it and bake in a preheated 400°F oven about 20 minutes, or until cooked. Run under the broiler for a couple of minutes to brown the top sides, if you wish. These may be served as is or added to tomato sauce to be used with a pasta. Heating the meatballs in the sauce will enrich the tomato sauce.

Each meatball		% of calories from fat 35	
Calories	62	Total Fat	2.5 g
Protein	7 g	Saturated Fat	0.6 g
Carbohydrates	3 g	Cholesterol	19 mg
Dietary Fiber	1 g	Sodium	33 mg

THIN SPAGHETTI WITH MUSHROOMS, YELLOW PEPPERS, AND SAUSAGE

MAKES 6 TO 8 SERVINGS

This recipe offers an excellent combination of flavors. The yellow peppers are attractive paired with the scallions, but you could use either red, green, or orange peppers if the yellow are not available.

1 link Italian sausage, casing removed
2 yellow bell peppers, cored, seeded, ribs removed, and sliced lengthwise 1/4 inch
3 cups (about 3/4 pound) sliced cremini mushrooms
1 cup thinly sliced scallions
1/4 cup finely chopped flat parsley
1/4 cup finely sliced basil leaves or 2 teaspoons dried
1 teaspoon dried rosemary, crushed
2 large cloves garlic, minced
3/4 pound thin spaghetti (use 1 pound if serving 8)
1 1/2 cups low-sodium, defatted chicken broth
1 cup freshly grated Parmesan cheese

❶ In a large, nonstick skillet, sauté sausage until it is no longer pink, breaking it up with the back of a wooden spoon, about 5 minutes. Transfer cooked sausage to a plate and set aside.

❷ Add peppers, mushrooms, scallions, herbs, and garlic to the skillet and sauté over medium heat until the peppers are done, 6 to 8 minutes, stirring frequently. Return sausage to the skillet.

❸ Cook the spaghetti according to package directions. Drain the pasta well and add it to the skillet. Add broth and 3/4 cup of the cheese. Cook over medium heat until all the ingredients are heated through and the sauce thickens a little, 3 to 4 minutes. Transfer to a large platter or to individual plates. Top with the remaining cheese and serve right away.

Each serving		% of calories from fat 27	
Calories	298	Total Fat	9 g
Protein	15 g	Saturated Fat	4 g
Carbohydrates	40 g	Cholesterol	20 mg
Dietary Fiber	5 g	Sodium	353 mg

VEAL MEATBALLS WITH TARRAGON

MAKES 16 MEATBALLS

Veal makes delicious meatballs; some people think it makes a lighter version than ones made with beef or pork.

1 tablespoon extra-virgin olive oil
1/2 cup finely chopped onion
2 large cloves garlic, minced
1 pound ground lean veal
3/4 cup freshly made bread crumbs
1/4 cup finely chopped flat parsley
1 teaspoon dried tarragon
1/4 teaspoon freshly grated nutmeg
1 large or 2 small eggs, lightly beaten
1/3 cup freshly grated Parmesan cheese
spray oil

❶ Heat oil in a skillet and sauté onion until tender, about 4 minutes. Add garlic and cook 1 minute. Stir and remove from the heat. Cool.

❷ Put the veal in a bowl and add onion and garlic. Add the bread crumbs, parsley, tarragon, nutmeg, egg(s), and Parmesan cheese.

❸ With splayed fingers, toss the meat lightly to mix all the ingredients. Do not overhandle. Divide the mixture into 16 portions and lightly form meatballs with the palms of your hands.

❹ Spray oil on a cookie sheet. Arrange the meatballs on it and bake in a preheated 400°F oven about 20 minutes, or until cooked. Run under the broiler for a couple of minutes to brown the tops, if you wish. These may be served as is or added to tomato sauce to be used with a pasta. Heating the meatballs in the sauce will add flavor to the tomato sauce.

Each meatball		% of calories from fat 47	
Calories	71	Total Fat	3.8 g
Protein	7 g	Saturated Fat	1.4 g
Carbohydrates	2 g	Cholesterol	38 mg
Dietary Fiber	1 g	Sodium	77 mg

CHAPTER 10
DELICIOUS AND YUMMY LIGHT PASTA SALADS

INTRODUCTION

Most of the recipes in this section take advantage of two good ideas: using tasty vegetables and fish or meat and combining them with low-fat dressed lettuces (and other vegetables) highly accented with herbs and spices. These great alliances are popular because they are easy to make and can be pulled together at the last minute. The markets are now filled with ingredients that were not so easily available a few years ago, such as radicchio, Belgian endive, and arugula. More than ever, supermarkets are selling prepacked salad greens, which can come in handy, even if they cost a few cents more. One of the more interesting packages is called mesclun, which is nothing more than mixed young salad greens. The caution, however, is to be sure that you get bright green color with crisp leaves; you don't want any signs of wilting or browning.

Low-fat salad dressings in supermarkets go a long way toward eliminating fat and calories. It's not easy to find good-tasting, high-flavor, low-fat ones, however. These dressings can be made at home, keeping in mind several principles:

❶ Try to reduce the amount of oil that you put into the dressing. Although the classic proportions are three parts oil to one part vinegar, you can surely get by on two to one and perhaps less if you use milder vinegars such as rice vinegar. If you use a more strongly flavored oil, such as hazelnut, sesame oil, or walnut oil, you may find you'll be satisfied with a ratio of one to one. Adding fruit juices or low-sodium broths to dressings will also stretch them, but you need to experiment.

❷ Grilling vegetables and then pureeing them concentrates the flavor so that it will provide a substantial foil for the acid in the dressing, besides adding body to the salad dressing.

❸ Cooking down fruit juices not only concentrates the flavor but also balances the sourness of the vinegars in the dressings nicely.

❹ Using a little (the emphasis here is on *little*) of a strong flavored food such as soy, Parmesan or goat cheese, peppercorns, red pepper flakes, or chilies will add a significant touch of taste.

❺ "Toast" spices such as fennel seeds. It is easy to do, just add them to a hot skillet, and when they begin to pop, they will release flavors that would otherwise go unnoticed.

Lastly, don't be afraid to try the newer ingredients you find in the markets. Perhaps we all know Vidalia onions from Georgia and the Walla Walla onions from Washington State, but how about the Texas Y-33s and the Hawaiian Mauis. It is true that these newer onions have a higher water content and will not store as well as the red, white, and yellow onions we use on a daily basis, but they are so mild that you can bite into them like a Fuji apple. Just adding them uncooked to any of these preparations will add an extra touch of freshness.

BASIC LOW-FAT ITALIAN SALAD DRESSING

MAKES ABOUT 2 1/2 CUPS

This dressing will keep several days in the refrigerator, but it is best to bring the amount of dressing needed for any particular recipe to room temperature before adding it to the salad. Please note the important direction of using the broth directly out of its container without adding water.

1 1/3 cups canned low-sodium vegetable or chicken broth, undiluted
1/2 cup white wine vinegar
1/4 cup fresh lemon juice
2 tablespoons dried Italian seasoning or 1 tablespoon each dried basil and dried oregano
1 tablespoon Dijon-style mustard
1 tablespoon sugar
1 tablespoon extra-virgin olive oil
1 teaspoon freshly ground black pepper
1/2 cup finely diced red, orange, or yellow bell pepper
1/2 cup finely chopped flat parsley
3 large cloves garlic, minced

❶ Put all the ingredients in a one-quart glass jar with a tight cover and shake vigorously until well combined.

The fat calories for the salad dressing are high, but when added to other foods, the fat calories may be significantly reduced. For example, spinach rotini with broccoli, basil, and balsamic (page 242) includes one cup of this salad dressing, yet the fat calories are 15 percent.

Each tablespoon		% of calories from fat 56	
Calories	8	Total Fat	0.5 g
Protein	0.2 g	Saturated Fat	0.1 g
Carbohydrates	1 g	Cholesterol	0.2 mg
Dietary Fiber	0.1 g	Sodium	14 mg

DITALI PASTA AND BROCCOLI SALAD

MAKES 4 SERVINGS

Ditali pasta is small tubular-shaped pasta that works well in salads. Broccoli, tomatoes, scallions, and pasta make a good salad combination.

1/2 pound ditali, cooked and drained
2 1/2 cups (cooked or steamed) broccoli florets
2 medium tomatoes, peeled, seeded, chopped 1/2 inch
1/2 cup thinly sliced scallions
1/4 cup finely chopped flat parsley
2 tablespoons extra-virgin olive oil
2 tablespoons balsamic vinegar
2 medium cloves garlic, minced
freshly ground black pepper
8 thin Parmesan cheese shavings

❶ Put all the ingredients except the cheese shavings in a large bowl and toss well. Be liberal with the black pepper. Leave at room temperature for 1 to 2 hours before serving.

❷ Divide among four plates, and add two thin pieces of cheese shavings on top of each serving.

Each serving		% of calories from fat 23	
Calories	343	Total Fat	9.2 g
Protein	11 g	Saturated Fat	1.7 g
Carbohydrates	55 g	Cholesterol	2 mg
Dietary Fiber	5 g	Sodium	84 mg

BOW TIES WITH SLICED ZUCCHINI IN GARLIC-BASIL VINAIGRETTE

MAKES 4 SERVINGS

Be sure to use small zucchini, and don't overcook the green peas. This is a very fresh-looking and flavorful salad.

3 medium garlic cloves, peeled and halved
1/3 cup low-sodium chicken broth
2 tablespoons coarsely chopped basil
1 tablespoon extra-virgin olive oil
1 tablespoon fresh lemon juice
1 tablespoon white wine vinegar
1 tablespoon Dijon mustard
freshly ground black pepper

For the salad:

1/2 pound bow ties, cooked and drained
1 cup thinly sliced fresh baby zucchini with skin on
1/2 cup cooked green peas
1/2 cup finely chopped red onion

❶ Put dressing ingredients into the bowl of a processor and process until the dressing is smooth.

❷ Combine salad ingredients in a bowl, add dressing, and toss well.

Each serving		% of calories from fat 16	
Calories	271	Total Fat	5 g
Protein	9 g	Saturated Fat	0.7 g
Carbohydrates	48 g	Cholesterol	0.4 mg
Dietary Fiber	5 g	Sodium	109 mg

CHICKEN AND PASTA SALAD WITH SPINACH

MAKES 6 SERVINGS

Thinly sliced fresh spinach adds great taste and color to pasta salads. Here it is added to a rather substantial pasta and chicken salad.

3/4 pound rotelle or similar sized pasta, cooked and drained
3 cups thinly sliced fresh spinach
3 cups fresh tomato cubes
1 1/2 cups diced cooked chicken or 1 can (12.5 ounces) drained and chopped
1/4 cup freshly grated Parmesan cheese
1/4 cup finely diced red or yellow bell peppers
1/4 cup thinly sliced black olives
1 bottle (8 ounces) fat-free vinaigrette

1. Combine all ingredients and toss well. This is best served at the time ingredients are tossed.

Each serving		% of calories from fat 18	
Calories	380	Total Fat	7.8 g
Protein	23 g	Saturated Fat	2.4 g
Carbohydrates	53 g	Cholesterol	40 mg
Dietary Fiber	4 g	Sodium	747 mg

ORZO AND VEGETABLES WITH SPICY LEMON DRESSING

MAKES 6 SERVINGS

Some years ago, when I was in Lecce, in the heel of the Italian boot, I had a salad similar to this one. Because the orzo and vegetables are a bit bland, they need a spicy, lemony dressing. What I remember about lunch that day, in addition to the salad, was the feeling of being in the middle of the Mediterranean—a great place to watch people.

For the dressing:

- 2 tablespoons grated lemon zest
- 1/4 cup fresh lemon juice (1 1/2 lemons)
- 1/3 cup low-sodium vegetable or chicken broth
- 2 tablespoons extra-virgin olive oil
- 2 large cloves garlic, minced
- 1 teaspoon sugar
- 1 teaspoon paprika
- pinches, about 1/4 teaspoon each, dry mustard, ground coriander, ground cumin, and red pepper flakes

For the salad:

- 2 cups orzo, cooked and drained
- 3 red ripe tomatoes, peeled, seeded, and diced 1/2 inch (page 73)
- 2 small Kirby cucumbers, peeled, and diced 1/2 inch
- 1 green bell pepper, seeded, ribbed, and diced 1/2 inch
- 8 scallions, including tender green part, thinly sliced

Continued on next page

MRS. CLEMENTS AND DRY MUSTARD

It is told that dry mustard was invented by a Mrs. Clements in Durham, England in the early 1700s. She would grind mustard seeds into a fine powder, just as was being done with wheat. The rest of the story has to do with the success of Durham's dry mustard powder, which sold not only in England but also throughout the world. No one seems able to explain exactly what special charm she had to persuade King George I to endorse her product.

❶ To make the dressing, combine all the ingredients in the bowl of a food processor, and pulse to combine. Leave the dressing at room temperature if ready to use within an hour. Taste for seasoning and add more pepper flakes if needed.

❷ Prepare the orzo and vegetables, but keep them separate.

❸ To serve, divide the cooked orzo among six plates. Arrange the raw vegetables on top. Spoon the dressing over the vegetables and orzo.

Each serving		**% of calories from fat 18**	
Calories	294	Total Fat	6 g
Protein	9 g	Saturated Fat	0.9 g
Carbohydrates	52 g	Cholesterol	1 mg
Dietary Fiber	4 g	Sodium	20 mg

FARFALLE AND PESTO SALAD

MAKES 4 SERVINGS

This recipe is one of my favorites. An interesting and tasty way to serve it is to put it on top of lightly salted sliced tomatoes.

2 medium cloves garlic, peeled and halved
1 cup packed basil leaves
2 tablespoons freshly grated Parmesan cheese
salt
freshly ground black pepper
2 tablespoons extra-virgin olive oil
2 tablespoons water
1/2 pound farfalle (bow tie) pasta, cooked and drained
1 cup green peas, cooked and drained
1/2 cup finely chopped red onion

1. Put garlic and basil in the bowl of a processor, and finely mince both. Add the Parmesan and pulse one or two times. Salt and pepper to taste. With processor on, add oil and water through the food tube.

2. Combine the pasta, green peas, and onions in a large bowl. Add the pesto and toss well. Adjust salt and pepper seasoning.

Each serving		% of calories from fat 24	
Calories	334	Total Fat	9.3 g
Protein	11 g	Saturated Fat	1.7 g
Carbohydrates	51 g	Cholesterol	2 mg
Dietary Fiber	6 g	Sodium	66 mg

FARFALLE, BLACK PEPPER, AND PARMESAN SALAD WITH RED ONIONS

MAKES 4 SERVINGS

The butterfly pasta, speckled with black pepper and bits of red onion, is attractive to look at, and the dressing is tart and tasty. This recipe makes a good lunch dish with a slice of toasted whole wheat bread followed by fresh fruit.

1/2 cup freshly grated Parmesan cheese
1/2 cup nonfat cottage cheese
1/2 cup skim buttermilk
2 tablespoons seasoned rice wine vinegar
1 large clove garlic, finely minced
liberal amount of freshly ground black pepper (about 1 teaspoon)
1/2 pound farfalle (butterflies or bows) pasta
1/2 red onion, sliced as thinly as possible

❶ Put the cheeses and the buttermilk in the bowl of a food processor. Add the vinegar, garlic, and black pepper and pulse three or four times to make a smooth sauce. Use immediately or store in the refrigerator for up to 48 hours.

❷ Cook the pasta according to package directions. Drain the pasta well and transfer it to a bowl. Add the onion slices and the mixed sauce and combine well. When serving, grind more fresh pepper on top.

Each serving		% of calories from fat 15	
Calories	281	Total Fat	4.9 g
Protein	16 g	Saturated Fat	2.7 g
Carbohydrates	42 g	Cholesterol	13 mg
Dietary Fiber	2 g	Sodium	359 mg

GARLICKY FUSILLI SALAD IN YOGURT CUCUMBER SAUCE

MAKES 6 TO 8 SERVINGS

Yogurt and cucumbers make a low-fat sauce but garlic, cumin, and Parmesan cheese are the taste factors in this really easy-to-make pasta salad.

- 2 large cucumbers, peeled, seeded, sliced 1/2 inch
- 4 medium cloves garlic, minced
- 1 tablespoon white wine vinegar
- 1 tablespoon cumin powder
- freshly ground black pepper
- 1 1/2 cups plain low-fat yogurt
- 1/2 pound fusilli pasta
- 1/2 cup freshly grated Parmesan cheese
- 1/4 cup finely diced dried tomatoes

1. In the bowl of a processor, add cucumbers, garlic, vinegar, cumin, and a liberal amount of black pepper, and pulse to puree. Add yogurt, and pulse just to combine. Transfer mixture to a large bowl.
2. Cook the pasta according to package directions. Drain the pasta, run it under cold water, and drain well again. Stir pasta into the yogurt mixture.
3. Fold in Parmesan cheese and dried tomatoes. Refrigerate for 3 to 4 hours to allow the flavors to develop.

THE GREAT FLAVOR OF CUMIN

Cumin is not as popular in the United States as it is throughout the rest of the world. In other countries, cumin is second only to black pepper. In the United States, cumin is used mostly in chili, but it is gaining popularity. In other cuisines such as those in Latin America, Asia, North Africa, and the Middle East, it is a kitchen staple. The best cumin I have tasted comes from Penzey's, a spice merchant in Waukesha, Wisconsin, where they grind it weekly. Cumin is available in seed and ground form.

Each serving:		% of calories from fat 17	
Calories	175	Total Fat	3.4 g
Protein	9 g	Saturated Fat	1.8 g
Carbohydrates	27 g	Cholesterol	8 mg
Dietary Fiber	2 g	Sodium	188 mg

PASTA, SWEET ONION, BASIL, AND CORN SALAD

MAKES 4 TO 6 SERVINGS

The corn must be young and freshly picked because it is added uncooked to the salad. If the corn is out of season, use frozen niblets but cook and drain them.

3/4 cup finely chopped fresh basil
1/4 cup white balsamic vinegar
2 tablespoons extra-virgin olive oil
1 tablespoon Dijon mustard
1/2 pound pasta, cooked and drained
2 medium tomatoes, peeled, seeded, and cubed
1/2 cup fresh corn kernels (off 1 ear of corn, uncooked)
1/2 cup finely chopped sweet onion such as Vidalia
salt
freshly ground black pepper

❶ For the dressing, combine 1/4 cup chopped basil with vinegar, oil, and mustard. Set aside.

❷ Combine remaining ingredients, including the remaining 1/2 cup basil, in a large bowl. Add dressing and toss. Adjust the salt and pepper seasoning.

Each serving:		% of calories from fat 25	
Calories	204	Total Fat	5.8 g
Protein	5 g	Saturated Fat	0.8 g
Carbohydrates	33 g	Cholesterol	0 mg
Dietary Fiber	2 g	Sodium	71 mg

"LUMACHINE" MEDIUM SHELLS PASTA SALAD WITH SNAPPER

THE FLAVOR OF DILL

I always think of caraway when I smell dill. Although its main function is to flavor pickles, dill also is used to flavor sauerkraut and vinegar. Dill is used a good deal in Russian and Scandinavian cooking. The feathery green leaves of the plant have a softer flavor than the seeds, but the seeds also can be used with the same foods. Dill seed is good in sauces, salad dressings, and marinades. Fresh chopped dill is paired with snapper, pasta, and onions in this pasta salad.

MAKES 6 SERVINGS

For the dressing:

1/2 cup no-fat or low-fat mayonnaise
1 tablespoon seasoned rice vinegar
1 tablespoon extra-virgin olive oil
1 tablespoon finely chopped flat parsley
salt
freshly ground black pepper
juice of 1/2 lemon (about 1 1/2 tablespoons)

For the salad:

1/2 pound pasta, cooked and drained
1 pound grilled or broiled snapper fillets
1/2 cup finely diced Vidalia onions
1 small celery heart, thinly sliced
1/4 cup finely diced bell pepper
1 tablespoon finely chopped fresh fennel ferns or dill
spray oil
18 drained capers for garnish

1. To make the dressing, put all dressing ingredients in a bowl, and stir until smooth.

2. For the salad, prepare the pasta and the fish. Lightly spray oil on the fish, and grill or sauté. Test with a wooden skewer. If the skewer penetrates easily, the fish is cooked. Break or cut the fish into small pieces.

3. Put pasta, fish, and other salad ingredients in a bowl. Add dressing and toss lightly but well enough to coat the pasta and fish mixture with the dressing. Garnish and serve.

Each Serving		% of calories from fat 13	
Calories	246	Total Fat	3.7 g
Protein	16 g	Saturated Fat	0.6 g
Carbohydrates	36 g	Cholesterol	19 mg
Dietary Fiber	2 g	Sodium	276 mg

ORECCHIETTE PASTA SALAD WITH ARTICHOKES

MAKES 6 SERVINGS

Orecchiette is in the shape of little ears, but you can use other small pasta shapes and get a good result. The artichokes, onions, peppers, olives, and Gorgonzola make this a delicious salad.

1/2 pound orecchiette pasta
2 cans (14 ounces) artichokes, drained well, dried, and finely sliced
2/3 cup fat-free Italian salad dressing, prepared
1/2 cup finely diced red or orange bell peppers
1/2 cup finely sliced red onions
1/4 cup thinly sliced cured Greek olives
1/2 cup crumbled Gorgonzola cheese
freshly ground black pepper

1. Cook the pasta according to package directions. Drain the pasta well and put it in a large bowl.

2. Add all the other ingredients. Toss well and serve on a large platter or individual plates.

Each serving:		% of calories from fat 17	
Calories	240	Total Fat	4.7 g
Protein	10 g	Saturated Fat	2.3 g
Carbohydrates	41 g	Cholesterol	8 mg
Dietary Fiber	5 g	Sodium	471 mg

ROTINI SALAD WITH CHICKEN, BEANS, AND RADISHES

MAKES 6 SERVINGS

This recipe is very low in fat and makes a great salad. The chicken breasts may be broiled and then sliced.

- 4 small boneless, skinless chicken breast halves, about 1 pound
- 1/2 pound rotini pasta, cooked and drained
- 1/2 pound fresh green beans, trimmed and cut in half
- 1 cucumber, peeled, seeded, and diced 1/4 inch
- 1 cup fat-free salad dressing, prepared
- 1 tablespoon orange zest
- 1 teaspoon dried dill weed
- freshly ground black pepper
- 1/2 cup thinly sliced fresh radishes
- 3 cups finely shredded Boston or Bibb lettuce

❶ Heat the grill. When the fire is ready, spray oil on the grid. Grill the chicken breasts 4 minutes per side. Remove, thinly slice, and set aside in a bowl. Add the cooked pasta and toss.

❷ Cook the green beans until tender, drain well, and add to the pasta. Add cucumber, salad dressing, orange zest, dill weed, pepper, and radishes.

❸ Distribute the salad greens to six plates and apportion the pasta salad over the greens. Serve at room temperature with crisped baguette slices.

ORANGE AND LEMON ZEST, A FRESH TOUCH OF FLAVOR

Zest is the thin, colored part of the peel from any citrus fruit. The zest can be cut easily from the skin of any citrus fruit with a vegetable peeler or paring knife, but be sure to avoid cutting away any pith, or bitter white part of the peel, with the zest. Zest gets its flavor from the essential oils in the outer part of the rind. Strips of zest, about one-half to one inch wide, can be cut from the peel, cut into thinner slivers, and cut again, crosswise, to mince the zest.

Each serving		% of calories from fat 9	
Calories	242	Total Fat	2.5 g
Protein	21 g	Saturated Fat	0.6 g
Carbohydrates	33 g	Cholesterol	42 mg
Dietary Fiber	3 g	Sodium	431 mg

PENNE PASTA IN PRIMAVERA SALAD

MAKES 6 SERVINGS

Make this salad with fresh zucchini only. The vegetables and pasta go well together and remind me of spring.

1/2 pound penne
2 tablespoons extra-virgin olive oil
1 tablespoon sugar
1 tablepoon finely grated lemon zest
freshly ground black pepper
3 tablespoons white wine vinegar
2 large cloves garlic, minced
1 cup tiny broccoli florets
3/4 cup zucchini, diced 1/4 inch
1 plum tomato, peeled, seeded, and diced
2 tablespoons finely chopped fresh flat parsley
6 tablespoons freshly grated Parmesan cheese

❶ Cook the penne according to package directions. Drain penne well, reserving about a cup of the cooking liquid. Add 1 tablespoon olive oil to the pasta, toss well, and set aside.

❷ Combine the remaining oil, sugar, lemon zest, pepper, vinegar, and garlic. Mix well.

❸ In a bowl, combine broccoli, zucchini, tomato, parsley, pasta, and dressing. If too dry, add one or two tablespoons of the cooking liquid. Toss well and divide among six plates. Sprinkle a tablespoon of cheese over each serving.

Each serving		% of calories from fat 28	
Calories	221	Total Fat	7 g
Protein	8 g	Saturated Fat	1.9 g
Carbohydrates	32 g	Cholesterol	5 mg
Dietary Fiber	2 g	Sodium	124 mg

SMALL PASTA, PEPPERS, AND ENDIVE SALAD WITH LOW-FAT "RANCH" SAUCE

MAKES 4 SERVINGS

You can use this recipe to fill a fresh tomato or half a cantaloupe or to serve it over an asparagus vinaigrette; there is enough here to serve six people easily. This is a tasty, fresh, summery type salad, and I like to make it with farfalle. However, you can use penne, medium-sized shells, radiatore, or rotelle.

For the sauce:

1/2 cup buttermilk
1/4 cup low-fat plain yogurt
1 tablespoon finely chopped flat parsley
1 tablespoon finely chopped fresh dill or fennel fern
1 tablespoon finely chopped onion
juice of 1 lemon, about 3 tablespoons
2 teaspoons sugar
dashes of hot pepper sauce
4 slices fat-free Swiss cheese, diced 1/4 inch
2 tablespoons freshly grated Pecorino cheese

For the salad:

2 cups uncooked small pasta, cooked and drained
1 red or orange bell pepper, cut into small cubes
1 fresh endive, trimmed and sliced into very thin rounds
garnish of fresh dill sprigs or fennel ferns

❶ To make the sauce, combine all the ingredients in a bowl and beat until well blended.

❷ To serve, put the pasta, peppers, and endive in a large bowl or platter. Add sauce, toss well, and add garnish. Or serve with other food inside a vegetable or fruit or on the side of grilled meat, poultry, fish, or another vegetable dish.

Each serving		% of calories from fat 10	
Calories	150	Total Fat	1.8 g
Protein	8 g	Saturated Fat	0.9 g
Carbohydrates	25 g	Cholesterol	5 mg
Dietary Fiber	1 g	Sodium	225 mg

WINE PASTA SALAD WITH TURKEY AND GRAPES

MAKES 4 SERVINGS

The various flavored pastas in the markets are truly amazing. Recently I discovered a pasta flavored with wine, both Cabernet Sauvignon and Chardonnay. They are worth a try, as faddish as they may seem.

1/2 pound wine pasta, cooked and drained, reserving 1/2 cup of the cooking liquid
1/2 pound turkey breast, cut into small matchsticks
1 cup small seedless white and red grapes (1/2 cup each), washed and dried
1/2 cup thinly sliced scallions
1/4 cup finely chopped chives
1/4 cup finely crumbled Gorgonzola or blue cheese
2 tablespoons extra-virgin olive oil
1/4 teaspoon salt
freshly ground black pepper

❶ Combine all ingredients, including the 1/2 cup of pasta cooking liquid, in a large bowl or a platter and toss well. Serve at room temperature.

Each serving		% of calories from fat 23	
Calories	407	Total Fat	10.7 g
Protein	24 g	Saturated Fat	2.5 g
Carbohydrates	53 g	Cholesterol	47 mg
Dietary Fiber	5 g	Sodium	273 mg

SPAGHETTINI AND SCALLOP SALAD IN BAKED WHOLE TOMATOES

MAKES 8 SERVINGS

This is a special salad for special times.

For the dressing:

3/4 pint low-fat sour cream
2 tablespoons horseradish
2 tablespoons Dijon mustard

For the salad:

8 medium-size, ripe, firm tomatoes
1/2 pound thin spaghetti, preferably #10
1 pound bay scallops
2 tablespoons low-sodium soy sauce
1/2 cup dry white wine
1/4 cup thinly sliced scallions including the tender green part
1/4 cup thinly sliced celery heart
8 scallions, trimmed, and quartered lengthwise

1. To make the dressing, combine all salad dressing ingredients, stir well, and set aside or refrigerate.

2. Bring a saucepan of lightly salted water to a boil. Add tomatoes for 15 seconds. Drain tomatoes, and put them in cold water. Core, peel, and scoop 2 melon balls out of each center. Discard the balls.

3. Arrange the tomatoes in individual ramekins, stem side up, and bake in a preheated 250°F oven for 30 minutes. Remove from the oven and drain carefully, by tilting the ramekin. Return the tomatoes in their ramekins to the oven and bake 30 minutes longer. Turn out, drain, and put a tomato on each of eight plates. After the tomatoes have cooled enough to handle, cut each tomato into four sections leaving the bottoms attached.

Continued on next page

THE STRONG BITE OF HORSERADISH

My parents always bought huge knobs of fresh horseradish from greengrocer markets in New York City. They would scrub them clean, and then grate them to use in a variety of ways. My mother and father took turns grating because their eyes teared. Horseradish was popular in our home, but I didn't know many people who grated fresh horseradish then, and I still don't. It has a really strong bite; I love it.

Like other radishes, it is a cruciferous vegetable, and according to some professionals, may help in the fight against cancer. It has a high content of vitamin C.

4. Cook the pasta according to package directions. Drain pasta well.

5. In a skillet large enough to hold scallops in one layer, add scallops and soy sauce, and sauté over medium-high heat to sear the scallops on each side, about 5 minutes total time. Remove scallops, and add the wine to deglaze the pan. The sauce should be lightly thickened. Use a rubber spatula to help clean the skillet.

6. In a large bowl, combine cooked pasta, scallops, and sauce from the skillet, scallions, and celery, and toss. Fold in the dressing.

7. To serve, fork and spoon the pasta salad to the center of each tomato with a fair amount of pasta outpouring one side of the plate (i.e., onto one side of the dish). Arrange 4 lengths (1 scallion in total) crisscrossed on the plate over the tomato and pasta.

BOTTLED HORSERADISH

Prepared horseradish is sold bottled in most supermarkets and usually comes in three forms: with vinegar and salt (sodium content is surprisingly low); with beet juice, which makes it red; and as a creamy sauce, which we will not use because it is made with mayonnaise. Of course, you can make your own horseradish by grating it fresh.

Each serving		% of calories from fat 18	
Calories	267	Total Fat	5.5 g
Protein	18 g	Saturated Fat	3.3 g
Carbohydrates	34 g	Cholesterol	34 mg
Dietary Fiber	4 g	Sodium	459 mg

SPINACH ROTINI WITH BROCCOLI, BASIL, AND BALSAMIC VINEGAR

MAKES 6 SERVINGS

The green pasta and the greens of the broccoli and basil, highlighted by the orange or yellow pepper make a beautiful presentation and tasty salad.

1 cup basic low-fat Italian salad dressing, page 219, made with balsamic vinegar
1/2 pound spinach rotini, cooked and drained
2 cups small fresh broccoli florets, steamed al dente
2 onions, thinly sliced
1/2 cup finely chopped fresh basil
1 orange or yellow bell pepper, seeded, and thinly sliced 1/4 inch lengthwise
freshly ground pepper
6 teaspoons Parmesan cheese, optional

❶ Make salad dressing using balsamic vinegar instead of white wine vinegar and eliminate the bell peppers.

❷ Combine all the ingredients in a large platter or bowl, toss well, and serve. Add the Parmesan cheese, if you wish.

Each serving		% of calories from fat 15	
Calories	177	Total Fat	3 g
Protein	6 g	Saturated Fat	0.4 g
Carbohydrates	32 g	Cholesterol	0 mg
Dietary Fiber	3 g	Sodium	9 mg

TORTELLINI PRIMAVERA SALAD

MAKES 8 TO 10 SERVINGS

I like to serve this salad in large green lettuce or radicchio cups. It is easy to find the two kinds of tortellini (one yellow, one green) in most refrigerated supermarket shelves.

- 1 package (9 ounces) fresh cheese tortellini (egg pasta)
- 1 package (9 ounces) fresh cheese tortellini (spinach pasta)
- 1 can (15 ounces) cannellini beans, rinsed and drained
- 1 can (14 ounces) artichoke hearts, rinsed, drained, and thinly sliced (see Note)
- 2 large tomatoes, peeled, seeded, and diced 1/2 inch
- 1 cup thinly sliced raw cremini mushrooms
- 1 cup thinly sliced Belgian endive
- 1/2 cup thinly sliced celery hearts
- 1/2 cup shredded carrot
- 1 1/2 cups basic low-fat Italian salad dressing (page 219)

Note: VIGO imports artichoke hearts packed in water and salt (a product from Spain) in 14-ounce cans. If you can't find this product or a similar one, use two 6-ounce jars packed by Progresso and others.

❶ Cook the tortellini according to package directions. (They should rise to the top, in 4 or 5 minutes, if cooked.) Drain tortellini, and transfer them to a large bowl or platter.

❷ Add all other ingredients. Stir well and serve.

Each serving		% of calories from fat 17	
Calories	193	Total Fat	3.8 g
Protein	9 g	Saturated Fat	1.5 g
Carbohydrates	32 g	Cholesterol	10 mg
Dietary Fiber	6 g	Sodium	825 mg

TRIPOLINI WITH FRESH TOMATOES IN A TOMATO-FLAVORED SALAD DRESSING

MAKES 6 SERVINGS

Tripolini looks like farfalle (bows or butterflies) except that they have rounded edges.

1 to 1 1/2 cups basic low-fat Italian salad dressing (page 219), changed as described below
1/2 cup tomato paste
1/2 pound tripolini pasta, cooked and drained
2 cups diced, skinned, and seeded fresh tomatoes
1/4 cup finely chopped fresh basil
1/4 cup finely chopped flat parsley
1/2 teaspoon red pepper flakes

1. Make the basic dressing, but add 1/2 cup tomato paste. Shake vigorously to be sure the tomato paste dissolves thoroughly.

2. Combine all ingredients and toss well. Serve this pasta salad warm or at room temperature with crisped pita bread wedges.

Each serving		% of calories from fat 10	
Calories	176	Total Fat	2 g
Protein	5 g	Saturated Fat	0.1 g
Carbohydrates	34 g	Cholesterol	0 mg
Dietary Fiber	2 g	Sodium	1,005 mg

BAKED PASTA WITH EGGS, PESTO, AND MOZZARELLA

MAKES 6 SERVINGS

This main course dish should be served with a fresh green salad or some steamed asparagus.

1 tablespoon extra-virgin olive oil
3/4 pound thin spaghetti, cooked and drained
2 packages (4 ounces each) egg substitute
1/4 cup pesto (page 109)
3/4 cup shredded nonfat mozzarella cheese
freshly ground black pepper

1. Lightly oil a 9 x 13 x 2-inch oval glass baking dish. Arrange the cooked spaghetti in it.

2. In a bowl, combine egg substitute, pesto, mozzarella, and a liberal amount of pepper. Pour this over the spaghetti, covering the pasta completely.

3. Bake in a preheated 350°F oven until the eggs are set, about 20 minutes. Serve hot.

Each serving		% of calories from fat 25	
Calories	348	Total Fat	10 g
Protein	15 g	Saturated Fat	2.7 g
Carbohydrates	48 g	Cholesterol	8 mg
Dietary Fiber	6 g	Sodium	95 mg

FETTUCCINE AND SPINACH BAKED WITH SMOKED MOZZARELLA

MAKES 8 SERVINGS

Here is a baked pasta dish you will cook more than once. It is substantial and needs only a salad to go with it. If you can't find smoked mozzarella use a low-fat plain one instead.

1/2 pound fettuccine
1 package (10 ounces) fresh spinach, rinsed, spun dry, stemmed, and thinly sliced
1 cup nonfat cottage cheese
1/4 cup freshly grated Parmesan cheese
1/2 cup finely chopped scallions
1 can (14 ounces) cannellini beans, rinsed well and drained
freshly ground black pepper
spray oil
2 cups basic low-fat marinara sauce (page 30)
1/2 cup thickly grated low-fat smoked mozzarella

❶ Cook the fettuccine according to package directions. Drain fettuccine and transfer to a large mixing bowl.

❷ Add spinach, cottage and Parmesan cheeses, scallions, beans, and a liberal amount of pepper. Toss to combine.

❸ Spray oil on a large oval glass or ceramic baking dish, about 9 x 12 x 2 inches, and transfer half of the pasta mixture into it. Pour or spread 1 cup marinara sauce over the top. Add remaining pasta mixture and top with the remaining sauce.

❹ Bake in a preheated 400°F oven until thoroughly heated, about 30 minutes. After 20 minutes of baking, sprinkle the mozzarella over all, and return it to the oven to cook another 10 minutes. Remove baking dish from oven, and let it stand for 5 minutes or so before serving.

Each serving		% of calories from fat 10	
Calories	252	Total Fat	3 g
Protein	16 g	Saturated Fat	1.5 g
Carbohydrates	41 g	Cholesterol	9 mg
Dietary Fiber	9 g	Sodium	204 mg

BAKED FETTUCCINE WITH MUSHROOMS AND GARLIC

MAKES 6 SERVINGS

This is a comfort food, and all it needs is a fresh green salad. It also works well as a buffet item, serving more than six if other food is available.

1 tablespoon extra-virgin olive oil
3 tablespoons unsalted butter
1 medium onion, peeled and thinly sliced
4 medium cloves garlic, minced
1 1/2 pounds cremini or button mushrooms, thinly sliced
2 tablespoons all-purpose flour
1 cup low-sodium, defatted chicken broth
1/2 cup nonfat sour cream
1/2 cup dry white wine
3/4 pound dried fettuccine, cooked and drained
1/2 cup finely chopped chives or scallions

1. Heat oil and 1 tablespoon butter in a large, nonstick skillet. Sauté onion 3 minutes until the slices are limp. Stir in the garlic and cook 1 minute longer.

2. Add the mushrooms and cook over medium heat, uncovered, until the mushrooms have released their juices, 10 to 15 minutes.

3. In a saucepan, heat the remaining 2 tablespoons butter. When butter is bubbly, add flour and whisk 2 minutes. Do not brown. Add broth and cook 2 minutes longer, stirring all the time. Remove from heat and whisk in the sour cream.

4. With a rubber spatula, fold in the mushroom mixture and wine. Add cooked fettuccine and mix well. Transfer to a buttered 9 x 13 x 2-inch oval glass baking dish and bake in a preheated 350°F oven until thoroughly heated, 20 to 30 minutes.

5. Garnish with the chives or scallions and serve hot.

Each serving		% of calories from fat 24	
Calories	375	Total Fat	10 g
Protein	12 g	Saturated Fat	4.3 g
Carbohydrates	58 g	Cholesterol	16 mg
Dietary Fiber	6 g	Sodium	41 mg

BAKED ZITI WITH THREE CHEESES AND ONIONS

MAKES 6 TO 8 SERVINGS

This layered and baked pasta dish is a favorite of mine. Ziti is a large tubular pasta, a popular shape with all the pasta manufacturers.

1 pound ziti
2 cups chopped onions
1 tablespoon extra-virgin olive oil
freshly ground black pepper
1/2 cup each freshly grated Pecorino and Parmesan cheeses
1 1/2 cups (1 pound) low-fat ricotta cheese
2 cups basic tomato sauce (page 76)

❶ Cook the pasta according to package directions and drain pasta. Combine the cooked pasta, uncooked onions, oil, and lots of pepper, and toss well. Transfer half of this pasta mixture to an oil-sprayed baking dish, about 9 x 13 x 2. Sprinkle half of the Pecorino and Parmesan cheeses over the pasta. Then spoon one half of the ricotta over all. Spoon 1 cup of tomato sauce over the ricotta.

❷ Repeat to make a second layer. Cover with foil.

❸ Bake in a preheated 350°F oven 30 minutes. Remove foil and bake 10 minutes longer.

Note: If you can get a Pecorino called Pepato, use it because this cheese is a variety spiced with peppercorns, further enhancing the sharp flavor of the cheese that goes well with a heavier type pasta such as ziti.

Each serving		% of calories from fat 15	
Calories	349	Total Fat	6 g
Protein	18 g	Saturated Fat	2.7 g
Carbohydrates	53 g	Cholesterol	15 mg
Dietary Fiber	3 g	Sodium	203 mg

PASTA AND BACON FRITTATA WITH MINT AND GREEN PEAS

MAKES 6 SERVINGS

1 cup small pasta, uncooked
2 containers (4 ounces each) of egg substitute
1/2 cup freshly grated nonfat mozzarella cheese
1/4 cup finely chopped fresh mint
freshly ground pepper or red pepper flakes
2 very thin slices bacon, thoroughly crisped and then crumbled
1 cup fresh or frozen green peas, cooked and drained
1/4 cup freshly grated Parmesan cheese
1 tablespoon extra-virgin olive oil
2 large cloves garlic, minced

1. Cook the pasta according to package directions. Drain pasta and set aside.

2. Combine the egg substitute, cooked pasta, mozzarella, mint, and pepper or pepper flakes in a large bowl. Mix well. Add crumbled bacon, peas, and Parmesan cheese. Mix again.

3. In a nonstick 9- or 10-inch skillet, heat the oil over medium high heat until hot (not smoking). Add garlic and sauté 1 minute. Pour pasta mixture in skillet and cook 8 minutes until the underside is browned. During this time, push the edge of the frittata toward the center of the pan with a fork to allow the uncooked egg to run over the edges; this will hasten the cooking time.

4. To finish the frittata, invert it onto a plate and slide it back into the pan. If it is too "loose," run it under the broiler for several minutes instead to firm the top.

5. Serve warm or cool. Serve with red, ripe tomatoes, sprinkled with a few drops of oil and some fresh basil.

Each serving		% of calories from fat 35	
Calories	128	Total Fat	5 g
Protein	9 g	Saturated Fat	1.7 g
Carbohydrates	10 g	Cholesterol	9 mg
Dietary Fiber	2 g	Sodium	264 mg

THE ANCIENT HERB MINT

The Latin *mentha*, or mint, has hundreds of varieties, wild as well as cultivated. The Romans used mint in their cooking and spread it throughout their empire. It still is a very popular herb throughout the world except, perhaps, in France, but I experience it often in Italy.

Spearmint is the everyday garden-variety that is curly leafed. This mint is used for drinks, jellies, sauces, salsas, and salads. Peppermint is the mint used in herbal teas and nonalcoholic beverages. Certain liqueurs are flavored with oil of peppermint, which is distilled from this variety of mint.

Mint adds considerable zest to pastas and other foods. When cooking pasta with snapper, use mint as a garnish.

BAKED ZUCCHINI WITH FARFALLE AND MOZZARELLA

MAKES 6 SERVINGS

This dish can be made ahead and reheated, but it is best right out of the oven. A crusty, warm loaf of bread and a crisp, green salad make a full meal.

spray oil
1 1/4 pounds zucchini (each 1 x 6 inches), ends trimmed and sliced lengthwise in 4
1 large onion, diced 1/2 inch
1 can (28 ounces) Italian-style tomatoes, put through a food mill, including their juices
2 teaspoons finely chopped fresh thyme or 1 teaspoon dried
freshly ground black pepper
1/2 pound farfalle, cooked and drained
1/2 pound skim milk mozzarella cheese, grated
1/4 cup freshly grated Pecorino cheese

❶ Lightly spray oil on a cookie or other flat baking sheet and lay the zucchini slices in a single layer. Spray oil the top of the zucchini slices. Bake about 12 minutes per side in a preheated 375°F oven. Set aside and leave the oven on.

❷ Spray oil a skillet and sauté onion until it becomes opaque, about 6 minutes. Add tomatoes and their liquid, thyme, and a liberal amount of pepper, and simmer 30 minutes until the sauce thickens.

❸ Combine the tomato sauce, cooked farfalle, and the mozzarella in a bowl.

❹ Spray oil a 2-quart baking dish. Lay half of the zucchini slices in the baking dish and cover with half of the pasta mixture. Repeat another layer of zucchini and pasta mixture. Sprinkle Pecorino cheese over all.

❺ Put dish in oven and cook 30 minutes until casserole is bubbling and thoroughly heated.

Each serving		% of calories from fat 24	
Calories	317	Total Fat	8.6 g
Protein	20 g	Saturated Fat	5 g
Carbohydrates	39 g	Cholesterol	25 mg
Dietary Fiber	3 g	Sodium	496 mg

LASAGNA WITH ROASTED TOMATOES AND ROASTED PEPPERS

MAKES 8 SERVINGS

Here's a lasagna dish with no ricotta cheese. It is filled with roasted peppers and tomatoes, and it is very tasty.

2 1/2 cups low-fat balsamella sauce (page 26)
8 sheets dried instant no-boil lasagna, each about 7-inches square
4 red or orange bell peppers, roasted (page 254)
4 medium tomatoes, roasted (page 255)
2 large cloves garlic, minced
1/4 cup finely chopped fresh basil or 1 teaspoon dried
freshly ground black pepper
1/2 cup freshly grated Pecorino Romano cheese
2/3 cup low-sodium chicken or vegetable broth

❶ Put a large spoonful of balsamella sauce in the bottom of an 8 x 8-inch glass baking dish. Lay one sheet of the lasagna on top. Lay some of the roasted pepper on top and add another large spoonful of balsamella sauce. Dot with garlic, basil, pepper, and cheese.

❷ Add more layers of pasta, alternating peppers and tomatoes as in Step 1. Dot each layer with balsamella sauce, garlic, basil, pepper, and cheese.

❸ Carefully pour broth into the edge of the baking dish. Cover with foil and bake 15 minutes in a preheated 375°F oven. Remove the foil and bake 10 minutes longer. Remove dish from oven and let stand 5 to 10 minutes before serving.

Each serving		% of calories from fat 28	
Calories	225	Total Fat	7 g
Protein	10 g	Saturated Fat	2.4 g
Carbohydrates	32 g	Cholesterol	11 mg
Dietary Fiber	3 g	Sodium	180 mg

ROASTED BELL PEPPERS

MAKES 4 SERVINGS

4 large red or orange bell peppers

❶ With a damp cloth, wipe the peppers clean. Place them on a flat baking tray and broil them slowly, under a low flame, until the skins are charred on all sides.

❷ Put the peppers in a brown paper bag, close the bag, and set them aside 10 minutes. Shake the bag back and forth to help loosen the skins.

❸ When the peppers are cool enough to handle, peel off the skins, and remove the seeds. Cut the peppers into strips or whatever shape is called for in a recipe and set aside.

Each serving		% of calories from fat 6	
Calories	44	Total Fat	0.3 g
Protein	1 g	Saturated Fat	0 g
Carbohydrates	11 g	Cholesterol	0 mg
Dietary Fiber	3 g	Sodium	3 mg

ROASTED TOMATOES

MAKES 4 SERVINGS

Roast these tomatoes in an electric oven.

4 medium tomatoes, cored and cut in halves
1 tablespoon extra-virgin olive oil
salt
freshly ground black pepper

❶ Arrange tomato halves, cut side up, in a glass baking dish. Lightly brush the cut surfaces with oil, a little salt, and a liberal amount of ground pepper.

❷ Bake 16 hours (put them in before retiring and take them out the next day—this is no trouble because the oven is at its lowest setting) in a preheated 150 to 170°F oven (usually the lowest oven setting). Do not turn the tomatoes; they should reduce by approximately half their original size. They should still be reasonably plump and moist and not totally dried as regular dried tomatoes. Use as needed in various recipes.

Each serving		% of calories from fat 59	
Calories	56	Total Fat	3.7 g
Protein	1 g	Saturated Fat	0.5 g
Carbohydrates	6 g	Cholesterol	0 mg
Dietary Fiber	1 g	Sodium	11 mg

ROLLED LASAGNA SHEETS FILLED WITH SPINACH, SAUSAGE, AND RICE

MAKES 12 SERVINGS

This recipe provides a different way to use lasagna strips. You can fill and roll lasagna with a variety of fillings and sauce them in many ways. Here's one of my favorites.

- 2 links Italian sausage, hot or sweet
- 1 tablespoon extra-virgin olive oil
- 1 medium onion, finely chopped
- 1/4 pound mushrooms, thinly sliced and cut in half
- 1 large clove garlic, minced
- 1 cup long-grain rice
- 1/2 cup finely shredded low-fat fontina cheese
- 1/2 cup low-sodium chicken broth
- 2 cups finely chopped fresh spinach (about 1/2 pound)
- freshly ground black pepper
- 14 lasagna strips (2 more than needed, but there in case of breakage)
- spray oil
- 3 cups tomato sauce (page 76)

❶ Remove the casing from the sausage links and break up the meat. Heat oil in a large skillet and cook sausage until it is well done. Transfer sausage to a large bowl. With a paper towel, remove most of the grease from the skillet.

❷ Add onion to the skillet and sauté until it becomes opaque, about 3 minutes. Add mushrooms and sauté 2 or 3 minutes longer. Add garlic and cook 1 minute. Transfer this mixture to the bowl with the sausage in it.

Continued on next page

❸ In 2 1/2 cups unsalted water with no oil, cook rice. Reduce the heat, cover, and simmer until the water is absorbed by the rice, about 15 minutes. Add the fontina cheese and stir it in immediately while the rice is warm. Transfer this to the sausage bowl. Add broth and spinach, and fold into mixture until well combined. Add a liberal amount of pepper.

❹ Cook the lasagna strips four at a time according to package instructions. Pat lasagna dry on cloth toweling. Spoon some of the filling on each strip and spread it to cover. Roll each strip and place it seamside down on a baking tray lightly sprayed with oil. Bake 15 minutes in a preheated 375°F oven. Serve one portion per plate with about 4 tablespoons of tomato sauce—one spoonful over the roll, the other three to each side of the roll on each plate.

Each serving		**% of calories from fat 22**	
Calories	238	Total Fat	6 g
Protein	9 g	Saturated Fat	2 g
Carbohydrates	37 g	Cholesterol	14 mg
Dietary Fiber	2 g	Sodium	167 mg

LASAGNA WITH GRILLED EGGPLANT AND ZUCCHINI

MAKES 6 SERVINGS

This recipe provides an excellent way to combine grilled vegetables with pasta. The vegetables develop a smoky flavor, and when put together lasagna style, they make the dish even more flavorful. You will enjoy this recipe and will want to repeat making it.

1 pound zucchini
1 eggplant, about 1 pound
2 red, yellow, or green bell peppers or 1 jar (12 ounces) roasted peppers
2 tablespoons extra-virgin olive oil
1/3 cup freshly grated Parmesan cheese
2 tablespoons finely chopped fresh basil or 1 teaspoon dried
1 tablespoon of finely chopped fresh oregano or 1/2 teaspoon dried
2 large garlic cloves, minced
freshly ground black pepper
4 cups low-sodium vegetable broth
8 sheets instant no-boil lasagna

1. Rinse and dry the zucchini, eggplant, and bell peppers. Slice off the ends of the zucchini and slice lengthwise in 1/4-inch strips. Do the same with the eggplant. When the fire is ready, grill the peppers and peel them, discarding the stems, seeds, and pulpy part of the ribs. Slice the peppers in 2- to 3-inch-wide strips. If using jarred peppers, drain them and set aside.

2. Add the eggplant and the zucchini slices to a lightly oiled grill, and grill both sides of the vegetables until tender when pierced with a wooden skewer. The eggplant will take about 4 or 5 minutes per side, and the zucchini will take about 3 to 4 minutes per side.

Continued on next page

❸ In a small bowl, combine cheese, herbs, garlic, and pepper. Stir well. Set aside.

❹ In a baking pan large enough to hold two lasagna sheets, add 1/2 cup of broth and fit two lasagna sheets into the pan. Cover with grilled eggplant and sprinkle one third of the cheese mixture over all. Place two more pasta sheets over the eggplant, pour 1 cup broth over the pasta, and lay the peppers over them. Add one third of the cheese mixture over all. Lay two more lasagna sheets, add another cup of broth, and arrange the grilled zucchini over the pasta. Add the last third of the cheese mixture.

❺ Add the remaining two lasagna sheets and carefully pour over the remaining broth. Sprinkle pepper liberally over the top of the lasagna. Bake in a preheated 350°F oven for 30 minutes or longer, until the pasta is thoroughly cooked. To test, run a wooden skewer through the layers of lasagna; if it penetrates easily, the pasta is cooked. Also, the lasagna should be boiling in the oven. Remove the pan from the oven and let sit for 10 minutes. Serve hot.

Each serving		**% of calories from fat 21**	
Calories	373	Total Fat	9 g
Protein	15 g	Saturated Fat	2.6 g
Carbohydrates	60 g	Cholesterol	8 mg
Dietary Fiber	6 g	Sodium	183 mg

MANICOTTI WITH TOFU AND BEAN FILLING

MAKES 8 SERVINGS

16 cooked jumbo manicotti shells
2 packages (about 10 ounces each) firm tofu
2 cans (14 ounces each) white beans, cannellini preferred, drained and rinsed
1 cup part-skim ricotta cheese
2 tablespoons crumbled crisped bacon (3 strips)
2 large cloves garlic, minced
1 tablespoon each, chopped fresh basil and oregano, or 1 teaspoon each, dried
heavy pinch red pepper flakes
2 cups low-fat marinara sauce (page 30)
3/4 cup freshly grated Pecorino cheese
1/2 cup finely sliced scallions

1. Cook the pasta according to package directions. Drain and dry pasta, and set it aside.

2. Process the tofu in a food processor until smooth. Transfer to a wide strainer; let drain 10 minutes.

3. Return tofu to the processor, and add beans, ricotta, bacon, garlic, herbs, and pepper flakes. Pulse on and off several times. Do not overprocess.

4. Spoon some marinara sauce on the bottom of a baking dish. Fill each manicotti with several spoonfuls of the bean mixture, and arrange manicotti side by side in the baking dish.

5. Cover the manicotti with the remaining sauce, sprinkle the Pecorino over all, and bake in a preheated 375°F oven until the top browns and the pasta bubbles, about 30 minutes. Remove baking dish from oven. Serve two manicotti per plate with a sprinkle of sliced scallions.

Each serving		% of calories from fat 28	
Calories	312	Total Fat	10 g
Protein	20 g	Saturated Fat	4.3 g
Carbohydrates	35 g	Cholesterol	24 mg
Dietary Fiber	6 g	Sodium	466 mg

TOFU

Tofu blocks, available in extra firm, firm, and soft, are sold individually wrapped or in large vats of water—I prefer the individual packets.

Tofu, if calcium fortified, is a good source of protein and calcium, and is considered a medium fat. One piece of tofu about 2 1/2 x 2 3/4 x 1 inch has 68 calories, 9.4 grams of protein, and 5 grams of fat; only 0.8 grams of the fat is saturated, and it has no cholesterol.

The downside of tofu is that it is bland; the good news is that tofu will absorb any flavor with which it is cooked. Tofu will take on the flavors of other foods.

Buy tofu in sealed and dated airtight packages. After you open the package, store unused tofu in fresh water, in a tightly covered container. If the tofu turns yellow and has a sour smell, throw it out.

SPECIAL LASAGNA WITH BALSAMELLA, RICOTTA, AND FONTINA FILLING

MAKES 8 SERVINGS

This dish can be made up to a day ahead of time and refrigerated. Remove it one hour before baking. If you wish to freeze this, wrap it well in foil, and when you are ready to bake it, no thawing is necessary. Cover with a fresh piece of foil and bake 350°F for one and a half hours. Remove the foil after one hour of baking and continue baking, uncovered, until lasagna is bubbling. Although this dish is higher in fat calories than most other dishes in this book, it is included for a special occasion and should be served with lettuces and vegetables with no-fat salad dressings.

16 to 18 lasagna strips (about 2 x 10 inches)
1 cup balsamella sauce (page 26)
1/2 cup shredded low-fat fontina cheese
1/2 cup freshly grated Parmesan cheese

For the filling:

2 cups nonfat-milk ricotta
1/4 cup thinly sliced scallions
1 tablespoon finely chopped flat parsley
2 eggs, lightly beaten
1 teaspoon sugar
freshly ground black pepper

For the tomato sauce:

1 tablespoon extra-virgin olive oil
1/4 pound Italian hot sausage, casing removed and meat crumbled
2 shallots, finely chopped
1 clove garlic, minced
1 large can (2 pounds, 3 ounces) Italian plum tomatoes, put through a food mill
2 tablespoons finely chopped fresh basil or 1 teaspoon dried
1 teaspoon sugar
freshly ground black pepper

Continued on next page

❶ Prepare sauce in a large saucepan by heating oil and adding sausage meat. Sauté about 2 minutes, add shallots and garlic, and sauté 1 minute longer, stirring all the time. Add tomatoes, basil, and sugar and bring to a boil. Lower the heat, partially cover, and simmer 40 minutes, stirring frequently. Add a liberal amount of pepper.

❷ Per package directions, cook four sheets of lasagna at a time until nearly tender. Have another large saucepan ready with a colander placed on top of it. Carefully empty the boiling water and pasta from the first pot into the colander in the second pot, catching the cooked pasta in the colander. Save the water for more uncooked pasta. Lay the cooked pasta on a cloth towel and pat it dry. Cook the remaining pasta strips four at a time until all are cooked. Set them aside.

❸ Combine all the ingredients for the filling in a bowl and mix until smooth. Set aside.

❹ Preheat the oven to 350°F. Spoon a small amount of the tomato sauce in the bottom of a baking dish, 9 x 12 x 3 inches. Arrange four cooked lasagna sheets over the sauce on the bottom. Add one third of the ricotta mixture evenly over the pasta; then add one third of the balsamella and one third of the fontina. Sprinkle about 1 tablespoon Parmesan cheese and a small amount of the tomato sauce over all.

❺ Add two more layers of lasagna sheets, ricotta mixture, balsamella, fontina, Parmesan, and tomato sauce, ending up with cooked pasta on top. Cover with more tomato sauce and sprinkle with the remaining Parmesan cheese. Bake for 50 minutes or until bubbling. Let the cooked lasagna stand for about 15 minutes before slicing and serving.

Each serving		**% of calories from fat 35**	
Calories	424	Total Fat	16 g
Protein	22 g	Saturated Fat	7 g
Carbohydrates	47 g	Cholesterol	85 mg
Dietary Fiber	2 g	Sodium	460 mg

PASTA AND TURKEY SAUSAGE FRITTATA

MAKES 4 SERVINGS

A slice of frittata with a green salad makes an excellent and satisfying lunch. The fennel seed flavors the turkey sausage to make a tasty frittata.

6 ounces turkey sausage
1 medium onion, finely chopped
1/4 teaspoon dried fennel seeds
4 cups cooked elbow or other small pasta
1 packet (8 ounces) fat-free egg substitute, thawed
1/4 cup evaporated skim milk
1/4 teaspoon red pepper flakes
1/2 cup finely shredded low-fat cheddar cheese

❶ Heat a large, nonstick skillet over high heat, and sauté the sausage, onion, and fennel seeds until the meat is no longer pink, about 5 minutes.

❷ In a bowl, combine cooked pasta, egg substitute, evaporated milk, and pepper flakes. Pour this evenly over the meat and onions in the skillet. Lower the heat to medium, cover the pan, and cook 5 minutes.

❸ Cook 5 minutes longer, covered, to set the top, or if you wish, run the skillet under the broiler instead. Remove from the heat, sprinkle the cheese over frittata, and serve when cheese has melted.

Each serving		% of calories from fat 21	
Calories	321	Total Fat	7.8 g
Protein	23 g	Saturated Fat	2.7 g
Carbohydrates	38 g	Cholesterol	32 mg
Dietary Fiber	2 g	Sodium	447 mg

PENNE AND BROCCOLI RABE BAKED CASSEROLE

MAKES 6 SERVINGS

Here is another comforting pasta casserole. This time it is enriched with broccoli rabe and cheese.

1 pound penne
2 tablespoons canola oil
1 large onion, diced 1/2 inch
3 cloves garlic, minced
1/4 cup all-purpose flour
2 1/2 cups low-sodium, defatted chicken broth
1 1/2 cups freshly grated Pecorino cheese
2 teaspoons dried oregano
pinch red pepper flakes
1 can (14 or 15 ounces) cut tomatoes, Italian style
2 cups cooked and chopped broccoli rabe
spray oil
1/3 cup fresh bread crumbs

❶ Cook the pasta according to package directions and drain it well.

❷ Heat 1 tablespoon canola oil in a skillet and sauté onion until it is transparent, about 4 minutes. Add garlic and cook 1 minute longer. Add flour, stir well, and cook 1 minute, stirring all the time.

❸ Add broth and cook until lightly thickened, 3 to 4 minutes. Remove from heat, and stir in 1/4 cup cheese, oregano, and red pepper flakes.

Continued on next page

4. In a large bowl, combine tomatoes, broccoli rabe, cooked pasta, 1 cup cheese, and skillet sauce. Spray oil a baking dish, about 8 x 12 inches, and transfer the pasta mixture to it.

5. Combine the remaining tablespoon of oil with the bread crumbs and the remaining 1/4 cup of cheese. Mix well and sprinkle over the pasta. Bake in a preheated 375°F oven 20 to 30 minutes until the pasta is bubbly and thoroughly heated and the crumbs have browned.

Each serving		**% of calories from fat 27**	
Calories	461	Total Fat	13 g
Protein	17 g	Saturated Fat	5 g
Carbohydrates	69 g	Cholesterol	28 mg
Dietary Fiber	12 g	Sodium	488 mg

THREE-CHEESE STUFFED SHELLS BAKED WITH TOMATO AND BALSAMELLA SAUCES

MAKES 6 SERVINGS

These shells make a wonderful buffet item, but they are also good served for lunch or supper, three per plate, with a fresh green salad.

18 large uncooked pasta shells
1 1/2 cups nonfat cottage cheese
1 cup shredded part-skim mozzarella cheese
2 tablespoons freshly grated Pecorino cheese
1/2 cup nonfat sour cream
2 egg whites, lightly beaten
1/4 cup finely chopped flat parsley
1 tablespoon finely chopped fresh oregano or 1 teaspoon dried
zest of 1 lemon
1/3 teaspoon freshly grated nutmeg
2 cups tomato sauce (page 76), heated
1 cup balsamella sauce (page 26), heated

1. Cook pasta shells according to package directions. Drain shells well. Set aside to cool.

2. In a bowl, combine three cheeses, sour cream, egg whites, parsley, oregano, lemon zest, and nutmeg. Mix well.

3. Fill each shell with teaspoonsful of the cheese filling and arrange the shells side by side in a baking dish large enough to hold them in a single layer (an 8 x 8 dish).

4. Spoon tomato sauce over all and spoon balsamella sauce, stripe fashion, over tomato sauce. Cover with foil and bake in a preheated 350°F oven until the sauces bubble and the shells are heated thoroughly, 25 to 30 minutes. Serve right away.

Each serving		% of calories from fat 20	
Calories	299	Total Fat	6.9 g
Protein	22 g	Saturated Fat	3 g
Carbohydrates	37 g	Cholesterol	19 mg
Dietary Fiber	2 g	Sodium	401 mg

SHELLS WITH SAVOY CABBAGE, POTATOES, AND FONTINA

MAKES 6 SERVINGS

This recipe provides a delicious combination of vegetables and pasta. It is best suited for cool and wintry evenings.

1 1/2 pounds medium shells

1 1/2 cups potatoes, peeled and cubed (1/2 inch)

1/2 head savoy cabbage (about 1/2 pound), thinly sliced as in coleslaw

2 tablespoons extra-virgin olive oil

1 tablespoon unsalted butter

3 large cloves garlic, minced

1/2 teaspoon dried fennel seeds

4 ounces shredded fontina cheese

❶ Cook the pasta according to package directions. Drain pasta and reserve the cooking liquid. Put drained pasta in a bowl and put cooking liquid back into the pot in which the pasta cooked.

❷ Add potatoes to cooking liquid and cook over medium heat, about 10 minutes. Add cabbage and cook 2 minutes longer. Drain potatoes and cabbage, reserving 1/2 cup of cooking liquid. Add potatoes, cabbage, and reserved cooking liquid to the pasta in the bowl.

❸ Heat oil in a large, nonstick skillet and melt butter. Add garlic and fennel seed, and sauté 1 minute, stirring all the time.

❹ Add pasta mixture to the skillet, add half of the cheese, and toss well. Transfer mixture to an oil-sprayed 13 x 9 x 2-inch glass baking dish. Top with the remaining cheese.

❺ Bake in a preheated 375°F oven until the cheese on the top melts, 5 minutes or so.

Each serving		% of calories from fat 25	
Calories	490	Total Fat	14 g
Protein	17 g	Saturated Fat	5.7 g
Carbohydrates	73 g	Cholesterol	27 mg
Dietary Fiber	6 g	Sodium	170 mg

CONVERSION TABLES

SOLID MEASURES

Here are approximate equivalents to measure items by weight, in both Imperial and metric. So as to avoid awkward measurements, some conversions are not exact.

	U.S. CUSTOMARY	METRIC	IMPERIAL
Butter	1 cup	225 g	8 oz
	½ cup	115 g	4 oz
	¼ cup	60 g	2 oz
	1 Tbsp	15 g	½ oz
Cheese (grated)	1 cup	115 g	4 oz
Fruit (chopped fresh)	1 cup	225 g	8 oz
Herbs (chopped fresh)	¼ cup	7 g	¼ oz
Meats/Chicken (chopped, cooked)	1 cup	175 g	6 oz
Mushrooms (chopped, fresh)	1 cup	70 g	2½ oz
Nuts (chopped)	1 cup	115 g	4 oz
Raisins (and other dried chopped fruits)	1 cup	175 g	6 oz
Rice (uncooked)	1 cup	225 g	8 oz
(cooked)	3 cups	225 g	8 oz
Vegetables (chopped, raw)	1 cup	115 g	4 oz

LIQUID MEASURES

The Imperial pint is larger than the U.S. pint; therefore, note the following when measuring liquid ingredients.

U.S. CUSTOMARY	IMPERIAL
1 cup = 8 fluid ounces	1 cup = 10 fluid ounces
½ cup = 4 fluid ounces	½ cup = 5 fluid ounces
1 tablespoon = ¾ fluid ounce	1 tablespoon = 1 fluid ounce

U.S. MEASURE	METRIC APPROXIMATE	IMPERIAL APPROXIMATE
1 quart (4 cups)	950 mL	1½ pints + 4 Tbsp
1 pint (2 cups)	450 mL	¾ pint
1 cup	236 mL	¼ pint + 6 Tbsp
1 Tbsp	15 mL	1 Tbsp
1 tsp	5 mL	1 tsp

...ES

...ed States, the following items are measured by weight. Use this ...n mind that measurements will vary, depending on the variety of ...e. Cup measurements are loosely packed; flour is measured directly from package (presifted).

	U.S. CUSTOMARY	METRIC	IMPERIAL
Flour (all-purpose)	1 cup	150 g	5 oz
Cornmeal	1 cup	175 g	6 oz
Sugar (granulated)	1 cup	190 g	6½ oz
(confectioners)	1 cup	80 g	2⅔ oz
(brown)	1 cup	160 g	5⅓ oz

OVEN TEMPERATURES

Fahrenheit	225	300	350	400	450
Celsius	110	150	180	200	230
Gas Mark	¼	2	4	6	8

LOW-CALORIE RECIPE INGREDIENT ALTERNATIVES

"TRADITIONAL"	LOW-CALORIE
Whole milk	Skim milk
(1 cup = 155 calories)	(1 cup = 86 calories)
Whole egg	Egg white
(1 medium = 79 calories)	(1 medium = 16 calories)
Butter	"Diet" margarine
(1/2 cup = 810 calories)	(1/2 cup = 400 calories)
Vegetable oil	Non-stick vegetable spray
(1 tablespoon = 120 calories)	(0 calories)
Mayonnaise	"Diet" mayonnaise
(1/2 cup = 788 calories)	(1/2 cup = 400 calories)
Sour cream	Plain, low-fat yogurt
(1/2 cup = 246 calories)	(1/2 cup = 72 calories)
Cream cheese	Neufchatel cheese
(4 ounces = 396 calories)	(4 ounces = 296 calories)
	"Light" (low-calorie) cream cheese
	(1/2 cup = 240 calories)
Whole milk ricotta cheese	Part-skim ricotta cheese
(1/2 cup = 216 calories)	(1/2 cup = 171 calories)
Flavored gelatin	Unflavored gelatin
(2-cup mold = 315 calories)	(2-cup mold = 23 calories)
Strawberries, frozen sweetened	Strawberries, frozen unsweetened
(4 ounces = 89 calories)	(4 ounces = 40 calories)
Pineapple canned in syrup	Pineapple canned in juice
(4 ounces = 89 calories)	(4 ounces = 37 calories)

TIPS FOR DECREASING FAT

1. Use more poultry and fish instead of red meat.
2. Broil, bake, steam, poach, or "oven fry" instead of pan frying or deep-fat frying.
3. Roast meat on racks to allow drainage of fat. Discard drippings.
4. Trim all visible fat.
5. Use nonstick skillets to minimize the use of additional fat when sautéing or browning.
6. When browning meat, spoon off or drain away all excess fat released ("pan broiling"). Blot cooked meat in a double thickness of paper towels to remove excess fat.
7. Substitute nonstick vegetable sprays for grease on baking pans and in casserole dishes.
8. Remove the skin from poultry (about 1/3 of the fat is in and immediately under the skin).
9. When purchasing canned fish (tuna, sardines, salmon, etc.), select items packed in water, mustard, or other oil-free dressings.
10. Chill meat drippings and remove the hardened fat that collects at the top before making gravy. Use the same technique to remove fat from stews and soups.
11. If onions begin to stick to the pan when sautéing, add a small amount of water and continue cooking until water evaporates.
12. Decrease the use of high-fat salad dressings, gravies, and sauces.
13. Use low-fat yogurt, low-fat buttermilk, and flavored vinegars to reduce fat in salad dressings. Try a mixture of half oil and half vinegar to decrease the amount of fat.
14. When selecting dairy products, choose low-fat or nonfat items.
15. For baking, substitute low-fat plain yogurt for sour cream.
16. Whip well-chilled evaporated milk to substitute for whipped cream.
17. Avoid nuts and seeds, which are high in fat and calories. Purchase dry-roasted, unsalted nuts to help decrease fat.
18. In baking, substitute 2 large egg whites for 1 large whole egg or 3 egg whites for 2 whole eggs.
19. Use unsweetened plain cocoa powder instead of baking chocolate.

NOTES ON FOOD STORAGE

FREEZER STORAGE

	RECOMMENDED STORAGE TIME	HANDLING SUGGESTIONS
Dairy Products		
Butter	6 to 9 months	Double-wrap or repackage all dairy products in moisture-vaporproof wrap or containers.
Margarine	12 months	
Ice cream, ice milk, sherbet	2 to 4 months	
Hard cheeses (brick, edam, cheddar, gouda, Swiss)	4 to 6 months	Cheeses will become crumbly in thawing. Plan to use them for cooking.
Fruits and Vegetables		
Fresh or frozen	8 to 12 months	Freeze in moisture-vaporproof plastic bags or containers. Do not freeze cabbage, greens, green onions, or radishes
Meat, Poultry, and Fish		
Beef	6 to 9 months	Remove fresh meat, poultry, or fish from store package; wipe dry, if necessary and repackage in moisture-vaporproof wrap.
Pork	3 to 6 months	
Variety meats	1 to 2 months	
Ground meats	2 to 3 months	
Fresh pork sausage	1 to 3 months	
Chicken, pieces	6 to 9 months	
Chicken, whole	12 months	
Turkey	6 months	
Lean fish (bass, cod, halibut, sole, swordfish)	6 months	Store purchased frozen fish in original wrap up to 2 weeks. For longer periods, double-wrap or repackage in moisture-vaporproof wrap.
Fat fish (catfish, mackerel, salmon, trout, tuna)	2 to 3 months	
Prepared Foods		
Meat casseroles	3 to 6 months	Be sure all foods are packaged in moisture-vaporproof wrap. Label packages with the type of food, number of servings, and date.
Meat loaves	1 to 2 months	
Meat roasts with gravy	1 to 3 months	
Breads	2 to 3 months	
Yeast bread dough	1 month	
Soups	4 to 6 months	

FOOD SAFETY

- Never forget the cardinal rule: When in doubt, throw it out.
- Keep hot foods hot—over 140 degrees. Keep cold foods cold—under 40 degrees.
- Do not let meats, poultry, fish or seafood, eggs, tofu, soft cheeses, or dishes made with any of these (raw or cooked) stand at room temperature for more than 1 hour—or refrigerate immediately on hot days. When grocery shopping, make the supermarket your last stop before going home, and buy perishable foods such as milk and seafood last.
- Pour leftover cooked foods into shallow containers and refrigerate immediately.
- Always thoroughly wash your hands with soap and water before handling food.
- Consider all raw meats, poultry, fish, shellfish, and eggs to be contaminated. After handling them, wash your hands and all surfaces they have touched thoroughly with soap and hot water. Do not allow meat or poultry juices to drip onto other foods.
- Thoroughly wash all fruits and vegetables, including berries. Once fruits and vegetables have been cut up, they should be refrigerated within 2 hours.
- Cook foods thoroughly. Red meats should reach an internal temperature of at least 160 degrees; chicken or turkey breast, 170 degrees; and poultry dark meat, 180 degrees. If you can't abide well-done steak or lamb chops, at least cook ground meats until they're no longer pink in the center. Cook eggs until the yolk is no longer runny. Either modify recipes that call for raw or lightly cooked eggs or don't use them.
- Be aware that it's best not to stuff poultry before roasting it; it's hard to get the stuffing cooked through without overcooking the meat. The safest course is to bake the stuffing separately. If you must stuff the bird, stick a meat thermometer into the center of the stuffing and do not remove the bird from the oven until the stuffing reaches 165 degrees.
- Keep raw and cooked meats, poultry, and fish separate. If you use a marinade for raw meat, boil it before you use it as a sauce for the cooked meat. Use clean utensils to move the cooked meat from the pan to a clean plate, not the same plate the raw meat was sitting on.
- Thaw frozen foods in the refrigerator, not at room temperature. In an emergency, you can thaw foods in the sink, covered with cold water. Replenish the water as it loses its chill. Thaw foods in the microwave only if you are going to cook them immediately.
- Do not pick and eat wild mushrooms, greens, berries, or other plants unless you absolutely, positively know what you are doing. Except for standard white mushrooms, cook mushrooms completely through.
- If you are canning foods, follow safe methods. Safety guidelines for canned foods change over the years, so consult a recently published book or pamphlet on canning. Only high-acid foods such as fruits can be safely processed in a hot-water bath. Process low-acid vegetables, meats, and other foods in a pressure canner.
- Wash cutting boards thoroughly with hot, soapy water after each use, or run them through the dishwasher (plastic, glass, or solid wood boards only). Air-dry or pat dry with paper towels. Occasionally sanitize the boards by flooding the surfaces with a solution of 2 teaspoons liquid chlorine bleach per quart of water. Let the solution stand on the board for several minutes, then rinse and air-dry or pat dry with clean paper towels. Once a cutting board cracks or becomes excessively nicked or pitted, throw it out. To play it safe, use one cutting board for meat, poultry, and fish, and a second one for fruits, vegetables, and bread.
- Remember that all food-safety rules are doubly important for the well-being of pregnant women, children, persons suffering from illness, and those over the age of 60.

Sources: U.S. Food and Drug Administration, U.S. Department of Agriculture, University of Illinois Cooperative Extension Service, National Food Safety Database.

SOURCES

If you'd like more information about a particular food-related subject, one of the following references may help. Today's transitional business climate means that there may be an occasional change in an address or phone number, particularly in listings for government agencies. The following list is arranged alphabetically by subject:

ARTICHOKES

California Artichoke Advisory Board
10719 Merritt Street
Castroville, CA 95012
(800) 827-2783

ASPARAGUS

California Asparagus Commission
4565 Quail Lakes Drive, Suite A-1
Stockton, CA 95207
(209) 474-7581

AVOCADOS

California Avocado Commission
1251 East Dyer Road, Suite 200
Santa Ana, CA 92705
(714) 558-6761

BEANS

National Dry Bean Council
1200 19th Street, NW, Suite 300
Washington, DC 20036
(202) 857-1169

BEEF

USDA Meat and Poultry Hotline
(800) 535-4555

National Live Stock and Meat Board
Beef Industry Council
444 North Michigan Avenue
Chicago, IL 60611
(312) 467-5520

CELERY

American Celery Council
P.O. Box 140067
Orlando, FL 32814
(407) 894-2911

CHEESE

National Cheese Institute
1250 H Street, NW, Suite 900
Washington, DC 20005
(202) 296-1909

CORN

National Corn Growers Association
1000 Executive Parkway
St. Louis, MO 63141
(314) 275-9915

DAIRY PRODUCTS

National Dairy Council
O'Hare International Center
10255 West Higgins Road, Suite 900
Rosemont, IL 60018
(708) 803-2000

National Dairy Board
2111 Wilson Boulevard
Arlington, VA 22201
(703) 528-4800

EGGS

United Egg Association
1 Massachusetts Avenue, Suite 800
Washington, DC 20001
(202) 842-2345

American Egg Board
1460 Renaissance Drive, Suite 301
Park Ridge, IL 60068
(708) 296-7043

FISH

National Fisheries Institute, Inc.
200 M Street, NW, Suite 580
Washington, DC 20036
(202) 296-3428

GRAPES

California Table Grape Commission
P.O. Box 5498
Fresno, CA 93755
(209) 224-4997

GREENS

Leafy Greens Council
33 Pheasant Lane
St. Paul, MN 55127
(612) 484-3321

HONEY

National Honey Board
421 21st Avenue, Suite 203
Longmont, CO 80501-1421
(303) 776-2337
(800) 356-5941 (Hotline)

LAMB

American Sheep Industry Association
6911 South Yosemite Street
Englewood, CO 80112
(303) 771-3500

MEAT

American Meat Institute
P.O. Box 3556
Washington, DC 20007
(703) 841-2400

National Live Stock and Meat Board
444 North Michigan Avenue
Chicago, IL 60611
(312) 467-5520

MUSHROOMS

American Mushroom Institute
907 East Baltimore Pike
Kennett Square, PA 19348
(215) 388-7806

NUTRITION

National Center for Nutrition and Dietetics
American Dietetic Association
216 West Jackson Boulevard
Chicago, IL 60606
(312) 899-0040;
(800) 366-1655

USDA Human Nutrition Information Service
6505 Belcrest Road
Hyattsville, MD 20782

OIL

Institute of Shortening and Edible Oils
1750 New York Avenue, NW
Washington, DC 20006
(202) 783-7960

International Olive Oil Council
(800) 232-6548

OLIVES

California Olive Association
660 J Street, Suite 290
Sacramento, CA 95814
(916) 444-9260

ONIONS

National Onion Association
822 Seventh Street, Suite 510
Greeley, CO 80631
(303) 353-5895

PASTA

National Pasta Association
2101 Wilson Boulevard, Suite 920
Arlington, VA 22201
(703) 841-0818

PEANUTS

Peanut Advisory Board
1950 North Park Place, NW
Atlanta, GA 30339
(404) 933-0357

PORK

National Pork Producers Council
P.O. Box 10383
Des Moines, IA 50306
(800) 937-7675

POTATOES

National Potato Promotion Board
7555 E. Hampden Street, Suite 412
Denver, CO 80231
(303) 369-7783

POULTRY

American Poultry Association
26363 South Tucker Road
Estacada, OR 97023
(503) 630-6759

USDA Meat and Poultry Hotline
(800) 535-4555

PRODUCE

Produce Marketing Association
P.O. Box 6036
Newark, DE 19714-6036
(302) 738-7100

SEAFOOD

National Seafood Educators
P.O. Box 60006
Richmond Beach, WA 98160
(206) 546-6410

TOMATOES

California Tomato Board
2019 North Gateway Boulevard
Fresno, CA 93727
(800) 827-0628

TURKEY

National Turkey Federation
11319 Sunset Hills Road
Reston, VA 22090
(703) 435-7206

USDA Meat and Poultry Hotline
(800) 535-4555

WINE

American Wine Society
3006 Latta Road
Rochester, NY 14612
(716) 225-7613

Wine Appreciation Guild
155 Connecticut Street
San Francisco, CA 94107
(415) 864-1202

NDEX

C

D

E

F

G

H

I

L

M

N

O

T